Red Sorrow

Red Sorrow

A MEMOIR

by
NANCHU

Arcade Publishing • New York

FIRST EDITION

Library of Congress Cataloging-in-Publication Data
Nanchu, 1953–
   Red sorrow : a memoir / by Nanchu
     p. cm.
   ISBN 1-55970-569-8
    1. Nanchu,1953– 2. China—History—Cultural Revolution, 1966–1976.
   3. Hong wei bing—Biography. I. Title
   DS778.N365 A3 2001
   951.05'6'092—dc21   2001022445

Published in the United States by Arcade Publishing, Inc., New York
Distributed by Time Warner Trade Publishing

Visit our Web site at www.arcadepub.com

Visit the author's Web page at www.geocities.com/rsorrow

10 9 8 7 6 5 4 3 2 1

Designed by API

EB

PRINTED IN THE UNITED STATES OF AMERICA

Contents

Author's Note

I started writing this book in August 1998. Memories, like a turbulent torrent, raged out of my heart and flew down vigorously on the page. Often my face was bathed in tears. But I dared not slow down. Our past cannot be forgotten; those who do forget must relive it. This mission has already been long delayed.

As a proud daughter of the Yellow River, I love you China. No matter where I go, I always do. This book is dedicated to my contemporaries who grew up in the Cultural Revolution, particularly those who sacrificed their young lives for their beliefs in those frenetic years, and those who still suffer today. With its publication, I, as a living witness, victim, participant, and survivor of the immense human tragedy, can relieve some of the burden that has long weighed down on me.

To protect people's safety, I have changed some of the names and the distinguishing features of individuals, locations, and institutions.

Acknowledgments

To Elizabeth Frost-Knappman, my agent, for believing in me, providing guidance, and lending me your strong shoulder along the way,

To Cal Barksdale, my editor, for contributing your intelligence, passion, and dedication unselfishly to this book and to his assistant, Danielle Durkin, for your precious work since the very beginning,

To Ann Marlowe and to the assistants at Arcade Publishing for your contribution,

To Zhongyi Wu, Donna Sparrow, Craig Dirgo, Bob Michael, and Ray Barbier for understanding, encouraging, and supporting me in the best ways,

Here are my sincerest thanks.

1

Dragon Calamity

1

The Rise of the Red Guards

In June 1966 I was only thirteen. My hometown, Shanghai, smelled like it was burning, and the air seemed to vibrate in the muggy heat. The North Train Station was a sea of faces and an ocean of red flags. Sirens blared, people bustled, and horses neighed. Dust raised by countless feet hung in the air like a foggy curtain. The vigorous Beijing teenagers poured into Shanghai by the trainload like swarms of locusts. In their green army uniforms and red armbands, the newly formed Red Guards quickly stationed themselves in the busy streets, stopping pedestrians. With rulers and shears in hand, they sliced open trouser legs less than seven inches wide. They severed pointed leather shoes, ripped up colorful clothing, whipped lovers who held hands, and shaved half the head of anyone with long hair — leaving the notorious "yin-yang head." They climbed the European buildings overlooking the Huangpu River, toppling their Renaissance-style sculptures one by one. From one of these buildings they hung a huge red banner proclaiming LONG LIVE THE RED TERROR.

The red cyclone arose just a few weeks after the Chinese Communist Party broadcast its May 16 Statement to the Nation, declaring the official start of the Great Proletarian Cultural Revolution: "A small handful of representatives of the bourgeoisie is lurking within our party, the government, and the army. These revisionists are conspiring to overthrow the dictatorship of the proletariat and turn this regime into a capitalist one. Some have already been exposed, but others, like China's Khrushchev, are still hiding among us."

★   ★   ★

On August 18, golden osmanthus blossoms gave off a rich perfume in the air. The flaming crimson leaves of maple trees on Western Hill danced in the sky. The capital city of Beijing was filled with a holiday atmosphere. Gongs and drums beat in the streets. Colorful balloons bobbed in the air. Glowing with health and radiating vigor, Chairman Mao appeared on the magnificent rostrum of Tiananmen, which overlooked the immense square. Smiling, he swept his huge hand toward the sea of cheering Red Guards, who were jumping up and down in the plaza below. He wore the red armband of the Red Guards on his green army uniform, demonstrating his unwavering support. In his strong Hunan accent Chairman Mao told them, "The youth of our country must care about its destiny. I call on you to spread the fire to every corner of the country and carry the Cultural Revolution to its conclusion!"

Chairman Mao stepped down from the rostrum of Tiananmen, crossed the Gold-Water Bridge, and walked with firm steps into the masses of Red Guards, who went wild with joy. Thunderous hand-clapping, heaven-shaking shouting, and the music of "Sailing on the Ocean, We Rely on Our Great Helmsman" moved the hearts of the Chinese people.

Four days later, the heat and humidity had turned Shanghai into a huge oven, even after sundown. The air stood still and leaves were motionless. The "concrete forest," as the city was called, smoldered. The hot breeze a small electric fan created leafed through the magazines on the desk again and again. In the kitchen, Mother was busy cooking dinner on the coal stove, her light blue polyester shirt sticking damply to her back. Beads of perspiration rolled down her face, which she wiped from time to time with a white hand towel. Father, in a sleeveless sweatshirt, paced back and forth through the apartment with his hands locked behind his back. In his small bedroom, Ming, my elder brother of nineteen, was stripped to the waist, sweat streaming down his muscular chest. One of the million Red Guards that Chairman Mao reviewed on August 18, he had returned home from Beijing just yesterday. Humming a song, he stuffed his army bag with his toothbrush, towels, clothing, and Mao's books. Tomorrow Ming would set off for Shaoshan in Hunan Province, Mao's birthplace, where the Red Guards would begin their Long Marches, traveling on foot to the remotest corners of the country and fanning the campaign to overthrow Mao's rival, President Liu Shaoqi, whom Mao had declared China's Khrushchev.

"Touch my hand one last time for good luck's sake," he said, offering his right hand.

That hand was tinged with good fortune, because Chairman Mao had shaken it when the Great Leader had mingled with the Red Guards in Tiananmen Square. Waving Mao's *Quotations,* Ming had jumped until his legs cramped, shouted until his throat bled, and cried until he had no tears to shed. Ever since, he had refused to wash his hand. The palm was already discolored, and dirt and grease filled its tiny wrinkles.

Dinnertime was always noisy: broad knives chopping on the cutting boards, metal pots and utensils clanging against each other, the radio playing revolutionary songs. It was an evening like other evenings, full of life. Mother had prepared light summer dishes: cucumber strips, green onion and tofu, and a pot of cooling green-bean soup. My younger brother, eleven-year-old Jie, and I scurried about, setting the table and arranging chairs. When he came into the dining room, Ming brought the electric fan and placed it on a shelf next to him. The colorful official portrait of Chairman Mao fluttered on the wall in the hot wind. As usual, Father began to make conversation at the dinner table.

No sooner had I swallowed a mouthful of food than the sharp, screeching sound of automobiles braking interrupted our meal. Footsteps thundered outside our apartment, and an earthquake of pounding and kicking rattled the door. Dishes and spoons trembled on the table. The head of the moving fan suddenly changed direction. The chopsticks dropped from Mother's hand. Father's eyes opened wide, and his face went ashen.

"I knew it would happen," he said to himself.

Hastily putting on a shirt, he walked toward the door, then froze halfway down the corridor, staring ahead vacantly.

"What's going on?" I asked Ming, shaking his arm in a panic.

He sputtered, breathing heavily through his open mouth. He jumped up and went to the window, and I followed. In the center of the courtyard, four strong headlights illuminated the pavement. We could see groups of young students in army uniforms running in all directions.

"It must be a Red Guard house search," Ming murmured in a broken voice.

The chill of fear gripped me. These days house searches were rampant in the city. Just last week the Red Guards had whipped to death an old landlady whose house stood at the edge of our residential area. But so far, all the targets of the Revolution had been former landlords, rich peasants, counterrevolutionaries, rightists, and capitalists — the party's historical enemies. My parents were veteran party members. How had the Revolution come to our door?

When angry voices threatened to break down the door, Father's trembling hand finally managed to turn the handle. Suddenly our home was filled with young Red Guards. They grabbed my parents and shoved them into the living room, forcing them down on their knees to face the east and repent to Chairman Mao. An enormous brush moved back and forth, painting their horrified faces with dripping black ink. Tall paper hats were set on their heads, sinking almost to their noses. These Red Guards belonged to Shanghai Hudong University, where father was the rector.

"Where do you keep your letters and diaries?" voices shouted.

Below the tall paper hat, Father's lips quivered, but the reply refused to come out. Instantly, a wide black belt was raised. CRACK! The whip struck Father's shoulder. CRACK, CRACK! It flashed up and down in the air, tearing away the paper cone on Father's head. The crisp sound was like a sharp knife penetrating my heart. The blood of rage rushed to my head. The Red Guard would whip Father to death. I remembered the old landlady who had vomited blood after the brutal beating, and, for a moment, I forgot that to resist the Red Guards was to resist Chairman Mao.

"Don't beat my father!" I yelled and shot like an arrow toward the young man holding the lash. The suddenness of the action surprised him; his arm fell to his side, the studded tip of the wide belt poised on the floor like the shining tail of a black snake. He stood there as though frightened, still as a piece of firewood. CRACK! As if coming from the ceiling, a lash struck my bare arm, leaving a thick welt. I raised my head. A tall girl with two goat-horn-like braids brandished a leather belt above me. My arm lost feeling and blood oozed, staining my skirt, yet my hands still clung tightly to the young man. Tears of pain blurred my eyes. In the mist I saw the girl cocking her arm again.

Mother jerked her head up and shouted from under the paper hat, "Don't worry about us! Leave the room right now!" Her pale lips trembled.

Within moments, my two brothers and I had been pushed into the narrow corridor. The wound continued oozing blood and irritated me. But I was glad that the beating had stopped.

Standing next to me, Ming panted like an old horse. His expression was a complicated mix of confusion, nervousness, and fear. Angry sparks also flickered in his dark eyes. His right hand held Jie firmly, while his left tightened into a fist, exposing blue veins. Ming's school bag still held several volumes of Chinese and English classics he had pocketed when he and his fellow Red Guard had raided his school library. They had burned thousands of books and sealed up the building, which had a venerable history of several hundred years. Just a few days ago, they had house-searched a capitalist and confiscated gold bricks and bars the man had hidden inside the walls. The informant was his own son, who in betraying his father hoped to win admission to the Red Guard organization. Ever since the beginning of the Revolution, sons and daughters had stood up to expose their parents, students beat their favorite teachers, best friends betrayed each other, and husbands and wives joined rival organizations and turned into deadly enemies. The Revolution, in its own unique way, excited and inspired men and women, old and young, all over the nation. This was what real revolution was all about, breaking down the old order and establishing a new world. People were convinced that a real revolution had to be an insurrection, an act of violence by which one class overthrows another. In Chairman Mao's words: "A revolution cannot be carried out in a gentle and civilized manner like hosting a dinner, writing an article, drawing pictures, or embroidering flowers."

In our home, the grave-looking Red Guards searched every corner, leaving nothing undisturbed. Their proud faces and spirited eyes revealed the thrill of newly gained power and independence.

"You son of a bitch!" Their voices thick, they yelled profanities to disguise their mild natures as courteous college students. They kicked at the doors and furniture and knocked down chairs. They glared at us, their postures as stiff as ramrods. Though their young faces revealed naïveté and childishness, these students, unlike the disorganized Red Guards on the streets, knew what they wanted. They were particularly interested in "ideological evidence": letters, personal notes, diaries, books. Anything disclosing my parents' ideological inclination and private thoughts was valuable to them.

In the chaos, our apartment became oppressive. The air seemed to be on fire. Scorching Tiger, as this weather was called, exhibited its full power. The wall behind me was hot, and the doors, chairs, tables, everything the hand touched, seemed to burn. We were soaked through with sweat from fear, anger, and worry, and the Red Guards too were drenched from their physical exertion and burning revolutionary zeal. When they had turned our home upside down, they continued their search in the bamboo-fenced front garden.

The creamy face of the building opposite shone a luminous sil-ver. The moon laid its frosty light on the plants and cast speckled cold shadows on the Red Guards, turning their faces light gray, like those of ghosts. Spades hacked aimlessly and pickaxes struck at random. Fist-sized toads jumped in fright. Disturbed insects hopped and flew for their lives. Heavy feet tore the lush plants and tramped them back into the soil. Hateful hands smashed the white and pink roses as the Red Guards dug down three feet deep to find "ideological evidence." Unsuccessful, they stormed back into the rooms and began ripping up the floors and battering the walls. New dust and old dust danced together under the lightbulbs, spreading like a cloud. Heavy breath-ing and the sounds of the pickaxes rose and fell.

As the frenzied wrecking went on, evening grew into night. Heat seemed to hiss in the air. Sweat stung the wound on my arm and dripped down to my fingertips. After declaring victory, most of the Red Guards left to assist with other house searches. Desks and chairs lay upside down. The small electric fan was dead on the floor. Landscape paintings in green and black had been torn to shreds. In front of my kneeling mother, a young man cut her wedding dress, embroidered with eight-cornered gold coins on purple satin, into pieces. He stamped on the satin strips as if crushing worms. Then he ordered Mother to get up and go with us children into the courtyard. Hands trembling, Mother removed the paper hat that was pressing on the bridge of her nose and drew herself up. She staggered but stead-ied herself quickly. Sweat cut many tiny ditches on her ink-darkened cheeks. Father raised his swollen face and attempted to stand up also, but a foot pressed him down hard.

2

Sword Out of the Scabbard

Bright stars, like shining eyes, blinked sharply in the dark sky. Silver moonlight sprayed evenly over the Chinese ivy twining with tiny purple and white flowers around the bamboo fences of household gardens. The trailing scent clung to the night air.

In the entrance to the Hudong University family housing, huge red flags surrounded a makeshift platform. Onstage the Red Guards were performing their famous Ardent Loyalty Dance, sweeping the enormous flags like hacking scythes from side to side. Other dancers placed their hands on their waists and jumped up and down like rabbits, stomping in unison with all their force and making a deafening sound. A cloud of dust rose under their hopping feet. Then all movement suddenly stopped. Bodies still, they gazed up to the sky, their faces solemn and eyes glistening. During the daytime they looked right at the red sun. In the evening they looked toward the North Star, which was said to be Chairman Mao guiding the Chinese people in the revolutionary direction.

Four Red Guards played a huge drum, drawing workers from outside the compound into the crowd. Climbing up and down the chain-link fence, clamorous youngsters took the chaos to be a holiday celebration.

Accompanied by the fast rhythm of the beating drums, Father and other school officials were brought onto the platform one by one. Two Red Guards twisted Father's arms behind his back and pressed his head down almost to his knees, forcing him to jog forward. This was the infamous "jet planing" torture. My eyes followed Father's distorted figure. My heart galloped in my throat. I held my breath tightly, my hands sticky with cold sweat.

The Capitalist Roaders, as they were called, nine men and one woman, "stood" in a row, their backs bowed at a ninety-degree angle so they could see only their feet and the ground in front of them. From their necks, the Red Guards hung two-foot-wide blackboards. As the biggest Capitalist Roader of the school, Father received a board bigger and heavier than the others. All of the school officials wore the yin-yang head, the newly shaved halves of their scalps glistening under the harsh light. Rings of flying moths and other night insects encircled the lamps, dazzling my eyes. The white bulbs reminded me of the merciless sun before it sank below the horizon. Long-horned grasshoppers hiding in the gardens raised such a racket that a new stream of sweat trickled down my forehead.

The hubbub stopped when General Ma, a slim young lecturer, stepped onto the platform. He was the commander of the Red Guards of the university and the mastermind behind tonight's sudden action. He was clad in a white shirt and green army pants. On his left arm he had pinned the conspicuous red armband with the prominent head of Chairman Mao.

General Ma raised his arms high in the air and shouted to the audience: "Tonight we have ended the rule of the Capitalist Roaders, the running dogs of Liu Shaoqi, China's Khrushchev. Our school will march along Chairman Mao's glorious revolutionary line to the final victory." His face was shiny with sweat when he finished. The drum sounded again; the hands and the red silk streamers on the drumsticks danced vigorously in the hot air.

The prearranged speakers began criticizing the school officials one by one, repeating the editorial in the *People's Daily:* "The capitalist class inside the party dreams every minute of restoring capitalism in our country and changing the color of the red flag. If this can be tolerated, what cannot?"

The purge of President Liu and government officials at various levels stemmed from personal reasons. In 1961, after Mao's disastrous Great Leap Forward movement caused the greatest famine in China's history, and about 40 million people starved to death, Liu Shaoqi assumed full responsibility for restoring China's collapsing economy. By implementing policies with greater profit incentive, he helped stabilize China's economy in just a few years and achieved significant growth. By 1965, one year before the Cultural Revolution, the country had climbed out of the deep valley of financial crisis. The satisfied public hung Liu's portrait side by side with that of Mao. Inside the Communist Party, Liu's reputation skyrocketed, and he was believed to be the right person to lead China. Liu's success angered and worried Mao. As people's lives were further improved, he grew more anxious. The conflict between Mao and Liu became both open strife and veiled struggle. One time, the weakened Mao said to Liu, "I am the chairman and you are the first deputy chairman. In nature there are unexpected storms and in life unpredictable vicissitudes. If I die, you won't know how to be the chairman. So it's better for me to hand over the power to you now and for you to learn how to be number one. My words don't carry weight in the country anymore." The embittered Mao finally found the opportunity for revenge in the Great Proletarian Cultural Revolution, for which he created the theory that inside the party there existed a bourgeois stronghold headed by Liu Shaoqi and a powerful capitalist line running from top to bottom. He knew this power struggle was life and death. The winner would be the king and the loser would go to meet Marx and Lenin.

While the speakers shouted themselves blue in the face, Father, who was half kneeling and half standing, shifted his feet frequently, his dangling hands swaying in front of his legs. His position made me afraid. Weighed down by the heavy board hanging on his neck, could he remain "standing" like this until the end of the meeting? How long would the meeting last? How many more speakers were after this one? I didn't care what they were talking about. I only wanted the meeting to be over soon so Father could stand erect again like a human being. With Father curled over on the stage, I felt guilty to be allowed to stand up straight. So I held myself as rigid as a tree, waiting, as if for a death sentence. My eyes never left Father for a second. Several times he tried to raise his back up a little but was quickly pressed down. Finally, unable to endure any more, he straightened his body, gasping for air, his ink-smudged face bloated and miserable. The Red Guard standing behind him immediately pounced on him and forced his head down to his knees, then yanked it up, then pressed it down and yanked it up again. The heavy board jumped up and down with the movement of Father's head. Fresh blood trickled from his nose and the corners of his mouth. Shaking with fright, I muted my cry by stuffing my mouth with a bloodstained handkerchief. Mother covered her blackened face with trembling hands. Ming and Jie hung their heads like hail-beaten crops.

The white moon in the starlit sky seemed to look down on us with indifference. Tree leaves never rustled once, and the air stood stubbornly still. The body heat radiating from the hundreds packed layer upon layer around the stage made breathing hard. Time froze. In this great stiffness, every minute passed like a year, and the loud harangues of the critics seemed to drag on into infinity. I closed my eyes tightly to shut out the scene. Then I heard a sudden thump. I opened them to see Father collapsed facedown on the stage. Some women in the crowd shrieked and little children in their mothers' arms wailed.

Several Red Guards quickly dragged Father behind the platform to the shadow of the enormous red flags that now hung spiritlessly in the heat. The criticism meeting resumed. The school officials bending over on the stage swayed like weeds moving in the storm. The boards dangling from their necks moved with them. The half-kneeling and half-standing posture they tried to maintain sapped their strength. But the Red Guards behind them kept on pressing their bodies down, slapping their faces savagely and warning them to be obedient. Sweat-soaked, their shirts clung to their skins. Perspiration dripped from their swollen faces. Then the woman official collapsed. She was quickly dragged offstage to the shadow of the red flags.

A pendulum clock struck unhurriedly: "Dong! Dong!" One time, two times. Then the sound rose from another, and another. Soon all the clocks inside and outside the compound echoed. One rose before the other fell. As if prodded by this chorus, the speakers finally shut their mouths. To the sounds of the last deafening slogans proclaiming the victory of Chairman Mao's revolutionary line, two Red Guards "escorted" my half-conscious father back to our apartment. Smeared with sweat, black ink, blood, and dirt, his face was almost unrecognizable.

It was late, almost midnight. Tires screeching, the automobiles carrying the Red Guards drove away. Lights were turned off one after another. Frightened people retired. The night finally resumed its usual quietness at this hour. Ming shouldered his army bag to leave. He would take the last bus back to his high school, located in southern Shanghai, and next day would join the Red Guards' Long Marches. Before he went, he stood in the corridor for a while, watching Father, who was groaning, then Mother, who sat in a chair like a clay figure. Ming's face was pained but stubborn. Maybe he had thought things through.

"I'm leaving," he said to me, handing me a piece of paper. "Give this note to Mother."

The first part of his letter was from either the *People's Daily* or *Red Flag* magazine: "This is a revolution unparalleled in human history. Navigating on the ocean, we depend on a helmsman. To make a revolution, we depend on Chairman Mao. We must hold high the great banner of Mao Zedong Thought and carry out the Cultural

Revolution to its end. This is the glorious mission that the people in China and the world give to us Red Guards."

Then Ming wrote in smaller characters: "My loyalty to Chairman Mao is primary. Everyone must make a personal sacrifice for the revolution. But to break with one's parents is difficult. I cannot turn the spearhead around to strike my family."

The door closed behind Ming, and with determined steps he walked across the porch. After that night, he seldom returned home.

3

Holy Months

The sun flared down and baked the asphalt roads into soft cakes. But hotter than the sun was the fervor of the ongoing Revolution.

In the following week, Father's love letter to his beautiful assistant was copied on full-sized posters and pasted all over, from the campus of Shanghai Hudong University to the fence of the family housing compound, and even on the door of our home. The Red Guards' surprise house search had indeed proved fruitful. At the bottom of Father's desk drawer they found a piece of "ideological evidence." The first two lines of the love letter, "Marxism is metaphysics; thou are my paramountcy," became the subject of household gossip and a children's chant. The words rang in my ears all day long. Father's secret love had shocked everyone in the family. Mother ate little for days. I felt deeply ashamed, and my cheeks burned whenever I met mocking eyes and pointing fingers, as if I were the one who wrote the love poem. I knew from people's angry looks that they hated me for my father's crime. Other children scorned my younger brother, Jie, abusing him like a stray dog.

In our neighborhood, General Ma staged frequent public humiliations in order to destroy Father's reputation and force him to confess that he was a Kuomintang spy and a shameful traitor like Liu Shaoqi.

Winds swept away the last threads of cloud, and the sky looked like a huge mirror, shimmering white. Father was kneeling on glass shards that sparkled like multicolored jewels in the bright sunlight. Our neighbors formed a dense circle around him under the naked sun, protecting their heads with newspapers and folding fans. Bare-headed and barefoot children ran about laughing, adding their chaotic energy to the scene. One heroic Red Guard, tired of beating Father with his hands, simply removed one of his cloth shoes and whipped Father's cheeks, battering him about the face and neck until they were black and blue. The shoe's sole must have come loose, and the nails cut into Father's face. Noise swirled from the crowd. I rested my head on Mother's arm.

"You have abandoned Marxism and Mao Zedong Thought, by falling on your knees before a woman's garnet skirt. You have betrayed your own wife because she is yellow-faced."

Under the scorching scrutiny of our neighbors, Mother kept her eyes glued to the ground, her hands stiffly folding and unfolding the corners of her brown jacket. Her face flushed and turned pale by turns. During the meeting she never raised her head once. She dared not look at the others. For a woman, any woman, there was nothing more humiliating than this. A lock of hair slipped from her smooth forehead and covered her sad-looking eyes. Mother nervously pushed it back. She was not a yellow-faced woman. Her skin was tight. She was only thirty-nine and still pretty, with two slim eyes, a delicate nose, and even lips. I wondered why Father craved another woman. Had he forgotten that this was a moral offense that could elicit the severest punishment? When he wrote the love letter to the young woman, had he been prepared for today? Father's wounded face jerked with pain. Although I felt sorry for him, his behavior disgusted me. I grasped the hand of my shamefaced mother: it felt clammy. Her fingers were rigid like five iron sticks. I couldn't tell at that moment whether she pitied Father or wanted the Red Guards to beat him to death. Father raised his yin-yang head stubbornly, his eyes smoldering.

"You don't look like you're repenting!" the Red Guard shouted angrily. Looking around, he picked up a rock from under an elm tree and, closing his eyes, took a deep breath to gather strength. Then he aimed at Father and threw it at his head. Blood spurted out of the fresh wound above Father's eyes, running down his face in rivulets. Still he refused to lower his head, and instead laughed at the cloudless sky as if asking why. The crowd stirred. Some applauded the Red Guard, while others yelled, "He deserves more. He deserves more!"

Encouraged by the clamor, several more Red Guards joined in. They rolled up their sleeves and rubbed their hands. Pushing Father to the glass-covered ground, they kicked and dragged his bloody body until he passed out.

Mother lost her composure and cried out fiercely. Jie fidgeted as if wanting to rush to Father's aid, but Mother held him back. My stomach churned. Fear crushed me.

That night, nightmares plagued me one after the other. I saw rods flashing above my head and blood flowing like rivers, crimson everywhere. I stepped back. Behind me was a cliff. I screamed in horror as I fell.

"Don't be afraid, Mother is here." Mother sat at my bedside, her warm hand smoothing my forehead. Her delicate eyes carried deep sorrow and pain, and her voice was thick. I buried my head in her lap, crying hysterically, my body shaking as I gasped for air. Mother gently stroked my back for a while. Then she stood up and opened a desk drawer. She gave me a small white pill, a tranquilizer, and I slept.

August, September, October, and November 1966 were glorified by the state propaganda as holy months. The flaming red leaves of maple trees on Beijing's Western Hill danced in the sky. The capital was again filled with a holiday atmosphere. Colorful balloons floated in the air. Glowing with health and radiating vigor, Chairman Mao appeared altogether eight times on the rostrum of Tiananmen and received more than ten million Red Guards from all over the country. The sky echoed with deafening cheers. And Chairman Mao's powerful words shook the land of China.

Following each of Chairman Mao's massive reviews during the holy months, Father was beaten. When the blood-colored sun hung in the middle of the blue sky, Liu Shaoqi and Deng Xiaoping, the Communist Party's general secretary and Liu's close ally, as well as many other government officials, were purged. The struggle was also extended to well-known artists, writers, scholars, actors, and actresses. On August 24, Lao She, the renowned author of the novel *Tea House,* drowned himself in a lake in Beijing. On September 3, the famous writer and translator Fu Lei and his wife gassed themselves to death in their Shanghai home. While red flags flew everywhere in the country, the prominent historian Wu Han, the pianist Gu Shangying, the actress Jiang Huizhu, and many others chose death.

The October wind stirred the yellow dirt, loosening and mixing it with the gray dust on the streets. Wind devils swirled the fallen leaves and tossed them willy-nilly, on roofs, in street corners, between fences. Before the latest wounds had fully healed, Father was ordered to take a huge bamboo broom in hand and clean the neighborhood streets every morning. He wore a ragged blue coat and wide-legged trousers with big patches on the knees. He was forbidden to wear a hat, so that everyone could see his yin-yang head. During the busy morning hours Father's eyes were dull and fixed, his head bent almost to his chest as he swept the sidewalks like a faceless specter. He did not want to be seen. He wanted the world to forget about him. Regardless, he caught everyone's attention. People detoured to pass near him, amused by his clownlike appearance. His yin-yang head was a wordless reminder that he was an enemy, the "stinking dog's dung."

Abuse quickly replaced curiosity, for Father was vulnerable. Men sneered at him, cuffing and kicking him. But he didn't stop thinking. He began to rise before dawn, when there was less traffic. Every morning I was awakened by his movements, even though he tried to be quiet. As I listened to the careful scraping sounds of sweeping outside the window, I tossed and turned as though I were resting on a bed of nails. Teardrops wet the pillow under my head as new worries preoccupied me. Would Father be safe down there? Would the early risers beat him still? I saw a silhouette standing in front of the window, peering into the gray dawn. It was Mother.

4

A Song of Loyalty

We found that General Ma's shadow followed us even into the privacy of our home. He knew everything we did. He knew that in our almost empty house Mother still had a lipstick in the desk drawer. He knew that sometimes Jie and I read hand-copied novels rather than Mao's writings, or played games with homemade chessmen and cards. Father often sat in his chair with one leg crossed on top of the other, drinking tea. Our family liked to talk at the dinner table. All of these trivial things would serve as the basis for fresh accusations against Father and bring him new troubles. General Ma was also aware that Father drank milk for breakfast. Since milk represented the Western bourgeois lifestyle, our supply was soon stopped.

Had General Ma planted a bug in our home during the house search? We scoured the rooms from the ceiling to the floor, from the holes in the walls to the cracks in the hardwood boards, but found nothing. If there were no listening devices, how did General Ma obtain his information? During this time, all of our neighbors and old friends avoided our family like death. In the past, when Father was powerful, ours was a much-visited house, and the courtyard was as crowded as a marketplace. But now visitors were so few that one could spread nets and catch sparrows on the doorstep. Since almost everyone avoided us, suspicion naturally fell on Ni, a young lecturer who lived a few doors away and was the only person who still visited us on a regular basis. The second day after the Red Guards' action,

Ni had brought over two big bowls of dumplings and watched until we ate them all.

One night, Ni came to collect the water fee. While she was chatting with us in her usual manner, her apricot-shaped eyes observed us carefully. For the first time I felt that behind her soft smiles lay something sharp. Father nonchalantly picked up a kettle and began watering the potted flowers in the corners of the rooms. As was his habit, he plucked the dead leaves, smoothed the good ones as if caressing them, and loosened the soil around the roots. The chrysanthemums were in full bloom, each golden petal competing for attention. Ni's gaze lingered on the flowers, her mouth half open in delight.

Soon, in front of the university canteen a new denunciation was posted, asking every revolutionary this very serious question: "How, under the iron fists of the proletarian dictatorship, can the Capitalist Roaders still have the heart to nurture their bourgeois attitude by taking pleasure in flowers instead of thoroughly confessing their crimes and repenting to Chairman Mao? Are we too soft on our enemies?"

The punishment came down hard after this, but Father learned his lesson. Whenever someone was at the door, he became "sick." He stopped whatever he was doing, put on a huge gauze mask, and hopped into bed, groaning miserably under his quilt. Ni never saw him out of bed again in our home.

The autumn rain continued falling, until the ground was sodden. One day General Ma himself visited our apartment. He came in broad daylight, when both of my parents were away. Without being invited, he took a seat beside the table. He reached into a pocket and took out a piece of paper, which he waved in front of me, saying that his thorough investigation had provided ample evidence that my father was a genuine traitor and Kuomintang spy.

General Ma cleared his throat three times before he went on:

"Today Chairman Mao asks us to overthrow Capitalist Roaders like your father. You must expose him and prove your loyalty to the great leader. There is no other way to test your heart." Ma observed me, his eyes piercing my chest.

So they'd proved at last that Father was a real traitor and spy! In my mind flashed the image of such an enemy — three-cornered eyes, thick jowls, trembling legs, a short neck like a tree stump.

No, my father doesn't look like that at all.

"He doesn't look like one, but he is one. Liu Shaoqi is the country's biggest traitor, and your father is a small traitor. Big wolf and small wolf, they are all wolves. Big Roaders and small Roaders, they are all Capitalist Roaders. Now, think carefully whether your father has ever said anything against our present situation. Think slowly and clearly." His eyes dug into me, demanding to know.

I knew this was a critical moment for me to show my loyalty to Chairman Mao, so I searched hard for anything suspicious I might know about Father. But my mind was as blank as a piece of white paper. I remembered nothing and could tell nothing.

General Ma looked disappointed. The corners of his mouth drooped. "Did he ever say anything against our great leader Chairman Mao?"

Did Father hate Chairman Mao? No! When the Cultural Revolution began, it was Father who removed Liu Shaoqi's portraits, leaving only those of Mao on the walls.

I shook my head vehemently.

"Has he ever bad-mouthed the Red Guards and our revolutionary action against your family?"

I remembered Father's pained face when the shoe nails cut into his flesh. But once, when Ming asked Father how he liked Ming's red armband, Father praised it and said it was the best one he had ever seen. The reason? Because the Red Guard characters were so big and showy.

Again, I shook my head.

"Then do you know if he hates the Cultural Revolution?"

Ever since the Revolution had begun in May, Father had carefully followed every step of its development. He read the *People's Daily* and listened to the Central Broadcasting Station with great attention. Having survived the horrible holy months, Father seemed to have accepted the fact that he was a Capitalist Roader who had committed serious crimes against our socialist country and our great leader Chairman Mao.

Silence.

General Ma stood up and stamped his muddy feet on the floor as if to warm them up. "All the evidence has proved that he's a traitor and a spy. You must draw a line between yourself and your father. Now is the time to show whether you're loyal to Chairman Mao or not," he warned before he slammed the door behind him.

I stood transfixed. The world had suddenly turned dark. Those words left me in serious doubt about Father's real identity. I didn't want to believe that he was a spy. But then I couldn't believe the Red Guard commander would just slander him for no reason at all. Maybe when Father betrayed the revolution, I hadn't been born yet. How did I know that he wasn't really a traitor? A feeling of contempt grew in my heart. General Ma was right. If our great leader asked me to place righteousness above family loyalty, then I should do it. I should do it because everybody else did it, because the whole country did it. Actually, it was the fashion to betray one's parents.

That evening, when Father came home, he shambled into the room, and his face looked drawn. He seemed more drained than usual. It must have been a long day of struggle. Yet my burning desire to find out the truth overcame any feelings of sympathy.

"Are you a spy?" I asked him sternly, not even giving him a chance to take a breath. I stared at him intently, like a cat peering at a mouse.

"What is wrong with you today?" he asked distractedly as he sat down at the dinner table, his eyes narrowing.

How pretentious he was! All enemies knew how to disguise themselves.

"Did you ever betray the revolutionary cause?" I questioned.

Surprised, my exhausted-looking father put down the bowl he had just picked up, his face flushed with anger and insult. He stood up and paced back and forth in the room with both hands clasped behind him. As if talking to himself, he wondered aloud how the interrogations had come to the dinner table in his own home and why the interrogator was his little girl.

When he finally calmed down, he stopped pacing. "Are these questions for a young child to ask?"

"Of course! General Ma said that the other children in the compound have all stood up to expose their parents. We also should make a revolution."

Father sighed deeply, and rubbed his face vigorously with both hands.

"Do you believe that I'm a traitor?" His voice cracked. He looked at me gravely, his eyes betraying unspoken feelings that I did not quite understand.

Father sat down again at the table, picking up his bowl. But he hadn't answered my question yet. I stepped forward and snatched it away from him.

Father's trembling hand slapped me on the face. A clear and loud sound. His hand was heavy. My ears buzzed. I covered my face and stepped back.

"Who are you? How do I know that you're not Chairman Mao's enemy?" I heard myself shouting, tears running down my hot cheeks. Another slap on my face. Blood oozed from my mouth. The room began to spin.

Mother rushed into the room and shielded me from Father's fist with her own body.

"Stop!" she shrieked at Father. "She is only a child. She doesn't understand."

Father narrowed his eyes, looking at me as if seeing a stranger.

Outside, it began to rain again. Impatient raindrops whipped the leaves on the tree branches, which quivered in the strong wind. Each October rainstorm chilled the air and slowly tamed the Scorching Tiger. It was well past dinnertime, but no one wanted to eat. The food sat cold on the table. Father wiped the blood from my chin with a towel. Under the yellow light, he and I sat near the window. His face was gloomy in the shadow, but his exhausted eyes glowed with excitement. In a wavering voice, Father began telling me the story of himself, the youngest son of a successful entrepreneur.

His father had operated several businesses in czarist Russia. The October Revolution of 1917 took away his entire assets, but he survived, escaping the country with several trunks of worthless imperial rubles. Ever after, the businessman guarded his rubles jealously and fantasized that the Soviet Union would give way to the old czarist days again and he would regain his lost paradise. His dream never came true, and he died bitter with resentment.

While studying at a university in Beijing, Father came to believe in the ideals of a communist society, in which everyone is equal and lives by the principle "from each according to his ability, to each according to his needs." He was outraged to see people freezing to death on the streets while meat and wine went to waste behind the vermilion gates of the rich under the Kuomintang regime. Father believed that China should model itself after the Soviet Union. Only in such a society could the people become masters of the country. Shortly thereafter, the Japanese occupied Beijing and the campus was no longer safe. The Chinese refused to be slaves of a foreign power; the resistance against Japan sprang up and never stopped for a day. Under the hammer and sickle of the party's flag, Father pledged that he would devote all his life to the communist cause and the realization of a classless society. From that moment on, he was a member of the party's underground movement in Beijing. This secret organization was directly under the leadership of Liu Shaoqi.

At the mention of Liu Shaoqi's name, Father paused. A cloud passed over his face. His eyes looked sad, and the crow's feet wrinkles around them deepened. Maybe he felt pity for the man, who had been brutally beaten and imprisoned soon after Chairman Mao's massive rallies of the Red Guards. In jail, Liu was not allowed to shave or groom himself, and his unkempt beard and hair grew long and made him appear almost like a wild animal. Father didn't know then that only three years later, in 1969, Liu Shaoqi would die in a prison in Kaifeng, Henan Province, after being refused treatment for diabetes and bearing unspeakable suffering. In 1966, following Liu's tragic downfall, government officials at all levels were tortured, exiled, jailed, and even murdered.

Father became restless. He stood up and, with his head lowered, began to pace urgently back and forth, his hands swinging at his sides. The uneven hair of his yin-yang head stood on end. Anger mixed with grief in his eyes. After a long while, Father slowed down. His facial muscles relaxed as calm returned.

"It was a belief, nothing but a noble belief, that an equal society would come into being, and communism would eventually prevail in the world," Father said fervently.

Outside the window, lightning flashed across the sky and thunder rumbled. Father continued his story. In 1949 the Chinese Communist Party launched the Land Reform Movement in his home province of Shandong. Land was confiscated from the landlords and rich peasants and redistributed among the poor. Father, already a diehard communist by then, made a special trip from Beijing to his hometown and helped give away his family assets to the poor villagers, leaving his own mother and sisters with nothing to live on.

"Now do you trust me that I'm a real communist, without personal interest?" Father asked, opening wide his tired, bloodshot eyes.

"You must be careful. Don't let yourself be used by others as a gun to shoot me."

The room was quiet except for the sound of the gently subsiding rain.

"You really are a traitor, not to the revolution but to your own landlord family," I said to Father, secretly rejoicing. He wasn't a traitor or a spy but still my good father. My knitted brows relaxed. That night, a big weight was removed from my chest.

5

The Dog's Son and Daughter

The year 1967 brought bitter weather to Shanghai. The cold northwest wind howled and sleet filled the streets with a treacherous layer of thin ice. Not long after the sound of firecrackers greeted the New Year, the city shook again with change. On January 3, the day was overcast. The turbid waves of the Huangpu River rolled uneasily. The Red Guards and industrial workers joined forces, arming themselves with safety helmets and iron bars. Together they seized by force the press buildings of *Wenhui Bao* and *Jiefang Ribao (Liberation Daily)*, the two biggest newspapers in Shanghai, replacing the staff with pro-Mao personnel.

On January 6, when the city was still enveloped in morning frost, the Red Guards and industrial workers closed all the major thoroughfares into the city. Wang Hongwen, a union leader and a member of the Gang of Four led by Mao's wife, Jiang Qing, held a rally of one million people in People's Square, during which he urged the Shanghai industrial workers to wrest all power from the municipal government. Like the whirling flows of the Huangpu River, the rebels stormed City Hall. The two virile brass lions guarding the building were knocked over. Amid deafening cheers, an enormous red flag was raised. Factory sirens resounded in the air above the river, hailing the glorious victory. A new regime, the Shanghai Revolutionary Committee of Chairman Mao, replaced the Liu-appointed municipal government. Mayor Cao Diqiu was placed on top of an ambulance and paraded all over the city. His silver hair flew in the freezing wind, and his words "I am not guilty" chilled the hearts of millions.

The Cultural Revolution gained momentum. Throughout the country, the notorious Shanghai January Red Storm moved the Revolution to a new stage, seizing power from Liu Shaoqi's government officials at all levels. Guided by Chairman Mao, the power struggle began at the grass-roots level in schools, hospitals, and factories and surged all the way up to municipal and provincial governments, and eventually to the core of the Chinese Communist Party. Millions participated. Tides rose; tides fell. Wind gathered; wind scattered. Shanghai mourned with the Huangpu River. The country sank into a deeper turmoil.

A cold wind drove most pedestrians from usually busy streets. Trees shivered. A fire engine's loud siren pierced the icy air. Disturbed from sleep, night-shift workers stuck their heads out the windows, like turtles emerging from their shells. Youngsters found a wonderful source of amusement as the glossy red fire truck threaded its way through the neighborhood and stopped in front of our apartment building.

Watching through the curtained window, I was stunned. Roped to the extended sky-ladder was a middle-aged man in a blue overcoat, his eyes half closed, his face pale and expressionless. Beneath his feet I saw Mother, secured to the ladder rungs with several leather belts. She clenched her teeth as if enduring great pain. Her lips were dark purple, and the corners trembled. Disgrace made her face miserable, and her disheveled hair blew in the bitter wind. Behind Mother fluttered an enormous red banner that read: RED GUARDS OF THE TRANSPORTATION ACADEMY. A group of warmly clad teenagers stood by the fire engine, their cheeks flushed.

The scene was so fantastic I thought I must be hallucinating. I rubbed my eyes and looked again. Mother blinked nervously. She was surely alive but suffering. I rushed frantically out the door to the front of our building, thinking I must save her somehow. But I stumbled and fell, and before I could get up and turn the corner, the motor started and the heartrending siren blared again. The fire engine pulled away, leaving a small crowd behind.

I leaned against the trunk of a leafless elm tree, letting the bitter wind bite me. A group of Red Guards who had been deposited by the fire engine were now painting a slogan on the sidewalk: "Down with An Hong, the Evil Hand behind the antirevolutionary current in our school!"

Seeing Mother's name, I became even more frightened. Each character they painted was as big as a man, and the entire slogan required a long stretch of concrete. The Red Guards intended for thousands of passing pedestrians to trample her name each day. Mother was only an ordinary school administrator carrying out routine duties. What wrong had she done to trigger this deep hatred? Until that morning when she left for work, no one had criticized her.

Mechanically I followed the Red Guards and watched as they hung a poster in large characters on our door. They pasted two long strips of paper across each of our windows to seal them. The neighborhood children helped out, handing brushes to the Red Guards and carrying the paste buckets.

My eyes flowed with tears. Was this going to be Mother's road to death? When living without human dignity became intolerable, desperate people sought an escape. Every day they jumped from tall buildings, lay under passing trains, or plunged into the ever-running Huangpu River. On the ferry ride between east and west Shanghai, I often saw bloated bodies floating on the surface of the muddy water and half-naked corpses tied behind the special city vessels that roamed the river in search of them. Death became so common that I saw it and heard about it almost every day.

By evening, Mother still hadn't returned home. The Red Guards told me that she was detained at her school and wouldn't be allowed to leave. Father hadn't come home either. He had been confined in the "cowshed" at Hudong University — a detention center for Capitalist Roaders — to receive additional criticism. Jie and I ate some leftovers and went to bed early. Listening to the sound of conversations through windows, I couldn't sleep. Fear and loneliness gripped me. I worried about the future we had to face in this hostile neighborhood. I even grew angry with my parents. Father had already disgraced our family and brought trouble upon us, and now it seemed so had Mother. In only a few months, the Red Guards had taken numerous actions against our family; we were the most notorious in this residential area. I knew that once the night was over, the neighborhood children would come back to torment us. Our survival would be even harder from tomorrow on.

The next evening, Mother returned home unexpectedly to collect some belongings and a change of clothes. In just one day, the ordeal had transformed her into a completely different person. She looked ghostly pale. Her cheeks were sunken and her eyes lifeless. Her once lustrous black hair had changed into unkempt gray threads overnight. She was no longer the quick-witted woman she had been, but instead appeared wooden and slow. Under the lamplight she sat and stared at the ceiling, drawing deep sighs.

"Am I the Evil Hand? Am I a counterrevolutionary?" she murmured. Then she became silent, losing herself in thought.

Mother came from the family of a Kuomintang army officer. At age sixteen she had run away from home and crossed mountains and rivers to search for the believers in communism. At the party's base in northern China, Mother met and married Father, who was attending the North China United University, an educational institution run by the party to train its officials during the wars against Japan and the Kuomintang. Now, after twenty-three years of loyal service, Mother wondered how she had become her party's enemy.

The next morning, she rose early. In the twilight she left with a small bag of clothes to catch the first morning bus. I watched as she moved slowly out the door. Now we were real orphans, without parents and without our elder brother, who hadn't returned since last August. I buried my head under the quilt and cried bitterly.

Because the schools had been shut down when the Revolution began, children had little to do and wandered the streets in gangs all day long, looking for ways to while away the time. When the Red Guards first began their actions, they had torn down the fence that separated Hudong University's family housing compound from the huge neighborhood of shabby apartment buildings beyond. We became easy targets for the children of the workers of the Shanghai Shipyards, Shanghai Steelworks, and other industrial facilities, who learned to hate us as Chairman Mao's enemies.

Now, with my parents gone, the children grew bold. They pounded and kicked the door of our ground-floor apartment at will. The vibrations were so strong that objects on the table jumped. At first, Jie and I thought that the Red Guards had come back, and we shook with fear.

When we became used to the daily harassment, the children grew more aggressive. They threw their shoulders against the door and tried to break it open. They launched frenzied attacks on the bamboo fence that surrounded our front yard, like soldiers charging the enemy's fort. They whistled and called out, and climbed nimbly to the top. Perched on this command post, they made machine guns with their bony hands and imitated the sounds of shooting. They threw rocks at the windows, cheering each time the "hand gre-nades" exploded on target. Less adventurous children stood below the fence, passing "ammunition" and "weapons" while shouting their support.

The shattered window glass splashed into the rooms, sending sharp-edged pieces onto the beds, the desks, and the chairs. The youngsters' ferocious taunts and threats terrified us. We hid in a small, windowless room in the back, trying not to provoke them with signs of our presence.

While both of my parents struggled as captives in their respective schools, I had to shoulder responsibility for the family. I had to mature faster to take care of Jie and myself. Father's salary had been completely stopped. I was forced to make ends meet with only Mother's, which paid mostly for my parents' food in their detention centers and my elder brother Ming's separate living expenses. The government had stopped subsidizing the Red Guards once Mao's reviews of them and their Long Marches were over, although it still supported their political activities. Jie and I had to survive on the little that was left over.

In the mornings and afternoons, I would pick up vegetable leaves from behind or under the stalls in the neighborhood market. I purchased the cheapest meat available, such as pig's heads and necks, which the citizens of Shanghai loathed. I learned to set aside my girl's shyness and adolescent pride and often begged the butcher for any scraps left over when he cleaned off the meat counter. My scavenging continued, day in and day out. Soon many of the women working in the market came to know me.

"Little Sister! Where is your mother? Why doesn't she come herself?"

"She is very sick," I answered, lowering my eyelids. Whenever people asked about Mother, tears would well up. Not only did other people see us as orphans, but that was how we felt.

A woman who wore a brown apron was particularly nice to me. While she was selling vegetables, she would often pull me to her side and rub my red cheeks and ears. "You're going to get frostbite," she'd say, blowing her warm breath on my frozen hands while caressing them with her own. She removed from her pocket a small jar of cream and applied it with her fingertips to my cheeks. Sometimes she would purposely drop good, choice vegetables for me to pick up. She'd let me know of any "special sale" offered only to market employees and would often reserve bargains for me. I couldn't afford to be lazy. I had to get food, no matter how far the store was and how long the line or how heavy the groceries for me to carry home. The hungry days we had experienced during China's greatest famine, from 1959 to 1961, were too horrible to relive.

As the Revolution continued, the children intensified their abuse. They took over the spacious front porch of our building, which was larger than many of their homes, and turned it into another command post. They stationed themselves there all day long, leaving only for meals. They knocked down the porch door, broke the windows, and to kill time wrestled with each other while waiting for us to come out. During these grim weeks we became the center of their lives, the source of entertainment, and targets on which to release their boundless energy. Without us, they would have been bored to death.

When we left our apartment, packs of children, like wolves sensing prey, swarmed in from all directions and followed us wherever we went. "The dog's son! Dog's daughter!" they taunted. They hurled bricks, stones, eggshells, and cabbage roots and spat at us, wetting our hair and faces. They brandished fists and kicked ruthlessly whenever they saw the chance. Jie became very timid, never daring to raise his head and look at people. He hunched his little back, like a turtle ready to withdraw inside its shell. He always took a side street whenever he saw people coming in his direction. He yielded the way to everyone. Nevertheless, the gang of children felt compelled to hit Jie whenever they could. In pain and anguish, he would cry all the way home, bruises and welts covering his thin body, while the jeering children chased at his heels. He couldn't express his anger in words. He learned to endure the beatings silently, as if he didn't exist in this world, as if nothing was happening to him.

Our situation became less and less secure. Once, when Jie and I were walking on the main street running through the neighborhood, an iron bar was thrown at us from a nearby balcony. I felt the wind of it and quickly pulled Jie aside. The bar fell with a big thump near the spot where we had stood. I looked up angrily but saw nobody, only heard the malevolent laughter.

The Lunar New Year of 1967 arrived amid celebrations and fire-crackers. But for Jie and me, it was cheerless and lonely.

Immediately after the festivities, Mother's school notified me to bring her thick winter clothes; she was sick. I hastily packed a cotton-padded coat, some pants, and a thick sweater into a bag and took Jie with me. The sky was dusky, and lined with white strips of cloud here and there. Skinny sparrows twittered, flitting from one electric pole to another. A thin layer of ice covered the roads.

We were led into a class building. As in all other schools during the Cultural Revolution, the glass of the windows was broken and the doors were pockmarked with big and small holes. An intense shiver ran down my body. The double doors at both ends of the long hallway had been torn off and were propped in the corners against the wall. The north wind rushed hard into one end and out the other, freezing even the slightest dampness on the concrete floor. So this was the place where Mother had been held in solitary confinement over the past month!

Stopping in front of a classroom, the Red Guard shouted, "An Hong! Come out! Your children are here!"

The door opened, and Mother shuffled slowly from inside. In the dark hallway, her rumpled hair seemed grayer than ever. Her eyes appeared distant and unfocused. She wore only a thin sweater inside a blue jacket. Her face was ashen and her lips dark blue. She was trembling with cold.

Mother was so surprised to see us that her body jerked. We rushed to hug her, but she remained stiff, like a statue. She didn't smile. She didn't even stroke our heads as she usually would.

For a long while, we stood in silence. Then her face tensed and her expression changed abruptly; misery and humiliation sparked in her eyes. In the harshest voice I had ever heard from her, she ordered: "Go home! This is not a place where you should be. Never come here again! Never! Never!" She paused, then cried in a muffled tone, "Leave! Leave now! Hurry! Get out of here!"

Her expression was brutally cold, devoid of any sign of affection. It hurt me deeply. How could our loving mother reject us? Didn't she still love us? I wanted to cry. How fast solitary confinement had changed her. Many years later, I still couldn't forget the way she looked at us then.

We fled the building as fast as we could and sobbed all the way home. This visit cast a dark shadow on our hearts. I wondered if Mother would ever come back alive and well.

Misfortunes always come hand in hand. In the following weeks, the Hudong University Red Guards drove us out of our spacious apartment and moved our belongings into the compound's storage room on the fourth floor — a small two-room apartment with thick dust disturbed only by mice and scorpions. Layers of cobwebs hung in the corners. The smell of mold was overwhelming.

As if measuring the size of the room, General Ma paced back and forth and commented, "This place is still too luxurious for your family when three generations of a worker's family are squeezed into one room and a dozen families have to share one kitchen and one bathroom."

Then he said, as though issuing a challenge, "Listen! From now on, your home coal delivery will be discontinued because the coal storage workers shouldn't be serving the families of Capitalist Roaders."

I sighed. Although we had always been afraid to go out into the hostile neighborhood, now we had to cross it many more times to get our coal. If we'd had a choice, we would have gone another way. But there was only one route to the coal store.

It took an adult three round rips to get a two-hundred-pound load of coal. The third trip was to return the empty iron baskets and the thick bamboo pole. But for Jie and me, the same load would take five round-trips, since we couldn't carry as much as an adult. For the entire afternoon, we would be plodding back and forth on the main road. As the saying goes, "The load is always lighter on other people's shoulders." Before, I never paid attention to the coal delivery workers who carried the iron baskets and climbed the stairways with heavy steps. Now the load weighed a thousand tons on our tender shoulders. We clenched our teeth and moved slowly, taking a rest every few steps. Sometimes, to reduce the pain on the shoulders, we simply held the pole in our hands. Along the way, gangs of children would follow us and do all they could to entertain themselves. Adults made gestures, grimaced, and gossiped to each other: "Look at those two! They must come from a bad family. It serves them right, the dog's son and daughter!"

Such remarks from the parents incited more violence from our tormentors. It was at this point I realized that simply withdrawing would only make things worse. I, as the elder of the two, had to take a stand.

One afternoon, as Jie and I inched our way forward under the heavy load of coal, throngs of teenage boys rushed us from every direction. Their eyes glowed in anticipation of action. In the past I would have raised an arm to shield my head and pulled Jie away, as when the children threw rocks or kicked us. But this time I stopped and met them face to face, my eyes burning with rage.

"Enough is enough!" I heard myself yelling at a boy who was shaking his fist at Jie. Without knowing where I found the strength or courage, I pushed him away and continued shoving him with such ferocity that he fell to the ground. With my eyes closed, I kicked him until my leg weakened, then changed to the other leg and went on kicking. The feeling of revenge was sweet. At that moment, I was the brave petrel from the pen of Maksim Gorky, flying between the roaring sea and the heavy clouds, longing for a fight and shouting for victory.

Overpowered by my unexpected resistance, the boy, who was taller than I, crawled away helplessly, grimacing with pain. The once truculent youngsters drew back. They looked at each other in bafflement. I seized the bamboo pole from the coal buckets and swung it hysterically. I must have gone berserk, like the soldier who can't stop killing in a bloody battle. The terrified boys fled. I chased after them, shouting in triumph, "If you dare touch us one more time, I will beat you all to death!"

The Cultural Revolution continued full steam ahead, sending the class enemies fleeing helter-skelter. Revolutionary songs punctuated the air. More and more of Mao's enemies were caught and punished. After inspecting south and north of the Yangtze River, the Great Helmsman himself said excitedly that the broad masses of people had been fully mobilized and the revolutionary situation was not only good but very good. Our victory was not only big, but very big. He encouraged the people all over the country to safeguard the revolutionary fruit and carry the Revolution to the very end.

When spring filled the air with warmth, I had no time for adolescent dreams. While other children played and laughed, I searched along the roadsides for wild plants that I could cook with rice to increase its bulk. I sought out plants with plain leaves and avoided the ones with frosty and bright foliage, which were signs of poison. I also hunted fat cabbage roots in the trash cans and cooked them on the coal stove. The indescribably awful smell would fill the rooms and upset our stomachs. Although a great hunger suppressant, the roots were difficult to digest and caused diarrhea and dropsy. In the evenings, when it was safest for us to go outside, Jie and I broke off branches of elm trees and ate the sweet new buds as if they were fresh fruit.

I would often follow a group of working-class housewives to a mountain of waste behind a nearby factory. With a U-shaped wire, I would dig out hazelnut-sized lumps of coal buried in the deep gray ash. I would return home coated with dust but happy to see a weak blue flame burning slowly in the coal stove and the cooking pot singing a soft song that, to my ears, praised my labor. With coal and food, Jie and I wouldn't need to linger on the streets, where hungry, dirty children from politically ostracized families usually drifted.

In July 1967 the Yangtze River glistened under the summer sun, flowing like a silver snake. Heartened by the excellent progress of the Great Cultural Revolution, Chairman Mao went swimming. In a buoyant mood, he breasted the risky water as easily as if he were walking leisurely in his Zhongnanhai Palace, setting a brilliant example for the country's young generation to fight on in the wind and the waves until the final victory.

Just days later, the setting sun painted the western sky. The clatter of wooden slippers filled the glowing neighborhood streets as residents filed out of their crowded homes. Scantily clad men and women fanned themselves zealously with big banana-leaf fans and smoked cheap cigarettes. Kids, their necks white with baby powder, chased one another through the throngs. Peddlers rapped loudly on the sides of the wooden boxes they carried on their shoulders, hawking tempting red-bean popsicles.

Heavy footsteps ascended the stairway and stopped in front of our door. Then came gentle taps, as if the knocker were afraid to frighten us. I listened, my heart pounding. I detected love, motherly love.

I ran to the door. Mother smiled at me, her eyes glistening. She was carrying bags of clothes. We stood there speechless. Then, as if awakened, I jumped to her and clasped my hands around her neck, laughing through tears. I hugged and touched her again and again to make sure that her arrival was real.

Solitary detention for six months had transformed Mother into a real "yellow-faced woman." She looked far older than her age. During her confinement, the obsessive, horribly crippling thoughts that had besieged her had developed into a mental disorder. Sadness and misery furrowed her face with wrinkles, both shallow and deep. Nevertheless, Mother had returned home alive. She survived the cruelest months of the Cultural Revolution when many others trapped in similar situations did not. This alone was enough for us to hang colorful lanterns in celebration.

6

The Death of Civilization

The sun and the moon shuttled back and forth. By late 1967 the Cultural Revolution completed its first year, and still there was no sign of an end. Schools across the nation remained closed, and children continued to hang out on the streets.

When the Revolution first started in 1966, our teachers had tried their best to keep the elementary school going despite the chaotic situation in the outside world. In a hoarse voice, my Chinese language teacher recited a Tang poem of a thousand years ago:

> Bright moonlight sprays before my bed,
> And I take it to be frost on the ground.
> Raising my head, I look at the moon;
> Bowing down, I think of my hometown.

Meanwhile, Chairman Mao's words, "There is no fault in making revolution! It is right to rebel!" rang out from the high-pitched loudspeakers in and around our school.

"Two yellow orioles sing in the green willow tree, and a line of white cranes flies toward the blue sky." The teacher's voice was drowned out in the Red Guards' ardent recitation of a poem by Chairman Mao:

> Wind and smoke rolling from the sky
> Awakening the workers and peasants by the millions,

We are of one heart.
At the base of Mount Buchou
Red flags dancing in riotous revelry.

Outside was a new world of revolution. The loudspeakers shouted all day long: "Capitalism and revisionism are threatening our country. China is in danger. Chairman Mao is in danger. All the young people must stand up to protect our socialist country and our great leader."

A white-hot heat burned inside me. How could I look on with folded arms? Although I was only thirteen in 1966, I felt I had to participate in the great revolution. I looked impatiently at my Chinese teacher. His silver hair represented tradition; his dry voice sounded like a monk's, insipid and boring. The young and dynamic voices of the Red Guards thrilled me, and I could no longer sit there like a "bourgeois lamb." I wanted to be a "revolutionary tiger."

But our teachers were stubborn. Every morning they showed up in the classroom before the bell rang. Their determined faces told us that they were not going to stop trying to teach us. We shouted that all teachers should be swept away from the classroom with the iron brooms of revolution. We banged on the desks and slapped the walls, making loud noises to frustrate their efforts. Yet their tireless tongues kept on wagging. Their hands continued to write math equations, the names of provinces, new Chinese characters, and more Tang poems:

Spring sleep is long.
And at dawn birds chirp everywhere.

Their grating voices shouted above ours in order to be heard. Their anxious eyes betrayed their inner worry for their naïve pupils.

Outside on the streets, the Red Guards were cleaning up the filth left by the old society. They toppled old road signs and destroyed the imposing temples, driving out the monks and nuns, whom they called symbols of China's feudalism. They invaded private homes and paraded all kinds of enemies in ambulances and fire engines, filling the city with the wail of sirens. Inside our small school, we could be stilled no longer. One day we pupils encircled a plump math teacher and pushed her back and forth in the ring as if she were a basketball. Our relentless laughter rang through the schoolyard as the woman screamed helplessly, trying to break through the human wall. Her face and hands received bloody scratches, her clothes were torn, and her hair was yanked out, leaving coin-sized raw spots on her head.

Within the next few days, we stormed the main office and forcibly removed Principal Zhang. At the subsequent criticism meeting, the leader of the school revolutionary rebels declared that the principal came from a bloodsucking landlord family. Before his voice fell silent, hundreds of students flooded the stage where Principal Zhang stood, forcing her to bend her head to her knees. The wave swept me with it and carried me up to her. Our anger toward the landlord class burst like an angry volcano. Hundreds of small fists landed on her body, hundreds of mouths spat on her. Her knotted hair became dotted with saliva. I saw a young boy holding a strand of the principal's hair, with a bloody piece of her scalp still attached.

Principal Zhang's eyes turned as dim as those of a dead fish. She looked like she was crying, but there were no tears. Then she seemed to be smiling. I felt chills running through my body, and for a moment I thought I was looking not at a living person but at a breathing corpse.

After the meeting, the school rebels locked the principal in a tool room, leaving the light on to prevent her from sleeping and to break her nerve. One night a few days later, as wind and rain swept across the city, Principal Zhang squeezed her battered body out the small window. The lightning flashing in the sky led her through the pitch black darkness to the familiar rails that she had crossed countless times on her way to and from school. She lay on the tracks, stretching out her arms to welcome the approaching train.

Our once well-organized school became a scene of desolation. The pupils damaged desks and chairs, smashed the windows and doors, broke the blackboards, and attacked those teachers who still attempted to teach. Then our school closed down.

From the start of the Cultural Revolution, the state-run propaganda machine had never ceased proclaiming that "the ignorant are the greatest" and "the more knowledge one has, the more counterrevolutionary one becomes." Lies told a thousand times became irrefutable truth. Looking back, New China's history was written with the intellectuals' blood. From the nationwide Elimination of the Counterrevolutionaries to the Antirightist campaign, from the Four Clean-Ups Socialist Movement to the current Cultural Revolution, in one campaign after another, those with learning had always been the targets.

Now the Chinese Communist Party called them the Filthy Number Nine of its ten great enemies — the landlords, wealthy peasants, counterrevolutionaries, bad elements, rightists, industrialists, Capitalist Roaders within the party, self-employed workers, intellectuals, and merchants. People became disillusioned with education in consequence. If years of learning would only cause the next generation to suffer, then what was the benefit in seeking it, and subjecting oneself to endless persecutions?

A Sunday in April 1967. Trees displayed their new branches in the warm spring air. A red banner flapped in the wind: THE ILLITERATE ARE THE MOST INTELLIGENT; THE LEARNED ARE THE STUPIDEST! In the courtyard of Hudong University's family housing, the spectacled professors and lecturers carried books, magazines, documents, science equipment, and tools from their homes and dumped them into a huge bonfire. Ashes flew like gray butterflies. Greatly relieved, the scholars declared that with no books to harm the brains of their children, the next generation would grow up to be splendid proletarians and the party's most reliable force. The youngsters sang and danced around the fire. Onlookers applauded with thunderous handclapping and vigorous shouts of support.

Falling slowly from the sky, the drifting black and white ashes settled quietly on the tree leaves, grass blades, and naked brown earth. Slowly but surely, this burning merged with another, an ancient scene of two thousand years ago, when the First Emperor Qin burned books and buried scholars alive to eliminate education and squelch dissent.

The black smoke swirled into our open windows and the ashes landed on the desks and chairs. Watching the shooting flames, Father couldn't hide his emotion any longer and pounded his fist on the table.

Now allowed home from his "cowshed" every Sunday, he saw how Jie and I were wasting our most valuable years in life doing nothing. Since part of his salary had been restored after the chaotic months at the beginning of the Cultural Revolution, I no longer had to pick up vegetable leaves or dig for coal among the ashes anymore. As we idled around the apartment, spending hours and hours sleeping, Father became anxious, like an ant running on a hot stove. He paced back and forth urgently. How, during these times, when the country condemned learning, hated knowledge, and praised ignorance, could he provide us with an education? Who was willing to teach? Even if someone were brave enough, did Father dare ask? If we were discovered studying, Father would be accused of new "crimes" and have to endure more suffering and beatings. I would rather have had no education at all than see Father suffer for me. Seeking an education was unsafe.

Another Sunday. The wind blew hard and rain came down in sheets, turning the world into a vast opacity. Father closed the windows and drew the curtains. Then he opened the boxes piled on top of one another in the corner of the room. He dug out some textbooks that had survived the house search and set them down in front of us.

"Laziness in youth means sorrow in old age. One inch of gold can't buy an inch of time. You will never have a second youth. So educate yourself when you are young. Read every chapter and do the exercises after each lesson. The day will come when education is important again," Father said firmly.

I nodded. I had already realized that having no school to go to was our biggest tragedy, and having no books to read seemed worse than death.

The next morning, Jie and I rose early. After breakfast I drew the curtain partly shut to block the view from the opposite building and sat down at a desk. As I leafed through the pages, words seemed to dance in front of my eyes. My concentration was rusty. The fountain pen weighed heavily in my hand. I felt as though I were sitting on a bed of nails. Every few minutes I stood up and wandered into the kitchen to find some distraction, like a piece of hot pickle. A bird sang outside. I tiptoed to the window and saw it perched on thin legs on the high-voltage power line, stretching its red neck and trilling to the air. I studied the clouds, wondering where they would go and what was beyond the edge of the sky.

Study used to be so effortless, but now it seemed close to impossible. It also made me anxious. I kept constantly in mind Father's warning that if someone came to the door, I should hide the books under my pillows. Fatigued, I would fall asleep. When I woke up, the sun was drooping, casting grotesque spots through the tree leaves onto the open pages of my book. I rubbed my eyes vigorously and, dutifully picking up the volume again, commenced reading from the last page. Jie was restless too. He could never forget his beloved comic books, which the Red Guards had confiscated during the house search. Turning inward, he drew pictures and talked to himself.

Self-education was not as easy as I first thought. It was boring and difficult. When I had questions, I had no one to turn to other than the outdated dictionaries. I often wavered, thinking that maybe it was true that education was useless and ignorance was glorious.

Without learning, I was still me, able to listen, feel, eat, sleep, and play. But I was Father's daughter, and I had to listen to him.

Days passed. The chair became comfortable. The textbooks were now new friends, who had turned the gray winter into warm spring. Words began taking root on the pages and brought me out of this grim world into the treasure-house of human knowledge. I learned about the Industrial Revolution that transformed the old feudal system in Britain into an industrialized economy and brought the world into the modern age; the French Revolution that overthrew the monarchy and established a democratic government upholding the equality of all citizens; the American Civil War, in which the industrialized North vanquished the backward South, abolished slavery, and liberated the black people; and China's Wuchang Revolution in 1911 that ended the country's two-thousand-year history of imperial rule and established a republic of the people.

Swimming in a sea of literature, I was moved by the great Tang poet Du Pu's beautiful verses and his deep concern for the poor:

> The autumn sky is high.
> The howling August wind
> Swirls away three layers of my thatched roof;
> Rain dripping on my bed.
> When will the day come
> When all the homeless have mansions to live in?

7

Unbridled

*A*fter an unbroken spell of wet weather, winter came again. Toward the end of 1967, the schools reopened when Chairman Mao called for all students and the Red Guards to return to the classroom to make revolution there. Now fourteen, I was assigned to the Red East Middle School near my home. The cold wind howled in the bare trees, and I became miserable at the thought of attending the same school as the children who had so ruthlessly bullied Jie and me.

I had never fared well in my elementary school. In 1961 our family had moved from the city of Harbin, the site of mass starvation since 1959, to Shanghai, which had suffered less severely. Although I always received good grades, my new classmates, who were not so malnourished as I, were never friendly. This was all because of my appearance. Prolonged hunger from the age of six had reduced me to skin and bones. My legs and arms resembled bamboo sticks. My face was so gaunt the adults looked on me with pity, saying they saw in me no more than an enormous mouth with huge, crooked teeth. The boys quickly nicknamed me the White-Boned Demon. I became accustomed to angry fists flashing in front of me and gazes condemning me with the thought "How could a girl look so ugly?"

Red East Middle School repaired its broken classrooms and welcomed the students back. At the thought that I would now have teachers to teach me, I cheered up a little, but school was in session only three days a week and two hours a day, and no academic classes were allowed. Miserable-looking teachers, with mops and brooms in hand, spent their time cleaning the bathrooms and the schoolyard. They did anything but teach. In the meantime, students held meetings to criticize them.

Soldiers wearing broad armbands were stationed in the building. After the January Red Storm they had taken control of schools, hospitals, and other cultural institutions where the intellectuals gathered. The soldiers ordered us, as new students, to set up Red Guard organizations. To gain respect from my new classmates so that my school life would be more tolerable, I adopted the most fashionable attire. I wore an oversized army uniform that belonged to Ming, fastened it with a black belt, and tucked my hair inside an army cap. My new classmates said that I looked like the real Red Guards they saw on the streets and elected me one of the five Red Guard leaders. Formerly an outcast, I felt surprised and enormously flattered. Beaming with joy, I returned home and looked in the mirror, which I seldom did, since it was the behavior of the condemned "petty bourgeoisie." The girl facing me was no longer a bag of bones with a huge, laughable mouth. Her facial features now seemed balanced. The once dry and drab hair was now smooth like black satin, shining with the luster of youth. Brightness had returned to the once spiritless eyes, and the face radiated a natural ruddiness. In the green army uniform pinned with a bright red armband, the girl glowed with life and vigor and fit well the ideal image of a heroic Red Guard making revolution on the streets.

The girl smiled at me self-confidently. I started to like her. It was a feeling that I had never before harbored. I had always hated my appearance, which brought me unspeakable suffering. In this world, I often thought sadly, no one other than my parents would want to look at me. Now, I had finally escaped the skeletal shadow that had haunted me for so long. Never before did I ever hold my head as high or feel as equal to the other girls as I did now. The power of youth burst into my darkened world and turned it into a bright realm of colorful flowers. The natural desire for beauty, which had long died in my heart, came alive again. I stroked my cheeks to make them redder and licked my cracked lips so that they were moist. I found a red crayon and painted my lips in front of the mirror. Then I quickly washed the color away. For the first time, I had vague thoughts about men, about being kissed lovingly and hugged firmly. But my face flushed with shame as I quickly shut away the "dirty" thoughts.

Fourteen years old. This was a time for high dreams and action. My body was light, lighter than a spring leaf. It could be easily blown away by a gentle breeze, not to mention a great revolutionary storm. This year, 1967, Lin Biao, Mao's immediate successor and the country's second helmsman, propelled the personality cult of Mao to its peak when millions of copies of the *Quotations of Chairman Mao,* which he had compiled, flooded the country. Mao badges were everywhere, and the state-run propaganda apparatus devoted its efforts to creating a godlike aura around the Great Helmsman. People stood in front of Mao's portrait waving the red-bound *Quotations,* wishing him a long, long life and his comrade-in-arms Lin Biao eternal health. The unrelenting propaganda convinced the nation that "Chairman Mao is our great savior. His kindness is vaster than the Pacific, higher than Everest." Many Red Guards even pinned Mao badges into the flesh of their chests.

The Red Guard movement, from its birth, put its faith in blood lineage: "A dragon breeds a dragon, a phoenix breeds a phoenix. The children of mice can only dig holes." Many of the very first Beijing and Shanghai Red Guards were the sons and daughters of top Communist Party officials such as He Long, one of the ten marshals of the People's Liberation Army. By contrast, the party had a deep distrust of the children of the Black Fives, the former landlords, wealthy peasants, counterrevolutionaries, bad elements, and rightists. No matter how hard these young people tried to prove themselves — and many betrayed their families and wrote pledges of loyalty with their own blood — the Red Guard organization steadfastly excluded them.

As the daughter of a Capitalist Roader, I was naturally politically suspect. In 1967 the investigation into whether my father was a traitor and Kuomintang spy intensified. Hudong University sent out team after team all over the country to find evidence that might incriminate him. The open-ended investigation lasted all ten years of the Revolution. Mother remained an "Evil Hand behind a black current" — in other words, a counterrevolutionary. Although I never thought of leaving my parents as Ming had or volunteered to denounce them in public like many youngsters, I did tell the school that I would draw a spiritual line between my family and myself. My parents understood me and supported my action. They asked me not to walk or talk with them in public, so they wouldn't tarnish my image as a Red Guard leader. Without a significant snag, I passed the political investigation into my family background. I was surprised it went so smoothly. Throughout the Cultural Revolution, I never knew whether I was from a revolutionary family or a counterrevolutionary family, for my parents were seldom a negative factor during any subsequent political background check.

Soon we, the Mao Zedong Thought Red Guards, were assigned our first mission — to catch Fan Lu, the biggest Capitalist Roader, former chief administrator of our district, and bring him into the daylight to face the Revolution.

Since Fan Lu usually remained in hiding during the daytime, we decided to search for him at night in the district government building, where he had been spotted recently in his old office. All fifty of us, wearing green army uniforms fastened with leather belts, arrived en masse at the district government building, a former American bank from the 1920s. It was a chilly night. The dim streetlamps surveyed pedestrians with a ghostly stare. In the cold wind, dead leaves drifted reluctantly to the ground, joining those that already lay in clusters at the curbsides. They crackled under our impatient feet. The mournful-sounding sirens of ships, big and small, sailing on the Huangpu River echoed wide and far.

We weren't surprised to see the main gate wide open, with no one guarding it. During the first few years of the Revolution, all government buildings were open twenty-four hours a day so the people could make constant revolution. We marched inside. It was quiet, fearfully quiet. There wasn't a soul in sight, only flickering lights dotting the deep corridors like eyes in a graveyard. The glass of the windows and doors had been shattered, and office furniture lay smashed and strewn everywhere. Some doors had been knocked down, and others bore punctures from being rammed or kicked. Abandoned paste buckets, long-handled brooms, workers' safety helmets, and iron and wooden rods were scattered on the worn marble floor. Thick layers of slogans, large-character posters, and banners covered the smoky walls. I shivered. This wasn't the once forbidding district building, it was an all-out bloody battlefield.

Following the January Red Storm, the Red Guards and industrial workers had assaulted the building to seize power. Battles raged back and forth over the next few months. Red Guards from different middle schools fought with former district employees over whether Fan Lu should be given a position in the newly established Revolutionary Committee. The Red Guards condemned Fan Lu as a loyal follower of Liu Shaoqi, China's Khrushchev. They said that Fan Lu was a die-hard Capitalist Roader, who must be overthrown. The other side claimed that he was Chairman Mao's good cadre and should be kept in power to lead the Cultural Revolution in this most important district of Shanghai. The two sides battled from the first floor to the very top, using mop handles, the legs of desks and chairs, iron bars, wooden rods, and spears as weapons. They shouted, "Beat me and kill me! But you can never bow our revolutionary heads!" "Let blood run! Let heads roll! We will never renounce Mao Zedong Thought!"

Ambulances waited outside to rush bloody bodies to the nearby hospitals. The youngest combatant was our age, fourteen years old.

Now fifty of us went through every floor, broke open every locked door, and searched the corners of every room. We shouted and stamped, making loud noises to encourage ourselves. The air was thick, making breathing difficult. From time to time I brushed aside the wet bangs that stuck to my face and with the cuffs of my coat wiped the sweat beading my forehead.

Time passed slowly. As the "Big Ben" of the Customs Building several blocks away struck twelve times, we regrouped on the top floor. No one had found Fan Lu or any other living being in this huge building. Exhausted, some of us lay down on the long, battered benches. Others even slept on the floor, which was specked with the earlier Red Guards' dried blood. Outside, the gauze of frost, as thin as a cicada's wings, fell on the city. The busy sirens died down, sounding only here and there when ships had to sail at this hour. The rolling Huangpu River lapsed into darkness, floating lights skimming over the surface.

Only a month later, we returned to search for Fan Lu again, but we didn't succeed that time either. When the Red Guards from Long Wind Middle School finally found him in the private home of an ardent supporter, a former employee, they beat him to death.

Gongs and drums greeted the year 1968. The Cultural Revolution, as praised in the New Year editorial of the *People's Daily*, surged forward. Day and night, we flocked into the streets and hailed the downfall of another top official or a clique of counterrevolutionaries concealed within the government and the party. Carrying huge red flags, we marched in the small lanes and on the big roads. Curious pedestrians stopped to watch and inflated our egos as the glorious protectors of Chairman Mao.

As our Red Guard organization expanded rapidly, we began looking for a headquarters. A girl recommended the house of her neighbor, a "rightist." The next day we went to the old man's house, which was located on a small, crowded lane near the bank of the Huangpu River. His home had a black-tiled roof and a whitewashed wall streaked with dirt. A cracked sink covered with dark green moss stood in the front courtyard. Weeds grew tall where feet couldn't reach. A deep red squat toilet painted with golden patterns sat in one corner. During the daytime, these wooden toilets were set neatly in front of every household to air in the sun. Such quaint scenery was typical of the older neighborhoods of Shanghai.

As we stepped into the well-lit formal room, I saw a bald man in his late fifties dozing on a bamboo chair, his face furrowed and his egg-shaped head glowing in the light. The room was warmed by natural "passive" heating, with the midday sun penetrating the windows and spreading warmth throughout the room. The Shanghai natives liked to crowd their homes with traditional furniture made of mahogany, but this room was almost barren, for it had already been searched many times before.

The girl stepped forward to talk to the old man, who had now been startled awake from his nap and was looking at us in alarm. A shadow fell across his face and he stiffened, then abruptly jumped to his feet and shook his head adamantly. "You know I have bronchitis. That room in the north is too cold during the winter. It doesn't see sunlight all year round. I am afraid those conditions are too harsh for my old bones."

He wavered, stressing the word "bronchitis" and coughing a few times, his voice old and cracking, his breath short. My sense of pity was touched. He was a sick man. When he spat, I saw threads of blood in the spittoon. The chill in the back room might kill him. Maybe we shouldn't occupy his sunny room, which, compared to the other one, was indeed heaven. But I was a Red Guard leader. Revolution was cruel, after all. It wasn't embroidering flowers or writing articles. It was a class struggle, a violent insurrection. One mustn't be too soft-hearted. As I reasoned within myself, the old man shambled with the assistance of his cane to the single bed and held the rusted bedrail firmly, panting from the exertion. But he quickly released his hand when several of my classmates unfastened their leather belts. Frightened, the crippled man pounded his chest, shook his head helplessly, and dragged his game leg to a corner, where he stood in silence.

We moved his bed into the cold, damp room. The boys hustled the man in and slammed the door. On top of a cracked hardwood table we set up an old manual printing machine that we could use to produce fliers to distribute on the busy streets and on campus. Cheers of jubilation filled the bright room, startling the golden cock that flapped in the front yard. The neighborhood children stopped to watch from outside the windows, pasting their tender faces on the glass and squeezing their noses into tiny pies.

Like unbridled horses running wild on the vast plain, like the swift torrents rushing down a mountain, we in our youthful vigor and feverish adulation of Mao had gotten out of control. Excited by the great social disorder and, most important of all, by our revolutionary beliefs, the Red Guards all over the country became unspeakably destructive. Red Guards resorted increasingly to violence, torturing countless innocent people to death. In the city of Chongqing, in Sichuan Province, the Red Guards attacked the People's Liberation Army and used tanks, heavy machine guns, and landing craft in their actions. Casualties in one fierce firefight were as high as six hundred. (Today, the Red Guard victims are buried in the nation's only Red Guard cemetery, situated near the site of the conflict. A mood of mystery and melancholy envelops the gruesome place.)

Despite repeated appeals from Chairman Mao, who asked the youngsters to use gentler methods to promote his revolution, the Red Guards were unable to rein in the violent confrontations and destructive activities. Voices of resentment rose from all sides. The Red Terrorists, as the Red Guards were called, became too revolutionary for the great leader. However, the Cultural Revolution must go on. Any obstacle in the way had to be removed. Chairman Mao began receiving workers and peasants. He told the country, "The working class must lead in everything." Forests of hard hands were raised high in the air. On July 27, 1968, the Great Leader sent his first Worker Propaganda Team to the rebellious Qinghua University in Beijing to restore order. Kuai Dafu, the belligerent general commander, ordered his Qinghua Red Guards to open fire, killing five members of the Worker Propaganda Team. Fresh blood of the workers was spilled. Mourning filled the country's top university. When the noise of the gunshots had died down, the red sun quivered in the broad sky.

8

The Fall of the Red Guards

September 1968. Maple trees on Beijing's Western Hill turned gold and red, illuminating half the sky. The red flags fluttered in the clear wind of the capital city. Scorching Tiger took over Shanghai, and cicadas drowned the city with a whining drone. In the insects' uproar, twenty-one-year-old Ming unexpectedly returned home from his high school. While he was taking off his army jacket, he declared that he was leaving Shanghai to settle down in the Heilongjiang Military Farms located along the Sino-Soviet border. He showed us his forefinger and told us that he had bitten it and sworn an oath to Chairman Mao with his blood.

Ming's belief was simple: Chairman Mao was the leader of China and the world revolution. Whatever he commanded, Ming would do. Now Chairman Mao had stood on the rostrum of Tiananmen calling upon the Red Guards to go to the countryside and be "reeducated" by the peasants. He stressed that this was an important step in smashing the "conspiracy" of the Americans and the Soviets, who were trying to impose capitalism and revisionism on China. It was also a strategic measure to reduce the huge differences between urban and rural areas and speed up the realization of communism in China.

"How can you tell if a youth is revolutionary or not? See if he is willing to connect himself with the laboring people," Chairman Mao said. "The countryside is a vast world where you can achieve many things."

The *People's Daily* echoed Chairman Mao's words, publishing an editorial entitled WE ALSO HAVE TWO HANDS, AND WILL NOT EAT FREE FOOD IN THE CITIES, urging the Red Guards to leave the city for the "emancipation of all mankind."

"Tell me about the Heilongjiang Military Farms!" I begged Ming, jealous that he would soon become a real soldier for Chairman Mao.

"You're only a little girl. It's not worth my time," he joked. But, unable to hide his excitement, he began recounting what he had heard at school: Replacing the former Heilongjiang agricultural farms on the Sino-Soviet border, the Heilongjiang Military Farms comprised six military divisions whose mission, according to Chairman Mao, was twofold:

1. to plough the virgin soil and grow food to support themselves, and

2. to defend the border against the Soviets in order to prevent our proletarian government from being turned into a revisionist regime.

Heilongjiang is a big province, one and a half times the size of France. The Heilongjiang Military Farms was the biggest operation of its kind in the country, taking up the entire province. The six divisions affiliated with the farms each had ten regiments, and each regiment had thirty to forty companies. The whole would accommodate approximately one million young people from big cities like Shanghai, Beijing, Tianjin, and Harbin during its ten years of operation.

If war with the Soviets broke out, the young people would serve as military reserves. In normal times, they were farm workers, earning a monthly salary of thirty-two yuan. It wasn't much, but still a big incentive. By way of comparison, those sent to a people's commune, composed of several agricultural villages, could earn only grain. Their life was extremely difficult.

In the Great Northern Wilderness, as the entire rural Heilongjiang was called, potatoes grew bigger than washbasins and ginseng the size of infants sprouted all over the land, said Ming in a quavering voice. One could hunt deer with only a stick and catch fish with a scoop net. Wild geese would land in the cooking pot all by themselves. Inspired by his lyrical description, I soared in my mind over uninterrupted green mountains and boundless black soil colored by red sorghum, green wheat, and yellow soybeans. I imagined living a military life and fighting against the Soviet revisionists. This was the dream of every young person during the Cultural Revolution, when the People's Liberation Army was ardently worshipped.

Father looked depressed. But he didn't display any sign of criticism of Mao's movement.

"Why do you have to leave home?" Mother finally asked, cautiously. "Since you are our eldest son, this year's graduation policy allows you to stay in Shanghai." Mother set down the towels she had been trying to squeeze into Ming's suitcase.

"I have already sent my blood pledge to Chairman Mao. I cannot and will not change my mind!" Ming replied in a high-pitched voice, his eyes shining with resolve. He carefully unfastened his Red Guard armband from his old army uniform and folded it slowly before he put it inside his duffel bag.

Three days later I saw Ming off at the naval base of the East China Sea Fleet. Besides using cargo and passenger trains, Shanghai also employed battleships to move the Red Guards quickly to northern coastal cities, where they were further dispersed to frontier villages. Smashing against the dark rocks, the breakers sent up a fountain of spray. White seagulls flashed between the sea and the clouds, singing and calling merrily. Waves churning with white foam splashed onto the dock as the rocking ship prepared to leave.

Sad-looking parents forced themselves to smile while choking back tears. In the crisp Shanghai dialect, they blamed themselves for not having gotten things ready for their children.

"The boy's departure came too suddenly. The quilt may not be thick enough against subzero temperatures. I didn't have time to darn the old sweater he's worn through," one woman standing next to me murmured to herself.

"Should I have bought that can of condensed milk? It would be nice for her to have when she falls sick. But the price was almost a third of my monthly salary," said another.

"He has no cotton-padded pants. What if he gets arthritis in the snowy weather?" a father sighed.

No matter how wonderful the description of the Heilongjiang Military Farms, it was a barbarous area nearly two thousand miles away. It was dangerous, a war front. It was too cold, colder than the Arctic in the parents' minds. But most of all, the majority of the children were only teenagers, too young for all the hardships.

"How long will my children have to stay there? A few months? A few years? Forever?" parents asked themselves. Chairman Mao had issued the orders but didn't provide the answers. Only time would tell.

However, Ming and the other Red Guards didn't appear sad at all. Bursting with youthful vigor, they grew impatient with the tears and the sentiments. Their eyebrows formed knots and their young faces showed contempt.

"Greeting the east wind, we are marching toward the sun. The northern frontier is our home," a resounding voice began singing solemnly, followed by many more, brightening the gloomy faces of the parents for a brief moment. The youngsters were eager to go. The night before, Ming had told me that we Red Guards were the real masters on China's political stage and what we did today would decide China's future. As a revolutionary, Ming was not prepared to return to Shanghai, the nest of comfort for spoiled flowers. The Sino-Soviet border was where he would shed his hot blood and devote his young life to Chairman Mao. There were green hills everywhere to bury loyal bones. Ming's dark eyes shone with heroic spirit, and his face was aglow with new dreams. Now, as the ship departed amid lingering sirens, I knew that he and his comrades couldn't wait for the new adventures.

One month later, we received Ming's first letter. The agricultural company where he'd been assigned was situated on the banks of the Ussuri, which separates the Soviet Union and China. Across the river he could see the Russians walking in their villages and hear dogs barking and cocks crowing. During peaceful times, when the river froze in winter, people could easily cross over. Historically, many Chinese and Russians had become kin through marriage. But now that relationship had soured. When the two sides fought major battles over the sovereignty of the Pearl Islands in the river, Ming and his young comrades took up machine guns and stayed in the trenches for days preparing for war, which was said to be imminent.

The departure of Ming and other senior Red Guards in September 1968 marked the beginning of the largest movement of youth in history, which sent 16 million young city people, or 10 percent of the entire urban population, to rural areas. The headquarters of the Red Guard troop at our Red East Middle School, once the busiest part of the school building, stood empty. The troop's general commander and deputy commanders had all left, some dispatched to the northern regions of Inner Mongolia and Heilongjiang, others to the primitive southern frontier in Yunnan Province bordering Burma, while still others went to the poor, mountainous areas of Guizhou in the deserted southwestern region. Without these senior leaders, the younger Red Guards ceased to engage in any more revolutionary activities and thus existed in name only. The Red Guard movement fell into disarray.

Graduation came in March 1970, when I had reached seventeen. The policy that year, "Red All Over," was the strictest so far: everyone had to leave Shanghai without exception. No one knew the real reasons behind the policy at the time. We learned later that the country's economy in 1970, four years into the disastrous Cultural

Revolution, was on the verge of collapse, and the cities had no jobs to offer the young people.

The classrooms became somber with dark clouds. Despite positive media reports about the heroic young people and their great accomplishments, our brothers and sisters in the countryside had not been sending any good news. The vast majority of the former Red Guards went to the people's communes located in the remotest corners of the nation. They toiled like beasts in the barren fields all year round, but the grain they reaped wasn't enough to last a year, or even half a year. To fill their stomachs, they had to do as the local peasants did, mix the grain with crop leaves. Having no place to call home, they lived in borrowed huts, drifting around in the production brigades rootlessly. The enormous discrepancy between their revolutionary idealism and the cruel reality of living at the bottom of society disillusioned these impassioned young people. Many committed suicide in their so-called Collective Homes.

A young soldier summoned me to his office. "The school assigns you to the Double Thunder People's Commune on Muo River, Heilongjiang Province," he told me. He sounded solemn.

My heart turned ice-cold. Tears welled up in my eyes. I could hear my own sobbing. I ran back home, took out a map of Heilongjiang Province, and found Muo River, the northernmost point in China right across from Russia's Siberia. I wondered what value my life would have there, where living was a mere struggle for survival. My heart trembled. A voice inside screamed, "No, you cannot accept this assignment!" I ran back to school. The soldier was surprised to see me again. He stood up, his face tight. He clasped his hands behind his back to show his authority.

"I want to go to the Heilongjiang Military Farms because my brother is there," I requested.

The soldier sat down again in his chair.

"You're not qualified. Only one person per family can go to the farms and earn a salary, and your elder brother has already used up the quota. Unfortunately, you have to earn crops in a people's commune. You'll eat what you grow, like most of the young people who already live there." He crossed his thighs and leaned back in his chair, signaling that there was no room for further negotiation.

I left the office without a word. The ten-minute walk from school seemed endless. I felt miserable for being so powerless at such a critical moment. The overcast sky hung low overhead, like the lid of an iron pot. Bean-sized raindrops whipped my face and soaked my hair. I broke into a run, deciding to challenge the decision.

I began writing to the farm's temporary recruitment center located in downtown Shanghai:

> How can a revolutionary live like a frog
> Watching the sky from the bottom of a well?
> My blood will conquer the evil spirit.
> My sweat will reflect the sunrise.
> Waving the red flag, I shout to the sky:
> My home is everywhere on the globe.

In April 1970, pearls of dew danced in the morning light. Tiny red flowers peeped from behind the leaves. Life was resurgent everywhere. A young man in a faded army uniform visited me at home.

"Lieutenant Colonel Lu of the Heilongjiang Military Farms asked me to come see you." He opened the army bag on his right shoulder and took out the thick pile of letters that I had mailed the recruitment center. "We need soldiers like you. If you have time, Colonel Lu would like to meet you tomorrow at Jinjiang Hotel."

Any time would have suited me! I leaped up, giggling with happiness. The young man's face broke out in a broad smile. Outside, pink rose blossoms poked through the bamboo fences, white willow catkins flew in the soft wind, and the gray-faced buildings glowed in the myriad of golden rays. Over someone's radio came Chairman Mao's words: "The world is yours as well as ours, but it is still yours after all. Like the morning sun, the youth are full of vitality. We place all our hopes on your shoulders. The world belongs to you. China's future belongs to you."

Between Fire
and Blood

9

Good-bye Shanghai

Graceful willows swayed their green silk ribbons in the spring breeze, which, like a pair of scissors, reshaped the landscape. Swallows in their black cocktail dresses twittered, flying back and forth to their new nests built under our eaves.

On May 15, I woke up early. I put on my shiny new green army uniform and a pair of green canvas shoes. I tucked my thick shoulder-length hair inside my army cap. On my chest I pinned a fist-sized silver head of Chairman Mao, the biggest I could find from among the hundreds of Mao badges at home. In a few hours I would leave home for Heilongjiang Military Farms, almost two thousand miles away. Father wanted to see me off at the train station. In June 1969 he had been transferred to Chongming Island on the East China Sea, where he was serving a term of hard labor to further transform his "capitalist ideology." But he'd requested leave to come home and say good-bye. He looked defeated, walking with his head bowed and his eyes gazing only at the tips of his feet.

On his way back to Shanghai he had written a poem for me:

> Today you are ready to leave,
> And full of will and spirit.
> Watching the rolling river running east,
> I realize that my little girl has grown up.
> But the road ahead
> Is full of dangers and hardships.

On your departure, I have only this for you:
Be cautious but courageous.

But when the moment came for us to leave, Father broke down and sat in a chair, weeping like a small child and covering his face with his hands. Mother said he'd better stay home, for he wouldn't be able to stand the strong emotions at the Shanghai train station. "A man doesn't easily shed tears until his heart is broken." It was the first time I had ever seen him cry. The harsh life on the frontier was well known. But he couldn't express his feelings in words; he was afraid that would discourage me from doing a good job in the countryside. His weeping saddened me. I felt a knife twisting my heart. Unable to say good-bye to Father, I quickly picked up my suitcase and went downstairs, with Mother following behind.

Clusters of yellow jasmine swinging in a neighbor's front yard bid me farewell. The thick elm trees shook their luxuriant leaves to say good-bye. Boisterous neighborhood children followed us for a while, knowing they wouldn't see me for a long time.

A holiday atmosphere surrounded Shanghai's North Train Station. Dozens of red flags and banners danced cheerfully in the warm wind, while gongs and drums reverberated in the air. Workers in blue labor uniforms patrolled the station to enforce discipline. Parents and relatives filled the platform.

A green train waited quietly beside the gathering, its sleek body stretching out into the distance like a giant serpent. I found my seat and opened the narrow train window, leaning out to talk to Mother, who stood below in the crowd. Mother had little to say except to exhort me again and again to take care of myself and write home often. I kept looking at my wristwatch. Time never seemed so precious before. When a clear voice came over the loudspeakers commanding all youngsters to get on board, the crowd stirred. Crying broke out both inside and outside the train. The station became like a funeral home. No one was sure what kind of life lay ahead; for some, this was to be a final farewell.

The train whistled, loud and long. Loudspeakers began playing "The East Is Red," which compared Mao to the sun. That light and upbeat tune contrasted sharply with the heart-wrenching cries. I stretched my arm out to reach Mother's hand, which felt hot, very hot. I held it firmly, hoping never to let it go. Another whistle, and the train jerked, moving forward slowly. Until the day I came back, if there was such a day, we could only live in each other's memories. Two lines of bright tears rolled uncontrollably down Mother's face, like pearls dropping from a broken string. My teary eyes were glued on her until she faded into the distance.

I was now truly on my own. I was no longer a Shanghai resident. Yesterday the neighborhood administration had canceled my residency. I would not be able to regain it unless the authorities allowed me to study or work in Shanghai. That possibility seemed remote, at least for now, when the government was sending millions away from the big cities. Yet I also felt relief — a new beginning, a new life was waiting for me. Like a brave young bird, I had flown into the sky with fledgling wings. The world awaited.

The special express charged full speed toward the north. For hours I looked out the window, anticipating my new life ahead. We passed fertile farmlands marked by webs of rivers and lakes, in the mighty watershed of the Yangtze, over the broad Yellow River, cradle of five thousand years of civilization.

Suddenly, the tall, silver-haired Lieutenant Colonel Lu gently patted my shoulder and asked how I was doing. Then, turning to his subordinates, he said, "This girl has done her utmost to get on today's train."

I stood up from my seat and saluted him, like a real soldier of the People's Liberation Army.

On the evening of the third day, the train glided slowly into our destination, Tashan, seat of the Fourth Division of the Heilongjiang Military Farms, located in the eastern part of the province. I peered out the window. It was a lonely station with grayish stone walls surrounded by bare earth and wastelands stretching from the railroads all the way to the edge of the horizon. Several peasants were loading sorghum on the backs of bony donkeys with long ears. While trees had already leafed out in the south, here they had just begun, reluctantly, with buds only the size of a fingernail. In the distance, rippled mountains stood against the vault of heaven, their peaks towering proudly in the cold sky. Except for the few dim lights flickering like ghosts on the deserted platform, and scattered local passengers carrying bags on their backs, I could see nothing else. The words "poverty" and "backwardness" popped into my mind. The Great Northern Wilderness stood in sharp contrast to metropolitan Shanghai.

I exited the train uncertain whether I should be excited or depressed at the thought that I'd be settling here for many years, perhaps the rest of my life. But no matter what happened, I would have to face it.

The new arrivals, numbering one thousand, drowned the tiny train station like a green flood. The company representatives were waiting for us at the station gate. To make themselves visible in the twilight, the men, in faded black and dusty gray, stood on huge rocks and tall stumps. Some even climbed trees. Holding loudspeakers close to their lips, they shouted out the names of their new recruits.

I and twenty-five others quickly gathered around Yi, the party secretary and top official of the construction company. He was a tall man in his late thirties. His highly arched eyebrows made him look like one of the majestic heroes in Jiang Qing's revolutionary Peking Operas. Speaking with machine-gun rapidity, he told us that he was a retired officer from the People's Air Force. I studied his army uniform, which, unlike our new ones, was genuine from his service in the military and had faded to a shade of yellow. His outfit reminded people of his proletarian blood and elite background, giving him an air of authority and power.

Yi led us into the waiting room, where we had to spend the night, as the trucks from the Seventy-third Regiment wouldn't arrive until the next morning. The floor was strewn with the local passengers' cloth bags, big and small, smelling exotic and earthy. Girls in gaudy garments buttoned at the left side leaned back in tall chairs, vigorously sucking on their small-bowled, long-stemmed pipes. They made noises in their throats like water boiling on the stove. White smoke threaded from the girls' pipes and hovered about the heads of the crowd. The thick cloud irritated my throat, and I couldn't stop coughing. The smell of coarse tobacco mixed with the unpleasant odor coming from unwashed human bodies, oily and impure, was stifling.

That night we had our first taste of the cold weather of Heilongjiang. Even in May, temperatures approached freezing at night. We had to put on our clumsy army overcoats, wrapping ourselves tightly in the unheated waiting room. Some girls jumped up and down to keep their feet warm. Spring was slow in coming to the desolate frontier. No wonder one ancient poem went this way:

> The bright moon emerges from behind the mountains,
> Moving among the ocean of clouds.
> The long spring wind blows ten thousand miles,
> But still cannot pass beyond the Jade Gate.

In this strange land filled with exotic smells, unfamiliar faces, and different accents, Father's childlike weeping and the bright tears rolling down Mother's face repeatedly flashed in my memory.

"Tonight's frost is the iciest, and my hometown's moon is the brightest. All my siblings are separated. Who will care about me?" Only after I left home did I realize how much it had meant to me.

The sun rose slowly from behind the ruffled mountains, casting its rays on the small Tashan train station. At 7:30 the trucks arrived, one after another, forming a long line like a shining dragon. Yi told us proudly that these trucks were the Chinese-made Liberation brand, so named to celebrate our independence from foreign assistance.

We climbed aboard one; the motor roared and the truck jolted along an unpaved road with its four wheels stirring up a column of yellow dust behind us. We complained about the pitching and bouncing, but Yi said we were lucky and should be thankful to heaven. In 1968, the year the first group of former Red Guards arrived, thousands of them had been trapped at the train station for days because heavy downpours had saturated the only road leading to the headquarters, making it impassable.

In the fresh morning breeze my hair flew wildly, sometimes blinding me. I devoured the scenery, which made me forget my homesickness and revived my dream of a new life. Beneath the sun, undulating mountains proudly showed off subtle shades of dark green, light green, bluish green, and yellowish green, all in wonderful contrast to the lustrous black soil, which the locals called Black Gold, the famous symbol of the Great Northern Wilderness. It was said that the Black Gold was so fragrant that it tasted sweet when savored slowly in the mouth.

Along the road, cultivated and uncultivated land merged into the blue sky, and the snow-moistened soil sparkled in the sun. The winds carried faint reverberations from the Russian-made tractors turning the new land. The glory of spring competed ferociously with the brilliant sunlight.

The truck made a sharp turn around a strange-looking mountain with a huge cleft at its top. "That's the Mount of Cracks, where we collect rocks in the winter for construction. Our company isn't far from here," said Yi.

"What does the construction company do?" I asked.

"We build everything from public lavatories to family housing for the regimental headquarters. We're a small company with seven platoons, over two hundred and fifty young people from the big cities, plus some one hundred locals. It's a true revolutionary melting pot, where you can be tempered into a real piece of gold."

In the distance, big and small lakes shining like pearls of various sizes were inlaid in a vast piece of velvet. A blanket of young wheat already covered some of the fields that stretched right up to the edge of the sky.

Yi continued. "Let me tell you about our Seventy-third Regiment. We're under the Fourth Division, guarding the east side of the border. Our regimental commander and his staff are all active military officers of the People's Liberation Army. The battalion and company leaders are retired officers like me.

"Our regiment has forty companies. Most are agricultural ones located far away, on the other side of the mountains. Only ten are industrial companies making bricks and tiles, processing food, building houses. You should count yourself lucky to be assigned to ours, since it's close to the center of the regiment. There are hospitals, department stores, even movie theaters." Yi pointed up ahead. Indeed, above the rise of the horizon appeared the silhouettes of chimneys and buildings.

10

This Broad Land

*L*ayers of white clouds drifted idly in the high sky, to wherever the winds would carry them. After three hours of plodding, the truck reached a crossroads and swerved to the right. In ten minutes it stopped in front of a mud-and-clay-walled structure with a light gray roof and a low wattle fence.

The rectangular building had only two rooms, each forming a wing, their doors facing each other across a central hall. Yi led us ten new girls to the room on the left side. There were two wall-to-wall brick beds, each ten yards long and two and a half feet high. They took up a huge portion of the room, leaving only a narrow aisle in the middle. One of the beds was already occupied. Ten floral quilts folded square lay in a line near the wall. Beneath each of them a sleeping mat big enough for a single person was spread out. Several new straw mats were laid on the clay top of the empty bed on the other side. This was to be ours.

The room was crowded. Wall-mounted shelves were packed with suitcases and bags. Dark towels, socks, handkerchiefs, and underwear hung on clotheslines. About two dozen basins were stacked in a corner. The dirt floor was damp and spotty with fresh sand.

"This is your new home. Arrange your beds, and I'll see you in the dining room." Clearly, Yi was not happy with our slow response to the new lodgings. He gave orders and left.

So this was my new home. But the room didn't have a single piece of furniture, not even a chair or table. The only place that belonged to me was my bed, a space one yard wide and one and a half yards long. I would spend much of my life there. I took off my shoes and slowly climbed on, arranging my bedding next to Xue, my former middle-school classmate, a skinny girl with big eyes and short hair.

One hour later, we began a guided tour. The construction company comprised a village of about thirty earthen houses built alongside the main dirt road. A horse-cart galloped, stirring up a long dust cloud behind it. The strong odor of the urine-soaked dust polluted the air. In the entire village, there wasn't a single paved road, not even a gravel one. Walking on the rugged track covered with dried footprints of both humans and livestock and the deep traces of wagon wheels, I could imagine what it would look like during the rainy periods.

Near the entrance to the company stood an L-shaped building, the only brick structure in the place. Located here was our canteen, with several run-down tables and a few chairs, some of which were missing legs. As we entered the kitchen, I saw a girl using a smoke-darkened spade to turn over chopped cabbage in a gigantic pot the size of a bathtub. The flames from the stove shot high, licking the sides of the pot. The girl's face was flushed with heat and her nostrils were smoke-darkened. The moment she saw us, her warm eyes turned serious. She tensed her face, looking official.

"Welcome! Welcome, our new Shanghai comrades!" The girl put down the spade and turned to face us.

"People call me Commander Gao. I am the cook squad leader. The company notified me yesterday of your arrival." She rubbed her hands on the grayish apron outside her oversized, blue, jacket.

"I know you Shanghai fellows eat rice, nothing but rice. Well, unfortunately, here firewood is as costly as cinnamon bark, and rice is as precious as pearls. The crop simply doesn't grow in this cold province. You'll have to learn to eat corn, sorghum, our everyday food. Don't starve yourselves. Human beings are iron, but only with food will they become steel." The girl's gaze became severe. Yi had already told us about the fights between the Shanghai youths and Gao's cooks over rice, the only staple food the Shanghainese ate. The serious-faced cooks placed a huge white basin of dark-purple steamed sorghum on the table along with a triangular bucket of boiled cabbage with slices of meat. Commander Gao said the meat was being served as a special treat for the newcomers. We should prepare ourselves not to see it for a long time.

There weren't enough chairs for everyone, so most of us ate standing up. The food tasted worse than wax and was coarser than sand. I swallowed the "stomach filler" as fast as it entered my mouth, pretending I enjoyed it. The other girls, who had never seen sorghum before, ate slowly, their faces uncertain. The boys frowned as though taking bitter herbal medicine, holding their breaths. Through the dusty windows, I saw Yi and an older man with splay feet approaching the building. Yi quickly came over to our tables.

"Our company is a revolutionary melting pot. Are all of you ready to settle here?" he asked, adjusting his army cap.

Chewing of sorghum stopped. I put down the spoon. We hung our heads like frostbitten eggplants. No one ate anymore. Yi became solemn.

"This place is not your great Shanghai. Life is still hard. For example, there is no running water here. We still drink from the well. We don't have much coal, so hot water is rationed. Each person is allowed only one basin a day."

What? Water is rationed? I was surprised.

Before Yi had finished, the older man, whose face resembled a dried walnut, broke in: "I would like to say a few words about the bathroom. There are no such things as flush toilets here, like you have in your great Shanghai."

He stopped abruptly, as if realizing that talking about the bathroom at the meal table wasn't very polite. But then he continued anyway.

"Have all of you been there yet?" His dull eyes stared at us.

Again, no one made a sound. The outhouse behind our dorm was a hut with a row of pits dug in the ground. It was so dirty that I could hardly find a clean spot for my feet. I had to close my eyes and hold my breath while flies buzzed around. Maggots as thick as a little finger wiggled everywhere. Some even tried to climb into my shoes. The experience of going to the outhouse was worse than a nightmare.

"Oh, I forgot to introduce myself. I am Old Tao, the company commander. Forty-five years of age, a retired Korean War veteran," the old walnut added quickly. He smoothed the silky goat beard on his chin, his toothless mouth moving on his wrinkled face.

"You'll need a flashlight. Carry it with you when you go at night. If you fall into the pit, no one will save you till the next morning." He and Yi laughed by themselves.

Both men had used the phrase "great Shanghai" as if coming from the city were something to be ashamed of.

Oh, food, water, and a bathroom! I sighed. Life was much harder here than I had imagined. Could I settle down here for the rest of my life, as Chairman Mao had asked us? My throat tightened. I missed home.

Like a huge fireball, the sun dropped behind the unbroken line of mountains, its last golden rays drenching the western half of the sky. The first wisps of smoke curled upward from the chimneys. The evening air was filled with the faint smell of corn porridge when we returned to our dorm. I climbed onto the huge, flat bed, sitting with my feet under my hips. Silence dominated the room. Some girls stared into the blankness while others began writing letters home. I closed my eyes and saw the fat maggots wriggling. Reminded by Old Tao, I couldn't forget them.

The tranquility was soon interrupted by bell-like laughter and the noise of conversation from outside. Several older girls stepped into the room. Expecting us, they nodded and smiled while taking off their hats, which were coated with dust. The girl who spoke in the Beijing dialect wore an oversized shirt and wide-legged pants. The trousers of the Shanghai girl were much narrower, and her army coat was patched. The Tianjin sister was clad in dark blue, her short collar standing on end. The pants of the girl from Harbin, the capital of Heilongjiang Province, were hemmed above the ankles and her coat had narrow sleeves and brass buttons. The Russians had built her city: were her clothes also Russian-influenced?

All of the girls were gray with dust from head to toe; their thick eyebrows had lost their original black. They must have been working in very rough conditions. Almost simultaneously, they grabbed the washbasins and hurried outside to receive their ration of warm water, which was just being delivered to the dorms.

There was no time to be shy. The girls quickly took off their dirty clothes and scrubbed themselves vigorously, passing the towels in and out of the basins, and splashing drops of water on the beds and the earthen floor. I took out a piece of paper and a fountain pen. While pretending to write, I watched them curiously, wondering how they managed to wash with only one basin of water. What they did was scrub their faces first, cleaning the eyes, nostrils, lips, and the backs of their ears. They rubbed soap on the wet towels and moved them fast on their tender chests. Their backs were zebra-striped with years of oil and dirt. Obviously, this kind of washing cleaned little. The northerners were the girls with broad shoulders, thicker backs, and more developed bosoms and hips. The ones with sloping shoulders, flat chests, and thin waists were the southern girls, nicknamed "soybean sprouts." In the brown water, they soaped their towels again. They moved to the lower part of their bodies and finally to their feet. Because the bed was too high to sit and wash both feet at once, they had to remain standing and immerse one foot at a time in the basins, which now floated with soap foam, bits of wood, and brick grit.

Washing up was the messiest time. The room was scattered with soiled underwear, smelly shoes, and dirty jackets, together with the tools the girls had brought back from the work site. Water splattered and formed small white-filmed pools on the muddy ground. The fragrance of the familiar sandalwood soap filled the air, reminding me again of home.

Another four girls returned and were soon followed by two more. They were just as eager to wash up, coming in and hurrying out of the room to fetch water, opening and closing the door repeatedly.

"Close the door! Hurry up and close the door!"

One girl scurried over to the door with both arms crossed in front of her chest. She had barely shut it when another girl kicked it open again, her hands full with a basin of water.

When I joined the washing army the next day, I became so obsessed with the door that I didn't dare take off my clothes. The boys in the opposite room will see me, I thought. I stood stiffly in front of my ration of water and moved the wet towel slowly under my clothes. Washing this way was difficult. But I soon found out that the biggest threat was not from the boys living across the hall — who, coming in and going out, looked at the ceiling like saints — but from Old Tao, the company commander. When most of us were in the nude, he would nudge the door open. With practiced skill, he would poke his bald head into the room while blocking the opening with his body, thus obscuring the view from the boys' room.

"Is Golden Bean back yet?"

The girls shivered at the man's thick voice. All movement stopped. The room went quiet as everyone held her breath.

Appearing to be greatly embarrassed by what he saw, the old walnut withdrew his body quickly and closed the door. Angry and disgusted the first time this happened, I looked at the senior girls for an answer, but no one met my questioning eyes. They resumed washing, grimacing slightly, but didn't register anger. No one talked about the problem, as if the old walnut had never peeped at all. He didn't look like he was new at it, though. The girls must have endured him for a long time. But with twenty people living in one room, it was impossible to lock the door, especially at washing time. I stopped moving the towel under my clothes. I couldn't continue. I was confused, but in the deliberate hush, I detected unspoken fear. I sensed it in the girls' downcast eyes and in the nervousness that hung in the air. All at once I understood that I had better keep quiet. I had forgotten for a moment who Old Tao was. In his hands, he held the power to decide our fates.

Fear Neither Hardships
nor Death

The next morning, I woke at 4:30, when the first light of dawn penetrated the darkness. Outside our windows, villagers called their backyard hogs to breakfast. An overwhelming sour smell of pig feed assailed my nostrils. In a minute, cocks crowed, dogs came running, birds chirped, and babies cried. I had to get up. Life started early on the frontier.

Sleepily we began work at the construction site. Old Tao gave each of us a carrying pole and a pair of buckets, which were so deep they reached my knees. Our job was to deliver mixed wet cement and bricks to the bricklayers, who worked on the scaffolds and were building a house for the Seventy-third Regimental Headquarters.

We were teamed up with six local peasants — our educators, as Chairman Mao called them. They were earthy people. Their skins were copper-colored from year-round outdoor labor. For lack of washing facilities, the men rarely bathed. Every day they wore the same patched cotton-padded clothes, which they fastened with straw ropes. The dark cloth was excellent for hiding dirt. Frequently I would see them use the front of their sleeves to wipe their mouths after meals. But compared to them, I was still dirty because I belonged to the "petty intellectuals," although I hadn't received any formal middle school education, not even for a day.

Chairman Mao said: "If you compare the unreformed petty intellectuals with the workers and peasants, you will find that the unsoiled petty intellectuals are not clean at all. The laboring people are much cleaner even if their hands are dirty and their feet stained with cow manure."

Work had to stop from time to time for us to worship Chairman Mao, no matter whether we were in the middle of mixing cement or erecting walls. Everyone, with Mao's *Quotations* in hand, stood facing the east, wishing Chairman Mao a long, long life and his immediate successor, Lin Biao, eternal health. Work also stopped for Daily Confessions. With guilt in their eyes, people voiced repentance to Chairman Mao for their selfish thoughts. "Our great teacher, great leader, great helmsman, and great commander, please forgive me for thinking about myself. Generation after generation, we will remember your kindness, for it is deeper than the sea and higher than the mountains." Everywhere the construction site echoed with Chairman Mao's slogan. "First, you must fear no hardships; second, you must fear no death." His thought continued: "All men will die. But the significance of death can be very different. To die for the people is weightier than Mount Tai, but to die for the fascists and for those who exploit and oppress the people is lighter than a feather."

Confessions could continue into the night. When I finally climbed onto the tall brick bed, all I wanted to do was to lie there forever and never get up. Every bone in my body was crying in pain, as if someone had whipped me hard with a wide leather belt. I struggled to open my eyes and saw that the older girls on the opposite bed had wrapped themselves in the heavy army overcoats and were sitting cross-legged like Buddhas. Some leaned against the wall, leafing through Mao's *Quotations*. Many were writing in diaries on their laps under the dim lights. But soon their heads began nodding as they fell asleep with the notebooks still open and fountain pens still in hand. Slight snoring rose and fell. My eyelids grew heavier and heavier. Everything blurred. "Comrades! Revolution is not done yet! We still need to work hard," deputy political instructor Wang Pei shouted in a sleepy voice.

Girls picked up Mao's books again, holding them closer to their faces. Rubbing my eyes vigorously, I opened my diary, and began confessing: Was there anything I said or did or thought during the day that hadn't been in line with Chairman Mao's teachings? Was I afraid of hardships or death? Did I think about myself too much? With one hand cupping my chin, I racked my brains. Some days, when I couldn't discover any evil thoughts, I would fill my diary with the most fashionable revolutionary rhetoric:

> If I die in a battle,
> Please tell my parents not to be sad,
> For I have shed my last drop of blood for the liberation
> of mankind.
> Tell them always to follow Chairman Mao.
> Only by following Chairman Mao
> Will we be invincible.
> Only by following Chairman Mao
> Will the world be made red all over.

> The east wind is blowing hard, the battle drum is beating. The Revolution is toppling the mountains and roiling the seas. But a few flies are wailing, and some termites are attempting to shake the big tree. This is their daydream, for the imperialists are declining day by day while we're getting stronger and stronger. But on the revolutionary Long March, we revolutionary youths should always be vigilant against the bombs thrown by the bourgeoisie, who never for a second abandon the goal of turning us into their predecessors.

In the following weeks I worked nonstop. When the fading, sicklelike moon hung in a sky as gray as a fish's belly, I began carrying loads heavier than my own weight, which was then about 115 pounds. Two knee-high buckets full of wet cement weighed at least 120 pounds. I didn't stop until the sickle of the moon had reappeared and stars twinkled overhead. The loose planks that formed our walkway bounced under my feet. The single step-plank that went from the ground to the scaffolding had no rails on either side. Once on this shaky incline, there was no way to stop or turn around. To me, it felt like the path to death. My legs became soft and my head grew dizzy. The empty space below seemed like a huge mouth opening to swallow me up. I had been afraid of heights ever since I could remember. But now I had to work in high places every day. Whether it was my shaking lips or my hesitant steps that betrayed me, Old Tao noticed my panic. He pointed his finger at the sky and proclaimed, "Remember what Chairman Mao says: 'Today's women occupy half the country's sky. Whatever a man can do, a woman can, too. There is nothing to be fearful of in this world, not even death.'"

One night a noise woke me. Xue, my middle-school friend, who slept beside me, was weeping. Seeing that I was awake, she put her head inside the quilt.

"What's wrong?" I asked, with my eyes still closed.

"My leg hurts so much, it's killing me," Xue choked out.

Resisting the urge to fall back asleep, I fumbled under my pillow for the flashlight. Xue pulled open her quilt. The dim light cast a yellow spot on her right kneecap. I pressed hard, leaving deep finger dents on the skin. I massaged her leg for a few minutes before falling back to a sound sleep. I was too tired. Xue's knee was red and swollen, but it didn't look as bad as my bleeding shoulders, which had swollen to the size of two steamed rolls. A careless pat on them would make me groan miserably. These days, I felt sore all over. My muscles and bones seemed to be detached from the rest of my body. I worked eighteen hours a day, seven days a week. Every day was a struggle; the burden of surviving had never been this heavy.

"Born untimely": *(clockwise)* the author's mother; the author at five; and her younger brother, Jie, three years old. The year this photograph was taken, 1958, Mao started the Great Leap Forward movement that would result in a nationwide famine in which forty million people starved to death.

敬祝毛主席万寿无疆！

Mao called on the Red Guards to "spread the fire to every corner of the country and carry the Cultural Revolution to its conclusion!" The slogan below his portrait reads: "We wish Chairman Mao eternal life."

The author's mother preparing for mandatory military training in 1966.

The author's father anxiously studying the May 16 Statement to the Nation, which initiated the Cultural Revolution, 1966.

Nanchu *(top left)*, fourteen years old, as a junior Red Guard leader, 1967.

Ming, the author's older brother *(in white cap)*, and his fellow Red Guards at the start of their Long Marches to the country's remotest corners to incite the people to overthrow Liu Shaoqi, 1966.

Nanchu, seventeen, leaving for the Heilongjiang Military Farms on the Sino-Soviet border during the Up to the Mountains, Down to the Countryside movement, 1970.

Self-reliance: Da Zhai, in northern China, was Mao's model commune for self-reliance. Here, ex–Red Guards from the cities are toiling in their spare time during the Da Zhai movement.

In her Peking opera *Red Lantern*, Madame Mao promoted the proletarian ideal of asceticism. The actor was rumored to be Madame Mao's lover.

Ming at the Usuri River, beyond which lies the Soviet Union, 1969. Chinese youths who crossed the river and were caught by the Soviets were often sent back to be executed by the Chinese government.

Eleven Shanghai youths refuse to evacuate the Yellow Mountain Tea Farm, 1971. Ex–Red Guards all over the country answered the call to "Devote your splendid youth to the people!"

"Fear neither hardships nor death!" Young girls from the cities gathering rocks for construction.

Nanchu, at eighteen, with Ming soon after the fire that nearly killed her, 1971.

Lin Biao *(left)* propelled the cult of Mao to absurd excess but later tried by every available means to assassinate the Great Leader.

Looking south toward home: Ming *(right)*, thirty-one years old and still in Heilongjiang ten years after leaving Shanghai, 1978.

Worker-peasant-soldier students on the men's and women's swim teams of East China Normal University, the base of Mao's educational revolution, 1973. Nanchu is standing second from the right.

January 1976: When Zhou Enlai died in the eleventh year of the Cultural Revolution, the nation could bear no more. Mourners bedecked the Monument of Heroes in Tiananmen Square with wreaths. In April, the ongoing memorial activities were repressed as a counterrevolutionary riot, and Deng Xioaping, the acting premier, was ousted for the third time.

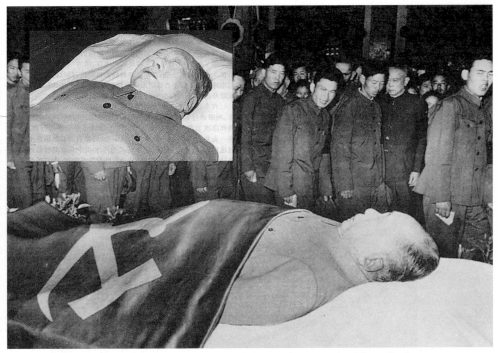

September 9, 1976: The Red Sun has set; God has died.

Nanchu wearing a black arm band, as everyone did after Mao's death, and standing by the Huangpu River to greet a new era, September 1976.

"May the laughing Buddha bless me!" Nanchu as a teacher at Shanghai University in 1978, when the political winds changed after Mao's death and she was regarded as politically dangerous.

At the University of Georgia, in the land of opportunity, September 1986.

A middle-aged member of the Falun Gong movement in Tiananmen Square, calling for justice and freedom of belief, 2001.

★　　　　★　　　　★

When the opulent green mountains turned red, yellow, and brown, autumn had arrived. The sky was especially high and bright. The golden wheat rippled in the transparent breeze. Clouds of black wood ears, a kind of edible fungus, grew as big as biscuits around tree roots. The hairy heads of "monkey mushrooms" hid behind the branches. Tender emerald fruit hung from the wild pear trees. Peasant children carrying cloth bags in all colors went to the mountains to collect hazelnuts. But the weather, like a newborn baby, changed expression without warning. It poured all day long, turning the fields into a huge swamp and beating down and burying the wheat in the mud.

"Seize food from the mouth of the dragon." Fifteen hundred of us were summoned from different industrial companies to march into the wet fields and salvage the harvest. Back pain and shoulder pain were forgotten as I dug, dragged, and cut the fallen wheat with my mud-stained sickle. Like a machine, I repeated the same monotonous movement thousands of times a day while fighting off blood-crazed insects that swarmed in the overcast weather.

At night the boys stayed in temporarily erected tents, the girls in the dining hall. We slept on the earthen floor with only straw mats under our exhausted bodies. The next morning, I woke up to find my undershirt wet with ground moisture. For more than a month we struggled in the huge "jelly pot." My hands and feet swelled from the long soakings in rainwater. My skin became white and thick with wrinkles and was so soft it tingled to the touch. The knuckles of my fingers were as big as chestnuts. I felt pain but wasn't concerned about it, since no one else seemed to be. Besides, we couldn't afford to show our worries. We were supposed to forget about ourselves and fight selflessly until our last breaths. Our bodies didn't belong to us but to the party and Chairman Mao.

No matter how tired we were, we still confessed to Mao at night:

How can I succeed in becoming a squad leader when I am the youngest? How can I become a real communist, who is loyal, candid, able to work independently, highly conscious of the complexities of class struggle, and always puts the interests of others before my own? I believe that age shouldn't be a problem, since the young have produced heroes ever since ancient times.

Abrasions and cuts from the sickle covered my hands, arms, and legs. Working even during my menstrual period, I felt cramped with pain and developed a strange disease: I would urinate at the sight and touch of water. My friend Xue's period simply stopped. It returned only many months later. Tormented by her leg pains, Xue always lagged behind. I would see her striking her leg with the sickle handle and wiping away her tears behind people's backs. During the last days of the harvest, we became so worn out that we walked on our knees in the muddy fields.

People began making fun of Xue because of her slowness and clumsiness. They said she was just lazy. But I knew that her health was deteriorating. Her once red cheeks had become colorless, and her entire right leg was now red and swollen. The pain crippled her.

Yi, the party secretary, finally agreed to let me accompany Xue to seek medical treatment at the divisional hospital in Tashan. The next morning, we walked one long hour, stopping repeatedly for Xue to rest, before we reached the transportation company, where a truck was waiting for us. A chubby Beijing boy looked us up and down from behind his steering wheel.

"What's wrong?"

"Leg pain," Xue said, bending down to blow the dust from a rock before sitting.

"Why does everybody have back pain or leg pain or hand pain?" the young driver, who obviously never had to work in the "jelly pot" like us, inquired with genuine curiosity. He said that just days ago he had driven several girls to the divisional hospital. Their fingers were red and swollen like carrots.

"Come on up!" He gestured for us to sit on the empty seat next to him.

With the lifting of the morning mist, a view of the countryside opened up under the bright sun. My mood became lighter than the floating clouds, for today was a day of freedom. I could escape the narrow step-plank and relax my strained body without being scolded for laziness. I actually had the time to smell the scents from the wild mountain, admire the beauty of the fallen leaves, and listen to the birds singing farewell as they migrated south.

Since it was such a fine day, the young man enjoyed himself too. He began driving "heroically." This was the common term used to mock young drivers who drove recklessly when girls sat beside them. We were blamed for causing nine out of ten transportation accidents at the Heilongjiang Military Farms. The eyes of the young driver shone with excitement and his upper body swaggered as he maneuvered the steering wheel. Pride beamed from his young face. The truck accelerated like a swift wind, and we bounced as though jumping on springs. My head hit the truck ceiling. Xue had to hold my arm to steady herself on the seat. Birds whirred past. A hedgehog rolled into a ball on the roadside. Poplar trees, brown valleys, and harvested fields flew by.

The truck finally came to a halt in front of a dome-roofed building at the bottom of a hill in Tashan. The gray-faced divisional hospital was once a Japanese biological laboratory during World War II. Smiling young nurses in white uniforms walked up and down the corridor with easy steps. Like us, they were also from the big cities. But through all kinds of networks, these girls, instead of doing physical labor, worked in the hospitals, holding jobs everyone wanted.

I helped Xue sit on a long bench in a doctor's office. She rested her head on the wooden back. Her face looked pale against the white walls. A middle-aged male doctor listened to her heart attentively, tapped her legs here and there with a small hammer, and flexed them. Xue's right leg made crackling sounds. She groaned, her face twisting with pain.

"You have rheumatism," the doctor concluded, his hand playing with the stethoscope hanging around his neck.

"How did I get it? I've just been here a few months." Xue opened her weary eyes wide. The disease frightened her.

"Like transplanted trees, youths from the south are vulnerable to the disease. But the direct cause must be that you worked barefoot on cold, marshy grounds or wet fields for too long." Having seen many young patients with similar symptoms, the doctor was sure of his diagnosis.

"We were soaking in water for a whole month during the autumn harvest!" I told the doctor. He nodded.

Nervously, I massaged my own hands and patted on my own knee joints. I pulled up my pants to see if my legs were red or swollen.

"Will I get better?" Xue asked worriedly.

"Only if you take good care of yourself. Don't sleep on a cold bed in any season. An unheated brick bed produces moisture harmful to the bones. Don't work barefoot under any circumstances and don't work too hard." There was compassion in his voice.

"But how can I possibly do that?" Xue cried in anguish.

And how could I? I asked myself too. Seeing to one's own well-being was selfish, and thinking about oneself was disloyal to Chairman Mao. And was I loyal to him? No! Because I couldn't keep from thinking about my own self. Because I felt every pain very distinctly. I stared at the ground. A big lump clogged my throat.

12

The Sugar Trap

After the harvest came September. Although spring, like a young bride, was always reluctant to show her shy face, winter, like an eager groom, was never timid in displaying his might. The howling northwest wind blew snowflakes as big as goose feathers, cloaking the vast land in silver. In October, temperatures plunged to forty degrees below zero. In this frigid cold, one's tongue could be frozen to window glass instantly, and one's bare ears could be frostbitten in seconds. Snow kept falling until it reached knee level. All transportation in and out of the regiment was curtailed.

It was five months since we'd come here. Our diet had been boiled cabbages, boiled potatoes, and boiled beets. We had not seen oil once. Now, the heap of potatoes piled in the corner of the canteen became hard frozen, like iron eggs. Even the waxy boiled cabbages were a luxury. In this weather, the kitchen served only soup consisting of a few vegetable leaves floating in a salty broth, three times a day. At mealtimes, the young men would strike their enameled bowls with their chopsticks and sing:

> Soup, we love revolutionary soup!
> Soup at breakfast, we smile at the morning sun,
> Soup at lunch makes us feel warm all over,
> Soup at dinner keeps us busy all night long.

Commander Gao, the cook squad leader, stood speechless. Her lips turned pale; her round eyes looked helpless. The canteen had almost nothing in stock. Snow, besides preventing us from gathering rocks on the Mount of Cracks, had halted almost all other normal activities. The cook girls, who no longer had much of anything to cook, sang in sincere and naïve tones:

> Although Golden Hill has no temple,
> Its beauty is too great for me to part.
> O, our great leader, Chairman Mao,
> Although I have never seen you,
> Your kindness lives forever in my heart.

The menu of soup, soup, soup sickened my stomach, and I lost a great deal of weight. My once full cheeks became drawn and lost their youthful color. As I suffered, I dreamed at night about cooked meat in every color — boiled white meat, brown meat in soybean sauce, and meat cooked with green onions. I saw myself sinking my teeth into a hog and eating it whole in one swallow. Then I woke up with a burning stomach and a mouthful of bitter liquid. Feeling the same way, Xue carefully removed from her trunk a tiny jar of rendered pork fat that her mother had given her at the train station. The small jar was a flame burning in the winter night. Resisting many greedy and begging eyes, she let only me share it with her. I placed the creamlike pork fat in my mouth and let it remain there, savoring it bit by bit until it melted in my throat.

One day I received a dinner invitation from Smallpox Lo, the deputy company commander. This local man got his nickname from the hundreds of big and small pits on his face left by smallpox during his childhood. Because of these blemishes, the broad-shouldered and solidly built Lo, in his late thirties, was still single.

"How nice! I can't wait. He's certainly not going to entertain us with salty soup." Xue, whom Lo had also invited, jumped up, forgetting her bad leg and falling to the ground. Her face colored. I pulled her to her feet and comforted her.

Lo lived in a small house at the end of a dirt road only a short distance from our dormitory. In his kitchen, which faced the front door, stood a clay hearth that served both as a cooking stove and a source of heat. On it a pot was sizzling. Black coal, yellow straw, and brown tree twigs made a heap in the corner. Behind the main door stood a large brown earthenware crock of water. The light in the room was dim, but it was warm and filled with a delicious smell. Various colorful New Year's posters depicting happy magpies, red peaches, and an old wise man with a long beard decorated the mud walls. Like everywhere else in the countryside of the northern provinces, a huge brick bed occupied the better half of the room. Spread at one end was a quilt with loud green peacocks and huge white roses against a dark red background, and in the middle of the bed stood a short-legged table. On it Lo had arranged tofu, dried bean curd with chives, and slivers of meat cooked with black ear fungus. We took off our shoes and sat on our legs around the table. My mouth watered intensely, and my eyes locked onto the food. Lo's greasy clothes, his dirty fingernails, and his cavity-filled teeth no longer bothered me at all.

"This is my poor stuff. Help yourself," Lo said, cordially initiating the dinner. His beady eyes flashed with warmth.

Although custom required that we, as guests, should decline three times before eating, we didn't wait. I gobbled up the food like a wolf out of the forest. I filled my mouth four times and swallowed once. Xue never raised her head, her chopsticks hurriedly moving around the dishes and her mouth chewing loudly. I laughed secretly at my poor manners, remembering the words of Confucius: "Only when one's stomach is full can he tell honor from disgrace."

Lo poured himself hard liquor in a crude bowl. Holding the bottom of the bowl, he drank slowly while watching us with half-closed eyes. Fishing around in his side pocket, he removed a piece of yellow-ish newspaper and a pinch of dried tobacco. Wrapping the dark-brown specks in the old paper, he laughed coarsely.

"You Shanghai girls are beautiful," he said, pointing to Xue. "Look at that skin. It's as fair as writing paper. Your eyebrows are like moth's wings. You girls are as charming as spring willows. It must be the water and the soil of the south. No wonder Great Emperor Qian-long searched for beauties in southern China." He tapped his ciga-rette on the table several times, struck a match, and lit it. White smoke streamed from his mouth and nostrils.

The room smelled strongly of alcohol and tobacco. Lo kept on drinking and smoking and praising. His pitted face was red and his eyes wild with animal desire. I felt the warmth spreading from his stout body. Lo's voice was deep and manly. Even his breath, mixed with wine and cigarettes, felt seductive. Xue, her eyes half closed, tilted her body toward him.

In this coziness, I forgot all about our freezing dormitory. The heated brick bed soothed my worn-out legs, and the food and the cordials warmed my heart. "Tulip wine flows, and the jade plate glows. With the host's hospitality, I forget that I am in a strange land." The gaudy quilt on the other side of the bed became even more vivid. The green peacocks displayed their fine tail feathers and began to dance. The white roses in full bloom illuminated the drab clay, which became more alluring than the emperor's dragon bed. All the plates and bowls were clean. I still didn't want to leave. Maybe this was a place I could call home.

Thinking about home, I lost myself in reflection. How were Father, Mother, and Jie? Did they miss me? Although the land here was frozen three yards deep, real winter never came to Shanghai this early in October. Now, it was chrysanthemum season there. Red, yellow, and golden flowers would be in full bloom in the front yard of our old apartment. Cupping my chin with both hands, I wondered:

Do Father and Mother know how much I've been missing them? Do they know how difficult life here is?

I couldn't help worrying about Jie, who was still small for his age of fifteen. He was only two years away from graduation. Where would he go? I hoped it wouldn't be here.

"Want more wine?" Lo asked me, half of his face shadowed in the dim light. The many pits on his rough skin deepened and darkened. I took a sip of the white wine from the bowl Lo handed me. It was strong as fire, scalding my head. Tears ran from my eyes. Suddenly I wanted to cry, to sob loudly in this mud house. I wanted to rest my head on this man's strong shoulder. I wanted to pour out my inner self to him, who had entertained us with good food tonight.

I looked at the clock on the wall. It was about nine. The villagers went to bed at seven. In winter, some retired right after supper. "Early to bed and early to rise" was the lifestyle peasants had observed for thousands of years. We should leave, I persuaded myself. But I didn't want to move my legs, which felt so warm and relaxed on the bed. I shivered when I thought about our dorm. The brick bed there was as cold as a casket. The company never assigned a special person to heat it in winter. Heating a ten-yard-long brick bed wasn't an easy job. After a long day's work, we were so exhausted that no one had the energy even if they had the skill. In this cozy comfort, how I wanted to lie down and sleep, just for one hour! But an inner voice urged me to get out. It was late. I reached under the table to tug at Xue, who had gulped two cups of wine and wanted more. I knew she was using it to quench her miseries and stop the leg pain.

But on her thigh my fingers met a strong and groping hand. Shocked, I drew back quickly. Through the window came the faint sound of the curfew bell. Two red clouds covered Xue's cheeks. Her dim eyes were tender. Her lips parted slightly. We should go. I pulled Xue's sleeve, but she looked at me reluctantly. I helped her get up so her good leg would touch the dirt floor first.

Lo staggered to the doorway.

"Come . . . back . . . again. . . . Next . . . Thursday, . . . how . . . is . . . that?" He smacked his lips.

Frigid air blew in my face as I opened the squeaking door. The ground was bright with the reflection of moonlight on the snow. Out of nowhere, a yellow dog ran up to us and sniffed our feet.

13

The Da Zhai Movement

Cold moonlight soaked the night. During the day, the weak sun couldn't break through the heavy clouds. Our village was immersed in the gray of a long winter. Spring was still, far, far away.

The next week we didn't return to Lo's house, for Yi called an urgent meeting to declare the beginning of the Da Zhai movement. Da Zhai was Chairman Mao's model commune, located on the sterile Yellow-Earth Plateau in northern China. Its success in transforming itself from a dirt-poor village to a "grain depot" proved the truth of Chairman Mao's words, "Mankind can outsmart nature."

Standing at the front of the stage, Yi did the calculation with his fingers. If one person in the company contributed five hours of his spare time a day to deliver manure to the company-owned field, then for five hundred people, including spouses and children, there would be 2,500 extra hours a day. With this huge supply of extra manpower, there was nothing in the world that couldn't be accomplished.

At 3:30 the next morning I awoke at the whistle and went outside. In the bone-freezing cold before the dawn, I shivered uncontrollably and quickly pulled down the flaps of my cotton hat. It was still dark, with only stars peeping at us in the sky. But on the trail leading to the company field a quarter mile away, I was surprised to see so many shadows moving. Yi's voice came from afar, offering a lively greeting to everyone he saw. He was already on his way back from the second trip. Had he slept at all last night? I wondered.

On the way I met all the company leaders, their wicker baskets topped with manure. Everyone was moving at full speed. Yi, with two baskets dancing on his shoulders, was in a fierce competition with my squadmate Lon, who was running neck and neck with the party secretary. Their sweaty heads were steaming in the frigid air. Girls ran after them, trying to catch up. Yi's inspiring voice pierced the thin air: "Comrades! Men should make ten round-trips and women at least seven."

In this competitive atmosphere, no one could afford to relax. Concealed behind my enthusiasm I harbored a deep fear of lagging behind, which would be interpreted as a lack of support for Chairman Mao's Da Zhai movement. I jogged with all my strength, the pole pinching my shoulders and the wicker baskets swaying up and down. One after another, I broke three carrying poles. As the saying goes, "In long-distance carrying, there is no light load." The load of manure weighed heavier and heavier on my shoulders like a growing mountain. Perspiration soaked my undershirt and sweater, and even penetrated my cotton-padded coat and pants. Salty sweat ran down my cheeks, and some froze at the corners of my mouth. But I didn't slow down. The company leaders would remember and record everyone's performance and punish those who were not "devoted." Yesterday they had permanently "lent" my friend Xue, along with a group of others, to an agricultural village located deep in the mountains fifty miles from the regimental hospital and a hundred miles from the divisional hospital. Although Xue had submitted the doctor's written diagnosis of rheumatoid arthritis, the company leaders still believed that she was simply lazy. Her future might be ruined. I had to keep trotting as long as I could still breathe.

When the day brightened, Yi called off the labor competition. Once I slowed down, the subzero temperature quickly hardened my sweat-soaked clothing and turned it into frozen armor, rattling with every movement. Miserable, I stiffened to avoid contact with the icy smoothness of my underclothes. My wet eyebrows and hair turned frosty. The only things not frozen were my feet and rubber shoes, since I kept on walking.

The day's formal work began on the Mount of Cracks. Drilling holes. Handling explosives. Hauling big rocks.

After dinner came another round of the Da Zhai movement. I dragged my tired body after the company leaders along the snowy trail. The northwest wind whined and the temperature plunged. Snow and frost swirled about us. Yi panted out a song from Chairman Mao's *Quotations:*

> We must rely on ourselves!
> This is called self-reliance.
> We are not isolated.
> All the laboring people in the world are our friends.
> We must rely on ourselves.
> This is called self-reliance.

My soul struggled and groaned in bitterness.

> Will conquers all.
> Since Yi is running, so must I.
> This is called self-reliance.
> I don't want to be sent away like Xue, so I must run.
> I must run. . . .
> This is called self-reliance.

The harsh reality began to filter through my diary entries too. I wrote in one:

> My back is so painful I can hardly keep it straight. My legs are so weak, it's like stepping on cotton. I don't know if I'll be able to carry anything tomorrow. There's not one second out of the twenty-four hours that belongs to me. I have devoted every bit of my life to the great, glorious, correct Chinese Communist Party.

Surviving the Da Zhai movement became everyone's primary concern. With sore backs, aching muscles, and weary bones, we persevered stoically for months. At night, when I took off my clothes, I saw that my body had changed: each shoulder was a hump of callus and muscle. My once thin legs now bulged with muscles. My once narrow feet had grown flat and broad, my toes spreading so they could stand firmly under heavy pressure. My once tender hands were now thick and hard with layers of shiny calluses, allowing me to handle rough materials without feeling pain. I was now shorter than when I first came; my growth had been stunted. Even worse, though I did not know it then, the heavy work was severely distorting my pelvic basin, leaving me with permanent physical damage.

The company leaders, who never worked during the day except in the morning and evening hours, were certain that using our spare time would bring about miracles. The company would soon become the second Da Zhai, and they would all be invited to Beijing to see Chairman Mao. However, as the movement dragged on, exhausted young people collapsed one after another. In the dormitories, the sick curled up under their quilts, and their loud coughing from pneumonia and bronchitis rose and fell day and night.

One afternoon, while carrying a huge rock, I collapsed. I wrenched both of my ankles, which at once turned bluish and swelled up. The next morning, I tried to get out of bed, but when my feet touched the ground it felt like I was walking on hundreds of knives, and I fell to the dirt floor. Realizing that my injury was serious, I sat all morning on the edge of the bed, staring dumbly at the smoke-darkened ceiling, depressed. At lunchtime Su, a plump Beijing girl from the cooking squad, stepped in, holding a bowl of hot noodles served only to the sick.

"You can't just sit there like a clay Buddha. You need to see someone right away or you'll get rheumatoid arthritis and become crippled." Her voice conveyed urgency and warmth.

Su was a cheerful girl with deep, smiling dimples at the corners of her mouth and thick braids past her shoulders. Both of her parents were veteran workers, the power base of the Chinese Communist Party. The family had never suffered during any of the political movements launched in New China. Her childhood was peaceful and uneventful. That may have contributed to her carefree personality, in contrast to my anxious one. After my school friend Xue left the company, I became close with this kind-hearted girl.

Su left and came back later. Her lunch over, she offered to take me to an expert in massage. She had found a pair of muddy rubber boots that she pulled over my swollen feet. She helped me put on my heavy overcoat. Then, holding onto my arms, she carried me on her back out of the dormitory. Breathing heavily, she set me down on the seat of an old bicycle. The sun was white, its rays soft on the skin. The two wheels milled the snow and rolled along the road leading to the mountain. Jackdaws flew low over our heads as Su faltered along. Finally she stopped in front of a lonely mud-walled hut near the foot of the mountain and rapped hard on the wooden door.

A small lady in her fifties answered. She looked neat, with her hair pulled back into a bun, and was wearing a faded blue jacket open at the side. Su carried me into the room and placed me on the brick bed.

The hut was a world of mud: the walls, ceiling, floor, windowsills, and the stove standing in the center of the room were all made of it. An aluminum pot fizzed slightly, its white steam floating in the air. A light odor of corn porridge pervaded the room. A big-bellied oil lamp was perched on the windowsill above the huge brick bed.

The small lady quickly pulled up my pant legs, revealing my injured ankles. The swelling had spread all over my feet, which shone like two purple balloons. She frowned, her nimble, long fingers skillfully probing here and there around the ankle. She lifted one foot onto her lap and started twisting, pressing, and rubbing vigorously with her powerful, bony hands. In agony with pain, I rolled on the bed while Su struggled to keep my kneecap pressed down tightly. The woman then grabbed the other foot.

In about half an hour, her iron claws suddenly relaxed and softened. She started caressing my foot, her fingers pushing the muscles in one direction. Her forehead was damp with sweat.

"I'm smoothing your veins so they won't become knotted," she said.

Her thumbs pinched and slid along the thick vein running through the ankle. Like kneading dough, she rubbed my foot back and forth with her palms, the bones crackling in her hands. At last she stopped.

From a dark cloth bag in the corner of the bed, she took out a handful of orange and brown herbs. She told me to mix them with white wine to form a paste and apply it to both ankles. That would remove blood stasis and promote circulation. She wrapped the herbs in an old piece of paper, the expression on her face as pure as jade and as calm as ice. The woman now smiled, showing her small white teeth.

I put a note of five yuan on the bed, nearly one-sixth of my monthly salary of thirty-two yuan, but she picked it up and pressed it into my hand.

"No! No! I can't simply watch a girl become a cripple, can I? I am also a mother. Your parents are too far away and can't take care of you. I'm just doing a little bit for them." She lowered the earflaps of my cotton hat and fastened the strings under my chin. Then she helped Su put me back on the old bicycle.

"Oh, I forgot something." She scurried back into the house. When she returned, she was carrying a basket of pink-shelled eggs. They were still hot. The locals raised hens in their backyards and collected the eggs one by one for the coming Lunar New Year. But she gave hers all to me. When I took the basket, the woman smiled from ear to ear. In this small lady whom I had never met before, I saw Mother again. She waved good-bye. The mud house faded in the twilight. But the bright plum flowers at the corner of the house still swayed in front of my eyes, like fire burning in the vast expanse of whiteness. This was the power of life. I truly admired their courage, blooming in the winter when every other flower had long withered.

The blue and purple slowly retreated from my swollen ankles, and the pain gradually eased. But I started running a fever and suffered severe chills. The next morning, Su moved me to her small dorm, which she shared with another cook. Because of their unique working schedules — early to rise and early to bed — the cooks had separate rooms. In her room next to the company office, Su said I could sleep on a warm bed for two and drink hot water from a flask she'd borrowed from the canteen.

The girls had gone to work, and the room was quiet and warm. I fell into a fitful sleep. As if in a dream, I felt a hand, a man's hand, gently touching my face and forehead. It caressed my long hair, which lay loose on the pillow. The hand was seductive, soft and greedy, arousing the long stifled desire within me. Lips pressed against mine. I became excited even in my sickness. I jerked and opened my eyes. In a blur I saw Yi's handsome face looming so close to mine that his breath, heavy with tobacco, overwhelmed me.

This was the most powerful leader in the company, more powerful even than the commander, and the very image of the party. I tried to sit up, but he pressed me down, looking at me sternly.

"Have you taken your medicine?" he asked.

"Not yet."

His eyes cast around. He stood up and went over to the battered table near the window. He took out a few pills from a paper bag that the clinician had left and filled a cup with warm water from the flask. He helped me sit up and take them. Yi extracted his own cigarette-stained handkerchief from his upper pocket and softly wiped my sweaty face and neck. He stared at my long-sleeved shirt sharply as if questioning why I wore clothes when sleeping. He didn't know that the long brick bed in our dormitory was always cold, so I had developed the habit of sleeping in my sweater, sometimes even in my cotton-padded coat and pants.

Yi sat beside my pillow, speaking in a low voice. His seemingly innocent touch here and there made me blush. I was ashamed of my excitement and dared not look at him; I didn't know what to do. Yi was married to a pretty wife and had a lovely daughter. I wanted to believe that the man in the prestigious army uniform acted out of no other motivation than concern for one of his young subordinates.

Yet, in my lonely heart, a longing rose. I flushed. Yi's face reddened. Roughly, he grabbed me in his arms and began kissing me. His hand reached for my collar to unbutton my shirt. As his fingers touched me, I felt them distinctly, each one desperate and hungry. They moved hastily down to my chest.

A fear suddenly seized me. In the man's powerful embrace, which was almost choking me, I became cold and stiff like an iron rod. I forgot about who he was. I forgot that he had every power to decide my future. All my initial longings turned into a wisp of smoke and disappeared into the air.

I broke free of Yi's arms and turned my back to him. I quickly closed and buttoned my shirt. An unpleasant silence fell upon the room, with the only sounds the crackling of twigs and the slight noise of his fingers angrily ripping the bamboo mat. After a few moments Yi left, slamming the door behind him.

Exhausted, I lay back down. That night my fever worsened. I had pneumonia and was rushed to the hospital.

I soon learned that Yi's attentions were not reserved just for me. Weeks later, rumors about him circulated wildly when my middle-school classmate Hua, a stout girl with a broad face and flat nose, received a big promotion. The long-tongued peasant wives sat under the midday sun at the south side of the brick building, gossiping with great fervor.

Hua had not been present in the mornings and evenings during the Da Zhai labor competition. Instead, she had worked in the warehouse, where she recently became manager. What's more, the wives claimed, the young girl didn't look like a virgin anymore. Her face had matured. Her breasts were tall and prominent and her hips round. The wives loudly asked passersby how Hua, who was not even admitted into the Communist Youth League, could become a manager, a job usually reserved for the elite Communist Party members.

As Hua's belly got bigger and bigger every day, gossip about the company leaders' sexual behavior spread further and faster than the northwest wind. Focus soon shifted from Yi to the deputy commander, Smallpox Lo, and other officials.

"I saw it with my own eyes," a young electrician said in a hushed voice, standing in the center of a curious crowd gathering in the dining room.

"What did you see?"

The young man covered his mouth and whispered, "I went to report to Lo that our electricity crew got trapped in the snow on the mountain. Through the torn windowpaper, I saw Lo's pants unzipped. Two naked girls were moving on top of him like dancing white snakes."

Girls covered their faces with their hands. The sex-hungry young men listened with mouths gaping, their tongues hanging. The accusation stunned me. I remembered the night when Xue and I ate in Lo's house, and the hand on Xue's thigh.

In the crowded dining room, Lo's two girls stood out like white lotuses, fresh and alluring. Working indoors in the small transformer station, they shunned storm and sun, and their clear skin contrasted sharply with my weather-beaten, sun-darkened complexion. They always appeared at ease because they didn't have to worry about heights or carrying excessive weights or handling explosives. Anger and despair gripped me.

Ever since the incident with Yi that day, I had a lingering fear that he would hold a grudge and that I might never escape the hard work I was doing. By now, I was the only city girl in the platoon still carrying the heavy building materials up to the high scaffolds during construction season and still blasting rocks on the mountain during winter. I had no hope of changing jobs anytime soon. I shivered at my gloomy future.

14

Asceticism — Spring Tide under the Iceberg

In January 1971, blizzards blasted and snow covered the land. The white flakes piled high on the limbs of the bare trees. Forming shadows in the cold moonlight, branches moved like monster's talons, raking upward to grasp the sky. In the wind, they shook like a horde of demons dancing in riotous revelry.

It was a Sunday afternoon. Having no clean clothes to change into, I planned to wash my heap of dirty ones on this bitter cold day. So I carried a bucket to the well to fetch water. It was one of those days when one's tongue could be frozen to the window in a second. Merciless winds solidified every drop of water. Layers of thick ice that had built up since the beginning of winter turned the area around the well into a rugged skating rink. A few yards away, I heard a girl screaming hysterically.

"Help! Help! Pin has fallen into the well!"

The back door of the canteen, which was close to the well, was kicked open and a broad-shouldered young man dashed through it. He faltered on the slippery path but managed to regain his balance quickly. While running, he yanked off his black overcoat and threw it on the ground in front of me. Reaching the well, he grasped the haft firmly with one hand and seized the worn-out wire rope with the other. He swung out to the center of the shaft and slid down. There was blood on the iron rope from the young man's torn hands. As I drew near, inching like an old lady with a pair of small feet, I heard the young man's deep voice coming from the bottom and echoing against the walls.

"Move your legs and sit on my shoulders."

The girl wept bitterly. The young man consoled her.

"Don't cry. What does Chairman Mao say? 'In times of darkness, we should see the brightness.'"

The weeping stopped. In a frightened voice, the girl said he was too tall for her to put her legs on his shoulders. He answered that he would lower himself further while he fastened the rope around his waist.

"Tan! What can we do up here?" shouted the anxious people gathered above.

"Pin! Be tough!" Commander Gao was breathless after her sprint from the kitchen.

At the young Tan's command, the people at the top turned the handle and pulled the pair up. The iron rope broke as they climbed out. The frightened Pin was carried off immediately. Grateful comrades covered Tan's dripping body with blankets and overcoats while heaping him with praise.

"What a brave young man!"

"Were you afraid when you jumped in?"

Tan smiled shyly. Looking at his brave face and firm jaw, his slightly upturned nose, and his frosty hair, thick and wavy, I felt waves of affection for him. I handed him a cup of hot water that I had fetched from the canteen. He stretched out his stiff hand but missed the handle, grasping my hand instead. As if from an electric shock, I recoiled, and the cup of hot water fell to the ground, spilling in many small, shallow rivulets.

"Sorry! I didn't mean to . . ." he whispered, his lips continuing to move as if he had thousands of words to say to me at once. His bright eyes were glowing like two torches, expressing unfathomable tenderness. I felt my heart thundering. I bent over to pick up the enamel mug in order to hide my blushing face.

"Tan! Hurry up or you'll freeze to death!"

People hustled him away indoors. Under layers of blankets and overcoats, Tan's legs wavered. Standing in the piercing wind, I watched his shape from behind. I forgot about fetching water. I forgot the knifelike cold. I kept thinking about his soft eyes. I wanted to follow him and hold his bleeding hands. When he disappeared in the twilight, I felt lonely without him.

Like a strong spring wind, Tan's story spread near and far in the barren winter. Tan was nominated for membership in the Chinese Communist Party, the highest honor a youth could win. But he was rejected twice. After the second rejection, we went to the company office to seek an explanation. Yi, the party secretary, stood before us. He said in a pained tone that it was Tan's father, an historical counter-revolutionary, who had ruined him. "Historical counterrevolutionary" referred to those people who used to work for the Kuomintang and Japanese and the businesses and institutions of Western countries. Tan's father had been a loan clerk in a British bank before 1949. During the Cultural Revolution, the label of historical counterrevolutionary was almost equal to a death sentence, one carried out in the slow form of daily persecution and humiliation.

"Do you know where his father is now?" Yi asked, clutching a hand-rolled cigarette between two brown fingers. "He's imprisoned in Qinghai Province." Yi emphasized the word "imprisoned," knowing the weight it carried. Qinghai Province near Tibet was infamous for its harsh treatment of political prisoners.

Crestfallen, we closed our mouths and bowed our heads, feeling deeply sorry for our comrade.

Soon after, Tan disappeared. Some said he went into the mountains. Others claimed they saw him go into the woods behind the village.

We searched for him all over. Again and again, I saw his lips parted with unspoken words at the wellside. He had meant to say something, but had stifled it instantly. Now I understood why, sensing the heavy weight he carried on his back. Why did his father's past have to pose such a great threat to him? I felt angry and retreated into a deep sorrow. Where are you, Tan? Do you see no way out but the one you chose? Please, Tan! Be strong and tough. Even in the darkness, there is always a streak of light. After today, there is always a tomorrow. Don't you see that?

A few days later, he came back. A hunter had saved his life. He had found the young man lying unconscious in the snow, in a valley, among the silent poplar trees. Footprints of deer had encircled him. Two red foxes had sniffed around him. The old hunter carried the unconscious body to his small hut and lit a fire to warm him. Several of Tan's toes were already dead, frozen black.

Afterward, Tan worked nonstop from dawn to dusk. He wouldn't accept his fate but tried desperately to challenge it. He severed all relations with his family and refused to write his father. He never went back home even when family visits were later allowed. It seems Tan had managed to escape from his father's evil shadow once. In his middle-school years, he was admitted to the Youth League and still wore its badge on his chest. But that was before the Cultural Revolution, before his father was sent to the Qinghai prison, in a period when the political treatment of youths like Tan was far more lenient under President Liu Shaoqi. Now, at the peak of the Cultural Revolution, the party refused to accept his loyalty. Yi made it clear that although Tan was a brave comrade, the party branch would never admit him as a member. Neither should he expect to study at a university, since he would never pass the political investigation of his family background. Because of his father's past connection with Great Britain, Tan, whom the party obviously suspected as at least a potential British spy, would be denied every opportunity open to other young people and would be the last allowed to leave this frontier village and return to Beijing, his hometown. As the future became clearer to him, a veil of sadness covered his bright eyes. Looking at them broke my heart.

I dreamed about the electric moment when Tan's hand had accidentally touched mine. I wanted to see him every day. When we met in a crowd, he looked at me, his dark, wavy hair flying joyfully in the wind. I would smile back. Then his sad eyes would glisten again. Love, like the life-giving spring wind, kissed our hearts. Shyly we stretched our arms to reach for each other, and timidly our steps moved toward each other, riding the wind of hopes and dreams.

But one cold night on the eve of the Lunar New Year, gunshots piercing the deep quiet shattered it all.

Awakened by the noise, I wondered if the Soviet revisionists, who were only a hundred miles away, had crossed the border. I rushed out of the dorm only to be told to stay indoors because fighting was going on in the company stable. For the rest of the night, machine guns stuttered and hand grenades boomed. Quiet came again only when day broke. I followed the other horrified young people to the stable. Fresh blood covered the white snow. Cartridge shells and fragments of hand grenades were lodged in the ground. Only one body remained. Beside it was a piece of paper: "It is all my fault for falling in love. I take complete responsibility. My behavior has nothing to do with the girl or with my family."

This corpse had been a handsome young man with heavy features, stiff hair that stood on end, and a wide, strong mouth, a comrade who worked together with me on the construction sites. He loved a girl from his hometown of Tianjin, the country's third largest city. At night they would meet secretly behind the company stable. But the night watchman surprised them. The next day, Old Tao, the company commander, called a meeting to expose and denounce the "crime."

In the crowd, those who knew more about the skirmish whispered that last night the young man from Tianjin had sneaked out of his detention room and stolen weapons from the company office.

From there, he went to Old Tao's home and killed the entire family on their brick beds.

"You forced me to do this! You forced me to do this!" Eyes shot with blood, he seized the stable where he and the girl had trysted and defended himself until the end.

The sun, which had broken through the winter clouds, disappeared again. Feathery snowflakes danced wildly around the dead man, cloaking him in their silver robe. The horror of it overwhelmed us. Surrounding his body, heads lowered, we gulped down sobs. We dared not shed sympathetic tears, although our hearts bled for the death of an innocent comrade. Tan's melancholy eyes looked worried, and his terrified face was paler than the snow. We tried to avoid eye contact. The northwest wind was brutal, stinging my skin like hundreds of tiny knives.

The following day was the Lunar New Year. Firecrackers jumped high into the sky. The joyous children in the village hung red lanterns and festoons to celebrate the nation's biggest holiday. But the dormitories stayed dead quiet. In the aftermath of the tragedy, the company leaders, on the warpath because of the death of Old Tao, were like crazed attack dogs, sniffing everywhere, more than ready to find and punish any "abnormal relations" existing among the hundreds of young people in the company. They read love letters at meetings, criticized any signs of affection, and forced "violators," placed in solitary confinement, to offer self-criticism and repent. The company declared that it was forbidden for a girl and a boy to meet alone at any time. If they had to meet, a company official was required to accompany them.

Around the same time, in contrast, the top revolutionary leaders indulged themselves in sensual pleasures and erotic adventures beyond the wildest imaginings of ordinary Chinese people. Chairman Mao danced and slept with countless beautiful women in his Zhongnanhai Palace. It was rumored that the great banner-holder, Jiang Qing, watched pornographic movies to stimulate her sexual desire and took lovers half her age, among them the star of her model Peking opera, *Red Lantern,* and the world table tennis champion. Of course, the leaders' private lives were kept top secret, and the Chinese people knew nothing about them. They became known to the public only after Mao died and his wife was arrested.

All over the country, crimes against the young city people proliferated. Based on incomplete statistics, the book *The Old Youth* records that, from 1968 to 1973, 3,400 cases of rape were reported in Laoning Province and 3,296 in Sichuan Province. Four hundred twenty-three suicides were reported on Xingjiang Army Reclamation Farms. In 1972, when a journalist from Xin Hua Press, China's official news agency, was covering stories in Yuan Nan Province on the Sino-Burmese border, he happened to witness many girls being guarded by armed militias and forced to collect heavy rocks. He was shocked to see teenagers doing such physically demanding and dangerous work. Was this reeducation? Back in Beijing, he wrote Chairman Mao. Somehow his letter touched Mao's heart. An investigation was ordered into the Yuan Nan Army Reclamation Farms. The following findings were the result: "Since 1968, there have been 1,034 cases of beatings, injuring 1,894 young people. Two were beaten to death. There were 286 cases of rape, resulting in injuries to 430 young women. Among the rapists, 7 are regimental officers, 25 are battalion commanders, and 202 are company leaders. As of this date, 29 of them have been dismissed."

That same year, in order to shore up the reputation of Mao's Up to the Mountain, Down to the Countryside movement, Beijing initiated a campaign to "kill the chickens in order to scare the monkeys." In Heilongjiang Military Farms, two active-duty army officers were executed. The commander of the Sixteenth Regiment and his chief of staff had sexually assaulted and raped as many as several dozen girls.

While revolutionary leaders indulged their appetites, we young people from seventeen to twenty-five lived like ascetics. We were forced to be saints. Whenever I saw Tan, my heart would cry miserably.

I wanted to embrace him so much, but at the same time I wanted to flee from him as far as I could. If I could have dug a hole in the ground and crawled inside like a little mouse, maybe from there I could have calmed down and looked upon him without fearing that my feelings would be discovered.

Many times I quietly slipped away to the woods behind our village. I rubbed my face with the snow, and ran aimlessly. Trees in various shapes bent over as if to comfort me with their branches. I admired them, for even they had the freedom to grow the way they wanted, while confusion and fear accompanied me always as I grew. I raised my head to the sky, thinking, Why did you give me such a strong craving to love and be loved? It must be evil if it isn't allowed and is condemned so strongly. But I can't get it out of my heart. What if I'm found out? Why do you let me live in such torment?

15

Dance with Fire

In spring 1971 the icy rivers and creeks swelled with melted snow. Government propaganda seemed to reach its highest pitch, cresting in a powerful new campaign to worship the godlike Chairman Mao. In an editorial entitled "Devote Your Splendid Youth to the People," the *People's Daily* praised Zhang Yong, a nineteen-year-old Tianjin girl who had plunged into an icy river to save a lamb that belonged to a people's commune in Inner Mongolia, where she had been sent and settled. She never emerged from the water. Citing her example, the *People's Daily* demanded unconditional sacrifice for Chairman Mao. The country's youths answered the call and their heroic deeds filled the national newspapers. Eleven youths from Shanghai refused to evacuate the Yellow Mountain Tea Farm during a devastating flood. Arm in arm, they formed a human wall against the torrent. Five Beijing boys were burned to death when they stood in the path of a ferocious mountain wildfire. They declined to fight it from the side — the act of a coward, they declared. Overnight, to die for Chairman Mao became the greatest honor.

In March I turned eighteen. The months that followed shone with radiance. Red and black butterflies fluttered about over the swampy ground and golden bees flitted from one wildflower to another. White- and red-headed birds ruffled their feathers to welcome summer.

Little did I know that the spirit of Zhang Yong would come to haunt me in the golden month of June. One morning, a piercing alarm woke us up before it was time. Wang Pei, the deputy party secretary and a strong Shanghai girl, was the first to jump out of bed and run outside. She was back in a minute, yelling, "Everybody get up! The repair shop is on fire! Let's go save it!"

I pulled on my clothes in a hurry and followed her to the scene of the fire. In the early dawn, the Great Northern Wilderness still slumbered in gray. But the siren penetrated the enormous quiet and awakened everyone. I saw a column of sparkling cinder-filled smoke swirling over the three-story building. By the time Wang Pei and I arrived, a small group of young men from the electricity platoon had already collected in front of the workshop. Wang Pei and I were the only girls.

Thick smoke surged out of the windows on the upper floors. Fanned by early morning breezes, a long tongue of violent flame licked the roof, making terrifying burning noises.

"There are some new machines and parts on the ground floor," one of the workers shouted.

Apart from some light smoke, the ground floor looked safe. Yan, the young squad leader of the electricity platoon, a typical northern man, tall and strong, yelled in his distinctive Tianjin dialect, "It's no use standing here watching. Time for us to repay Chairman Mao's great loving kindness. Let's learn from Zhang Yong! Come on!"

And with that, the stouthearted squad leader jumped through the open window into the workshop.

"Learn from Zhang Yong! Learn from Zhang Yong! Revolutionaries don't fear death; cowards don't make revolution." A few young men echoed Yan and followed him through the window.

"Yes, it's time to see if we're loyal to Chairman Mao or not!" And a few more jumped in.

And what about me? Should I learn from Zhang Yong? Was I loyal to Chairman Mao? I felt ashamed to be standing there watching. I wanted to follow my comrades, these courageous young men, yet my legs were as soft as noodles. I couldn't lift them. I couldn't make myself. The roaring of the violent flames scared me, and I wanted to run away. But I looked at Wang Pei, who was standing next to me. Her uncombed hair was as messy as a bird's nest. Her crooked front teeth protruded from her mouth. She was a party member and the only company official in the crowd. But at this moment, with her arms crossed in front of her, she just stood there, her face calm as a lake. Maybe a party member and an official didn't need to learn from Zhang Yong. A feeling of contempt rose from the bottom of my heart and quelled my fear. She was supposed to be in the vanguard, but at this critical moment she was acting like a coward. I never knew that she was this selfish and insensitive. Taking a deep breath, I jumped through one of the open windows. Immediately, I felt liberated from my burden.

Inside the huge workshop, only light smoke oozed from overhead. I ran over to the young men and tried to help, but I couldn't join in. I only reached their shoulders in height. So I turned to the lighter machine parts scattered around the floor and carried them to the window to pass to people outside.

Things went smoothly, and I made a dozen trips. The smoke didn't bother me at all. The transient peace gave me the feeling we had plenty of time to remove our country's valuable property. Focused entirely on what I was doing, I forgot that the ferocious fire, which had started below the roof, was devouring its way down to the ground floor.

Though exhausted, the young men still yelled at the top of their voices: "First, you must fear no hardships. Second, you must fear no death." Outside, the gray light of dawn drove away the darkness and poked through the windows, illuminating the walls and heralding another bright new day. Everything seemed so normal, as if we were carrying out an ordinary task. But amid the fracas of the young men's shouts, I heard people outside cry in panic, "Get out quickly! The fire's come down! Get out quickly! Hurry."

I rushed to the young men and screamed, "Get out quickly! The fire's come down!" No one paid any attention. No one seemed even to notice my existence. Sweat soaked their clothes, drops of perspiration dripped down their young faces, which were blotchy with dust and oil. The sharp edges of the machines had ripped their clothes on their shoulders and arms, exposing muscle. Under the pressure, they moved in unison, slowly but firmly. Step by step, they marched toward the main door.

I bent over to grab the last two machine parts, one in each hand, and decided it was time to get out. Although small, the parts weighed me down. As I tried to stand up, I heard a huge boom as if heaven had fallen in. The burning floor upstairs ignited the ceiling. A big wind gushed in and sucked down blazing beams. When they hit the concrete floor, they made dreadful loud breaking sounds. The sawdust used as ceiling insulation rained down like a cloudburst, ignited, and exploded into violent flame. In a split second, every inch of air was on fire. Flames shot through the entire space.

I was stunned by the suddenness of it. Before I had time to react, a burning beam struck me on the head and knocked me to the floor semiconscious. But the whistling fire singing in my ears quickly revived me.

"No, I cannot lie here." I struggled to open my eyes. My vision was blurred. The only thing I saw was flickering flames, big and small, dancing around. Everywhere was fire, fire, fire, in orange red, golden red, and crimson, red in all shades. Leaping flames, like thousands of forked dragon tongues, long and short, licked and greedily devoured everything in their way. They sang merrily and rhythmically.

I struggled to stand. As I rose, my movement stirred a draft, attracting the roaring flame. I could hear my long hair burning, making the most terrifying hissing sound I had ever heard. As flames caressed my hands, the skin peeled quickly, like translucent plastic wrap, from my arms all the way to the fingertips. Hot tongues touched my face, like needles pricking into the flesh.

The workshop was now a huge oven. The heat forced me to run aimlessly in search of an escape. Where was the window? Around me I could see nothing but an ocean of golden redness. Hot beams, giving off red smoke, kept falling from above, bringing with them new showers of sawdust. Blazing wood scraps found their way under my clothing through my open collar and burned my back. Wet, sticky blood ran down from my injured head, which felt like it would burst open with pain. My mind seemed like a desert. I tried frantically to distinguish, amid the flames, where the exit was, but I could see nothing and remember nothing.

Where were the young men? My eyes searched desperately. It was a search for hope, a longing for life. "Help! Help!" I cried. But my voice was drowned out in the bellowing fire. My tears were sucked away instantly by the scorching heat. Time slipped away, one second, two seconds, three seconds . . . a minute, and it had never been this valuable. Now, it meant life and death to me.

"Help! Help!" I yelled in pain, horror, and desperation. No one answered. Flames began to swallow my clothes, and I knew that I would soon be burned to death.

I began hallucinating, seeing water in the roaring red blaze. I thought I felt the cool blue water embracing me from all sides. No more excruciating heat. No more dancing golden dragons. No more pain. I swam in a broad blue sea. The pleasant salt breeze massaged my face softly, playing with my long black hair. One moment, I was flying above with the snow-white seagulls. The next, I was on a fishing boat, sailing on the mirrorlike surface. In the sunshine, in the cloudless sky, came into view the arch of a rainbow. Intoxicating melodies rose from all sides. . . .

During this hallucination, my heart filled with enormous happiness. As if guided by design, my aimlessly running feet found the right direction. My once confused mind became crystal clear: If I continued moving ahead there was a window. Fire still blocked the way, but I knew an exit was right there waiting for me. I ran forward;

the fire grew weaker. I made a right turn. I saw an open window, just a few steps away — the only window in the big workshop that still hadn't caught fire.

I made a run for it. I grasped the hot frame and stuck my body through, crying for help. People rushed to me. Many hands dragged me out and set me on the ground. Horrified people beat my clothing and rolled me over. Someone poured cold water on my burning back.

I don't know how long I lay on the early-summer ground before I was lifted onto a horse-cart. In the rhythm of galloping, I fell unconscious.

16

The Price Paid

I dreamed I was hiding behind huge trees on a green mountain, peering at the white-bearded, silver-haired sages playing chess on a flat rock, drinking and laughing. Birds cheeped and mountain flowers sent forth their fragrant aroma. I watched and watched until I dozed off. When I awakened, withered leaves blanketed the mountain and the luxuriant summer was gone. Back at the village at the bottom of the mountain, I couldn't find my past. Everything familiar had disappeared. A hundred years had passed. The world had changed.

I woke up. The pain in my head was extremely sharp, as if someone were stubbornly drilling a hole. My back was burning. I tried to open my eyes. But my face and head were wrapped in several layers of bandages, leaving only two holes for nostrils to breathe through and one for my mouth to take in liquid. I attempted to move my arms, but I was too weak. They were heavy, weighed down with tons of bandages that fatigued me. A thousand tiny knives cut through my throat. I wanted water badly. I tried to make a noise.

"She has finally come back!"

Through the thick bandages, I heard a remote but excited voice. It was a male's nasal voice inflected with a heavy local accent. I heard four or five other voices around me.

I licked my lips dramatically to attract their attention.

"Give her some water!" ordered the first voice. I learned later that it belonged to Dr. Ge, a middle-aged man with bushy hair and thick sideburns. He was a retired military doctor from the Korean War, in charge of the medical group saving my life.

A spoonful of clear water was cautiously placed into my mouth, then another. Water, a lifeline at any time, alleviated the scorching pain of my throat and refreshed my consciousness.

"How do you feel now?" Dr. Ge asked with concern.

"Fine!" I meant to say. But hardly did I utter the word than I was seized with a fit of dizziness and started throwing up. Bitter liquid gushed out. I turned my head so I wouldn't choke myself. Towels patted my chin and neck.

"She has suffered a concussion. Vomiting is a sure sign," Dr. Ge explained in a whisper to his staff, touching the left top of my head. "Her hair was dirty with wood powder and dust from the collapsed ceilings, so we shaved it to the scalp to prevent any possible infection."

I listened with curiosity and a sense of strangeness, as if the story were about someone else. Gradually their voices faded, moving farther and farther away. I fell asleep again.

When I woke, the strange feeling was still with me, that during my sleep a hundred years had passed outside the hospital room. Were it not for the excruciating pain that reminded me every minute of the nightmare I had gone through, I would still have believed that I was the woodsman of the green mountain, watching the sages.

I would rather live in a fantasy world than face the reality: 50 percent of my body was burned. The burns covered my face, neck, hands, arms, and back. Each day, the bandages had to be taken off and changed. Soaked and stiffened with blood and secretions from my skin, they stuck to my raw flesh. To remove them was like peeling my skin piece by piece and cutting into my flesh bit by bit. Worst of all, the hospital had no morphine or painkiller of any kind. I had to bear the agony totally on my own.

I tried not to scream, because I felt ashamed to make loud noises in the small hospital. But every morning when the nurses forcefully unwound the blood-hardened bandages, I couldn't stop myself.

Other patients gathered outside my room, watching through the small window in the door, sighing and sobbing.

A few days later, because of my unrelenting severe headache, Doctor Ge ordered the bandages removed from my head and face. The strong swelling prevented me from opening my eyes. But I could tell how shocked my young comrades were when they came to see me. I heard nervous throat-clearing, nose-snuffling, and comforting words offered in a tearful voice. I heard people run precipitately from the room to allow the door and walls to muffle uncontrollable sobs. A peasant wife murmured to a nurse, "The girl was not bad looking before she was burned. What a pity! What man would want her now?" Obviously she didn't consider me a sentient person anymore.

Alarmed by all this, I sank into a deep depression. While still fighting for my life, I was now forced to worry about my appearance. Day after day, the psychological burden seemed to grow more oppressive than my physical pain. I asked Dr. Ge how seriously I was burned and whether the injuries would forever affect my face. But he simply hemmed and hawed, and pulled up the sheet to cover my naked shoulders. His evasiveness worried me even more. I asked again. This time Dr. Ge told me that the burns were third degree. He spoke reluctantly.

"What does that mean?"

"It means that fire has already hurt the muscles, which usually results in scars."

"Big scars? Horrible scars?" I heard my voice breaking.

"Many are small."

"Small? Tiny?"

His voice halted. An uncomfortable silence set in. He tucked the corners of the white sheet tightly under my back as if fearing I would catch cold. I thought of Wang Pei and her indifferent mien and folded arms when the young men had jumped into the smoking workshop. I began to admire her cold-bloodedness, which neither passionate revolutionary slogans nor the party's earnest exhortations could stir. Why was I so enthusiastic? I wasn't even a member of the Communist Youth League.

I was only eighteen. How was I going to face the rest of my life?

I kept my worries to myself, but couldn't help the tears pouring from my swollen eyes. Only then did the visitors realize that beneath the badly scorched surface, there was a soul, a real soul, who still knew, felt, and suffered.

Under the torment of pain, I couldn't eat or sleep. Dr. Ge knew this was dangerous and decided to free me from the daily changing, abandoning the bandages altogether. Instead he applied a layer of thick antibiotic ointment on the burned surfaces, hoping that the skin secretions would dry up faster and the wounds heal faster when they were in direct contact with the air. The nurses were ordered to sanitize the room thoroughly, and visitors were prohibited.

Now I could rest and eat again. Soon the swelling receded and, as the skin secretions ceased, a layer of hard shell — eschar, in the medical terminology — formed.

One morning when I woke up, I opened my eyes. The sunlight glared, and the whiteness of the nurses' uniforms hurt. The first thing I asked for was a mirror. The nurse was reluctant. I insisted. I am not going to be frightened, I indicated. "Are you sure?" She looked at me with concern. Yes! I nodded. She left the room for a minute and came back with a hand-sized mirror. She put it between my two palms, which were unburned. Trembling, I moved it in front of my eyes and took a glance, just one glance. The mirror dropped, tumbled to the cement floor, and broke. Through a mist, I saw a monster — a hairless head with a bloated face covered with charred pine-tree bark. Eschar pulled down my lower eyelids, exposing the red inner skin.

The flames had turned me into an ugly creature. No one, not even myself, could tell that the horrible image in the mirror was that of a young girl of eighteen. Where was my youthful skin? My two arched eyebrows? My red lips? On my face I saw nothing but scorching darkness. Could I still dream my beautiful adolescent dream about Tan, the precious knight on a white charger who resided in my heart? Not one minute passed that I didn't think about him. It must have been this wonderful feeling that had sustained me so far. Tan and his friends had come to see me the other day. I could tell from his quavering voice that he was suffering. But now I dared not think about him anymore. A monster could not love an angel. Maybe I should have died in the fire.

The stories about me, the only girl to dash into the burning shop to save communal property, filled the local media.

In my hospital room, I heard a loudspeaker outside. The regiment's Mao Zedong Thought Propaganda Team had turned my story into a song of political instruction:

> Thunderstorms are rolling and
> Red flags are flying.
> Today let me sing about a girl.
> The girl's aim is high,
> Higher than Mount Everest.
> The girl's will is strong,
> Stronger than century-old rocks.
> . . .
> Let fire ravage her face,
> But it can never destroy her red heart.

The singing was delivered with great emotion and accompanied by the clear clicking sounds of two pieces of bamboo struck together. Looking at my eschar-covered arms and hands, I managed a wan smile. I still felt saddened over the death of two other young people, who had been trapped in the fire and never made their way out. The young men I had followed were also hospitalized here, suffering from burns of various degrees. Because of limited space in the wards, they were all put in one big room. Unsanitary conditions caused serious infections that endangered their lives and later left horrible scars on their faces and hands.

By contrast, the speed of my recovery astonished Dr. Ge. The anxious expression departed little by little from his harrowed face. His once unkempt hair became smooth and cleanly parted. Then the hospital ran out of penicillin. An emergency call was made to the divisional hospital. No luck, it was fire season. Dr. Ge asked me if my parents in Shanghai could help.

"No!" I cried.

Dr. Ge was puzzled. This was not an unusual question. He didn't know that I wanted desperately to hide my injury from my parents. What could they do except worry themselves to death? But bad news travels fast. Despite my efforts to block the information, the story quickly reached my parents' ears via the families of my schoolmates and Shanghai's largest newspaper, *Wenhui Bao*. The paper ran a story calling me the "fine daughter of the Shanghai people," and later sent a script of Jiang Qing's *Red Lantern* to encourage me on the road of revolution.

In the next few days I received a letter from my anxious father:

> You are our beloved daughter. Our entire family sends you our fondest wishes. You must treat physical injuries as if you are dealing with an enemy. If you cannot beat them spiritually, they will overwhelm and crush you. If you are tough, your body will yield endless power to fight. My dear child, you must be strong.

He told me that Ming, who was only a hundred miles away, would come to see me soon. Father's letter brought me new hope. At the moment, I badly needed Ming, who at twenty-four was six years my senior. I had a thousand things to talk to him about: my pain, sadness, fears, dreams, and especially my future appearance, maybe even Tan. But Ming did not come. Instead I received a letter from him:

"You should fear neither hardships nor death." . . . While I'm very worried about you, I also have my job to do. There is no doubt that revolutionary work is more important than a personal matter. So, I've decided not to go see you. But no matter what happens, you must bear Chairman Mao's instructions in mind and conquer all difficulties with his thoughts.

Choking with sobs, I gazed at the green mountain range rising and falling in the distance. My mood had never been this low. The horrible face I saw in the mirror the other day haunted me like a ghost. Whenever I closed my eyes, I saw it. It gnawed at my heart, my mind, and my nerves. I imagined myself sitting on the regimental platform, reporting to hundreds or thousands of young people how I became the person they saw. The young faces below would fill with a mixture of horror, pity, and distaste. Human memories were short. Very soon, people would forget what I did for the country, but they would always remember how horrible I looked.

My evenings became as empty as deep canyons as I lay under the yellow light. Other than the footsteps of the night-shift nurses walking up and down the corridor, there was only the long, endless quiet that slowly seemed to engulf me. I could not lie still. I rolled and tossed, wanting to find a mirror that I had neither the intention nor the courage to use. I needed to know if my face would look "normal," and I wanted the answer immediately. Without it, every minute was torture. I started hating Ming for his altruism, although I fully understood him. If I were he, I would have done the same. Hadn't we been taught to put the interests of Chairman Mao and the party before our own and those of our family, even before our own lives? After all, we were all products of the heroic age of the Cultural Revolution.

17

The Beauty of a Goddess

Fifteen days later Mu, a paralyzed girl, was moved into my ward. She was transferred here after being treated unsuccessfully at the general hospital of the Heilongjiang Military Farms in Harbin.

With a new roommate, I felt some solace. Bathed in the bright sunlight, Mu was the most beautiful girl I had ever seen. Her creamy skin revealed tiny veins underneath. When she smiled, her perfect teeth looked like two rows of pearls. Mu's shoulder-length hair was as dark as shimmering coal. Her eyebrows arched like willow tree leaves. Like diamonds, her apricot-shaped eyes sparkled darkly.

When the nurses lifted Mu in their arms to change her dirty sheets or to wash her, I couldn't tear my eyes away from her graceful body. As if inspecting a piece of art, I would gaze at her snow-white arms, smooth shoulders, long legs, plump milk-white breasts. Tragedy established a link between us. While I worried about myself, I also felt deeply sorry for Mu. Poetry and literature proclaimed that absolute beauties were always short-lived and ill-fated. Mu was proof. She was injured during Chairman Mao's movement to prepare for war with the Soviet Union, when he called on the people to "store grains widely and dig air shelters deeply." As the territorial dispute between China and its northern neighbor escalated, all along the border the atmosphere was tense. The armed sections of every company practiced military drills. One day in 1971, shrapnel from a grenade struck Mu in the head. The injured girl was placed on a tractor, the only means of transportation available in the mountain village. Slowly but steadily, the tractor bumped along the rough mountain trail. Forgetting his own danger, the driver had but one goal in mind: to rush the beautiful girl to the regimental hospital and save her life. It was an all-night drive. When he finally arrived the next morning, Mu's condition was grave. Her head injury had worsened. Her life was saved only after she had been transferred to a dozen local and provincial hospitals, but she remained paralyzed. According to her doctors, her original injury was not as severe as the harm caused by the rough transportation, which had damaged her brain.

I would watch Mu inspecting her left hand, the only limb she could control, inch by inch for long periods of time. As if talking to an old friend, she whispered to it, mixing her words with hysterical laughter and muffled sobs. Her hand was her friend, a friend who would never betray her. It would always listen to her, be with her, for better or worse, for life and death.

Once I got past the life-threatening stage of my fire wounds, I was able to get out of bed and move about the room. Soon I roamed around the small hospital. Being able to walk made things worse for me. When strangers bumped into me, they seemed to tremble. They slid away with their bodies pressed against the wall. Deeply hurt, I stopped leaving the room and confined myself to bed for days. I became weary of my never-ending fight with injuries, the world around me, and even my own physical body, which was ugly, a darkened husk. Depressed, I felt that energy had been drained out of me and blood had dried up in my veins. Sometimes, merely keeping my eyes open was a great burden. All I wanted to do was lie peacefully without pain, any kind of pain. I lost my appetite, thinking I could go on and on without eating. One night, after tossing in bed for hours, I got up and took three sleeping pills that I had accumulated. But a voice inside kept insisting, "It's not enough! You need more! You need more!" I went to search Mu's bedside table, my clumsy hands knocking things onto the cement floor. Mu stirred.

"Do you have any sleeping pills?" I asked her impatiently. "I can't sleep at all."

"Ring the bell. The nurse will give you one."

"One isn't enough. I need more." The little voice inside me urged again. Mu seemed to understand. She looked at me sadly. I saw her sparkling diamond eyes moisten. My miseries were written all over my face and in my eyes. She could read them clearly.

"Don't stand there like a wooden duck," Mu said. "Sit down."

I sat on the floor beside her bed, holding her lifeless hand in mine, while her other hand stroked my hairless head softly.

"When the black bark falls off, your face will look much better. You just have to be patient." She comforted me like an elder sister. Hope returned like a clear spring, bringing with it the power of life. After all, I was only eighteen and life had just begun. I pressed my scorched cheeks firmly against hers, and I could feel the miserable soul of a beautiful girl whose future was much dimmer than mine. But no matter how cruel life was for her, she never mentioned death. Only nineteen, she continued to hope that one day she would stand up and leave this hospital.

It was very quiet, just after midnight. All the nurses had already retired to their own rooms. There was no sound except the elegy of the wind as it passed through the leaves of the trees. Inside the poorly lit hospital room, I sat by Mu, waiting for the morning to come before the sleeping pills finally took effect and put me to sleep the whole next day and night.

Eventually several places cracked open on my face, exposing pinkish new skin beneath the eschars. I felt a terrible itching, as if millions of tiny worms were gnawing away underneath the dark shell. It made me restless. Dr. Ge had me wear a pair of thick gloves even during sleep to make sure my hands wouldn't scratch my face. Although it was a good sign indicating that the eschars would soon fall off, the itching became unbearable. The tiny worms seemed to have proliferated everywhere inside my body, making it impossible for me to eat or sleep or think. My tongue became numb, and thin blood vessels crisscrossed my eyes. Dr. Ge looked at me with great pity, since he had no medicine for my discomfort. To help me with the battle, he brought a basket of boiled eggs from home.

"Do you know that the eggs laid by my hens taste sweet? I put sugar in the chicken feed. You must taste one first before you believe it," he said, trying to be humorous as he peeled the eggshell.

Over the next few days, bit by bit, the eschars, which once clung so tightly to my face and hands, loosened and started falling off. At first they fell one or two pieces at a time, here and there. Then even the slightest facial or body movement would bring down a rain of them. My heart became heavier than ever, as I waited anxiously to see my true face behind the mask. I prayed, "Please, please help me one more time. Return my original face. Do not leave me with horrible scars!"

In the following days, eschars fell in landslides. One time, as I was eating, the chewing movement brought down a huge piece from my forehead that fell into the soup bowl, where it floated like a fish. Black scraps were everywhere on my bed and clothes. Finally the itching stopped.

One sunny morning, Dr. Ge walked into the room with light steps. He examined my face carefully, then, with a pair of tweezers, pulled off the last big piece of eschar dangling on my cheek. Dr. Ge smiled from ear to ear, his eyes gleaming with delight.

"Miracle! It really is a miracle, considering you had third-degree burns!" he almost yelled.

From under his white uniform he took out a square mirror and placed it in front of me. In the bright sunlight pouring through the window, I looked. The charred leather mask was gone. In its place was a young face, glowing with tender new skin smooth as water and delicate as pink satin. The once turned out eyelids had returned to their normal positions. Although many brownish scars covered my eyelids, the bridge of my nose, my cheeks, and my forehead, these defects did not ruin my face.

I saw myself smiling sweetly. It was a smile of relief, a smile of victory. I wanted to sing a happy song.

> Let me beat one thousand golden drums,
> Let me play one thousand silver flutes.

Mu cried. I hugged her, gluing my face tightly against hers until my newborn skin burned with pain.

Since Mother was coming soon, and I didn't want her to feel saddened by seeing me in the hospital, I asked Dr. Ge to release me. But looking at my scorched hands, he was reluctant. He agreed only after I explained my reason and only on the condition that I come for a checkup once a week. "Your hands, especially the right hand, are far from well. You shouldn't touch water or any construction materials. Stay indoors for at least six months away from sun, wind, rain, snow, frost, and extreme temperatures."

Mu cried bitterly. Our friendship forged in times of misfortune was priceless. As I promised her I would, I came back to visit regularly. The last time I saw her was two years later. Her face expressionless, she asked me to sit down at her bedside. Her long black hair had lost its luster and looked like withered grass, its ends split badly. It hadn't been cut for a long time. Her once creamy, tight skin was waxen and sagging. Her beautiful apricot-shaped eyes were no longer sparkling like diamonds. They were sunken and aged.

Indifferently she told me to lift the white sheet covering her. It was heartbreaking to see that her once full and healthy body was now reduced to the size of a child's. Her round hips were gone. Her breasts were two empty bags hanging loosely on her chest. Her entire body was purple and blue owing to poor blood circulation and bedsores. I couldn't believe it was the same body that I had seen two short years before. Mu, the girl with bones of jade and clear skin of ice, was suffering from severe muscular atrophy and neglect. Nurses had been ordered to change her position often and to stretch and massage her legs, arms, and hips in order to prevent such a thing from happening. But if they were busy with other things, they often skipped Mu's treatment. The hospital staff knew that she, an orphan whose Christian parents had died at the beginning of the Cultural Revolution, was the most vulnerable person in the world — paralyzed, with no relatives to speak for her. The hospital could do whatever it wanted. Anything they did for her was a favor.

Later, after I left Heilongjiang, I wrote Mu several letters, but I never received any answer. I surmised that she could get no one to write for her — or, more likely, she no longer lived in this world.

18

Mother's Heart

In mid-July, just a few days after I left the hospital, the wind whipped up into a summer storm. The rain kept pitter-pattering, washing the mountains and fields afresh and dressing them in new clothes. After the rain the sun shone again and drops gleamed on the roofs, leaves, and blades of grass. Mushrooms in hues of milky cream, grayish brown, and blood red sprang up around the trees and in the wasteland.

My travel-weary mother arrived at our small village bearing two suitcases of canned food and medicine. The moment she saw me, her worried face opened with broad smiles, and her knitted brows became even. She narrowed her eyes and looked at me closely. As soon as we entered the small room that Yi had assigned us during her stay, she removed from her purse several cotton balls. She dipped them in water and gently rolled them on my face.

"In the corners of your mouth are some yellow crystals. Here, on your forehead. Also there behind your ears. Your eyelids are wrinkled. On the nose. . . . You're lucky the brown scars are shallow and don't look horrible. Oh, you have no eyebrows. What about your hair? Was it shaved or burned away?"

Mother's trembling fingers examined my face inch by inch. She held my right hand, which was still wrapped in pine-tree bark, stroking it lovingly. Through the thick eschar I couldn't feel her touch, but I could see the tears forming in her eyes.

"You're suffering." She took out a handkerchief and wiped her eyes and nose. Her voice was trembling.

"Actually, I didn't feel much pain," I said to console her, but my throat tightened. I turned away to pour a cup of water. There were no words in the world that could describe the suffering I had experienced. And the psychological torment was the worst. But after having come through fire and blood, I was stronger and maturer now. Mother should be at ease with me. I had grown up.

I wiped my eyes and set the cup of water in front of her. She was unpacking her suitcases and didn't seem to have noticed my emotion. Mother said that before she saw me, she had already prepared for the worst. The Shanghai doctors told her that if the fire had ruined my facial muscles, skin transplant surgery would be necessary. Usually doctors would take the skin from the patient's inner thighs to cover the burns. So Mother, preparing to offer her own skin for transplant, began massaging her belly, her best skin, with alcohol many times a day to keep it elastic. She didn't stop, even on the crowded train.

She laughed good-humoredly. "I was so embarrassed. Imagine a woman opening her shirt from time to time to caress her belly. People thought I was crazy. Men cast sidelong glances at me. Some even turned their backs. Women stared at me critically. I thought they would report me. But I couldn't care too much. You are my priority."

"How is Father?"

"When he heard the news, he fainted in the cotton fields on his Chongming Island farm."

I could imagine Father's misery — and I felt guilty. He had said in his most recent letter that he would come visit me. But he must have changed his mind at the last minute, fearing he might pass out again on seeing me burned like a charred tree trunk. My eyes were wet. I held my brave mother's arm. Whatever happened, she was always tough and optimistic. She was the pillar of strength in our family.

The canned meats Mother brought provided huge relief. I gave a few cans to Su, who was like a sister.

A few days later, Yi asked me to show Mother around. The political instructor wanted her, as a representative of the parents of Shanghai, to report to the Shanghai people how good life was here when she returned home.

A thin trail of gray smoke swirled from a clay chimney. The smelly dirt road smoldered under the summer sun. Mother's clean cloth shoes were soon covered with a coat of fine dust. As we strolled around the village, chicken and geese scurried ahead. Barefoot children, sucking wild green onions, gamboled around us. Their curious eyes followed Mother closely, a woman from a big city in a faraway place.

From the loudspeakers installed on the trees, a voice called for attention and announced that a summary execution was about to be carried out. Who was it this time? How unlucky that it should happen during Mother's short stay here. This was something she didn't need to know. I turned to her apologetically. But holding our breaths, we listened.

Following routine, the denunciation came first. The "criminal" was a Shanghai boy from a regiment located by the Ussuri River. He had two counts against him. His first "crime" was seeing a girl and refusing to stop when asked to. His second "crime," by far the more serious, was that he swam across the Ussuri River to the Soviet Union one night; he had betrayed the motherland. But even the Soviets didn't appreciate a traitor. They sent him, together with other defectors, back to China.

Nervously I looked at Mother. She lowered her head, her eyes staring at the shadowy ground under her feet. I shivered, clinging tightly to her arm.

The loudspeaker boomed, "Do you have any last words?"

A long silence. Then came a voice conveying a heartrending naïveté: "Would you give me a piece of candy? Thank you . . . Tell my mother that I'll miss her, always! Tell her that I'm sorry I can't perform my filial duties," the voice choked out.

Mother was in tears. We waited in silence, anxiously. A flock of crows hovered over the treetops, cawing noisily. These were unlucky birds, but recently, out of nowhere, they had infested our village.

BANG! BANG! BANG! Three gunshots ruptured the morning calm. Mother's face turned waxen.

"Is he from the Fifty-second Regiment? That's Ming's regiment." As if awakening from a nightmare, Mother cried, "Send a telegram to Ming! I must see him no matter how busy he is."

Ming arrived in a week. He was handsome, his skin tinged olive from outdoor labor and his body well-built and healthy. Mother wanted to know everything about his life. But the first thing she asked him was whether or not he knew about the execution of the "traitor." Ming said it was common for young people in his regiment to escape to the other side of the Ussuri River for personal or political reasons. Some were shot to death before they crossed the border; others, if they didn't drown, would often be sent back by the Soviets. But still, death could not stop the exodus. Young people nourished all kinds of fantasies about the Soviet Union, which they picked up from its movies and literature. They thought the land across the Ussuri River was heaven on earth, a place where they could escape political persecution and their miserable lives here in Heilongjiang Military Farms.

Mother and Ming spent many sleepless nights talking. Often they were still talking when I woke up. One night I heard Mother tell him, "Observe the rules. Don't see girls — better not to look at them at all. It is best if you're blind to this matter. It was a girl who led to the death of the 'traitor' boy. A girl will ruin you also. Wait until the day when you can return to Shanghai. But here, no matter what happens, never attempt to cross the Ussuri River."

Ming was strangely silent for a long while, then he replied in a low voice full of guilt, "But I already met a girl."

As if electrocuted, Mother sprang up. "Why are you doing things that aren't allowed? Haven't you learned from the example of the 'traitor' boy?" she said severely.

"But the girl I met is my battalion commander. She selected me from among hundreds. We share a common belief — to realize communism in the world. Besides, this shows the party's utmost trust in me. How could I decline?"

After a long silence, Mother asked Ming if he had forgotten his goal of attending college. At that time, at the recommendations of local leaders, a few colleges were admitting a small number of unmarried students from the countryside, who would study certain critical subjects such as foreign languages, teaching, agriculture, and Chinese traditional medicine to meet the government's urgent needs.

Ming replied that he wanted to become an electrical engineer, so receiving a college education was imperative.

"But you must have hope. You must wait, wait for new policies. If you marry a local leader, then you will never go to college," Mother said.

After a long silence, Ming agreed to stop the relationship with his commander. He left in a few days. New worries crept to Mother's face. Ming seemed to have carried away part of her heart.

The homesick Shanghai youth crowded into our small room during the evenings. The first parent ever to visit the company, perhaps the whole regiment, Mother was for them the perfect person to whom to express their pent-up feelings. They squatted on their heels with bowls in hand, noisily eating supper while asking her questions about the Cultural Revolution in Beijing and Shanghai.

"People in the cities live in the modern world. Here we have no daily newspapers, no movies, no books, so we live in ignorance, out-and-out cavemen," they mocked themselves, with pained expressions.

One evening after the sun had set, Mother and I sat chatting on the bed. She began repeating the same thing she had said many time before: "Don't see any young men! Don't fall in love with any of them! Like girls to Ming, boys to you are the root of all trouble."

Since I met Tan only in my dreams, I could honestly tell her that I wasn't seeing anyone. She expressed relief. She said she trusted that a girl had more self-control in dealing with her feelings than a boy.

Embarrassed, I changed the subject.

"Mother, we want you to go before the Shanghai Revolutionary Committee and convey the reality of our lives here. Are you afraid?"

"Am I afraid?" She shook her head. As the first parent to come here, she said, she felt an obligation to do whatever she could for the Shanghai youth.

I looked at her with admiration. She was a brave woman. I started telling her some of our woes.

I told Mother that we had turned the once empty headquarters of Seventy-third Regiment into a prosperous center. Red brick family housing, special quarters for the ranking army officers, theaters, swimming pools, department stores, tall office buildings, a hundred-foot-high chimney used to heat private shower rooms. . . . Year in and year out we broke our backs, but we ourselves still lived in the same earthen houses under the rawest conditions. There were still twenty people occupying one room, ten people sleeping on one bed. We still washed our bodies with a basin of rationed water and still ate boiled vegetables and salt broth.

"Look," I said, "the livestock live better. They have special people to take care of them, comb their hair, feed them soybean cakes, breed them in mating season. If they were in danger, we would save them, sacrificing our own lives. There are so many of us, but not as many animals. The country has millions and millions of youths, but not millions and millions of cows, or horses, or mules, or donkeys, or hogs."

"Don't say that! What if you let your thoughts be known?"

Once, the company leaders held a special meeting to find out who owned a forbidden copy of the novel *Shanghai Morning,* written by Zhou Gucheng. A hand-copied version of *Song of Youth* by Young Muo, the story of a girl in search of the Chinese Communist Party, was labeled pornographic. Romantic songs with lines like "In this beautiful, quiet night when only my violin is singing, I want to write a letter to a girl far away, but there is no mailman to deliver it" were criticized as decadent. One could be beaten for singing, "The moon has risen in the sky, but why is there no cloud? If you wait, the cherry flower will bloom all by itself." The company leaders claimed that class enemies hid in dark corners and sang corrupt tunes to poison our minds — to make us homesick and lovesick. Why did such capitalist garbage remain? They recited Chairman Mao's words that we must want to struggle, dare to struggle, and know how to struggle. They quoted Lenin, saying that when the old society died, it didn't want to be put inside a coffin. It preferred to continue spreading its foul smell in order to poison everyone. "Comrades! We need to clap you hard on the shoulders to wake you up. We need to shout in your ears, 'The class enemy is killing you with an invisible knife.'"

Mother couldn't help laughing. "Are things really so serious? Just a few love songs!" Tired of sitting on her legs, she got up from the bed.

"But they said it was the subtle sign of class struggle. A real communist can always smell it and sense it, even if he can't touch it."

But in one respect we were lucky, I told Mother. The officials had never suspected our diaries, which they thought must be full of confessions to Chairman Mao. But other than the burning revolutionary rhetoric, my several notebooks were filled with beautiful poems, secret love messages left at the well or other places, and complaints about our situation.

The night wind knocked on the door and windows like a naughty child. My grievances continued pouring out in an angry flood. I told Mother that I saw no straight road ahead of me. My future was dark since the time I offended Yi.

Mother stopped me. What she cared most was that I be able to leave this place and return to her side. In a hushed voice she said, "You must always hide your real self from the company leaders. What else can you do when they decide your fate? Endurance and patience are our virtues. Those who don't know how to endure will ruin themselves. This is a miserable nation at a very miserable time. Do we have any other way?"

Without our realizing it, the night passed. Cocks crowed. The villagers rose to feed their hogs and chickens in their backyards. Dogs scampered, birds chirped, and babies cried. Another day began.

Twenty days passed. In August, when the soybeans in the vast fields turned golden and began ringing their tiny bells for harvest, Mother had to leave. She was still the "Evil Hand behind the black current" and would have to continue confessing her "crimes" in her school. At our company, she had already seen and heard enough. And as the first parent representative, she was determined to serve as a messenger, a bridge linking the sons and daughters with their beloved parents. She would have a lot of homes to visit, many packages to deliver, and the Shanghai Revolutionary Committee to talk to. Our situation here must change.

Yet she was reluctant to part. In this Great Northern Wilderness, she had left two of her three children. No one knew when they would return home, safe and sound. For Ming, who was already twenty-four, the situation here seemed too complicated to sort out, and for me, only eighteen, it was worse. On the day of her departure, Mother rose early and washed several basinfuls of my dirty clothes. She washed my head and cleaned my body thoroughly. My hands were still not supposed to touch water, so bathing remained difficult for me. Mother's eyes were like two peaches, red and swollen from excessive crying. Lines of anxiety deepened around her mouth. I felt this separation harder than the last one in Shanghai's North Train Station. I didn't know when or even whether I would see her again. Until the day we were reunited, we could live only in each other's thoughts. At the Tashan train station, Mother made me leave first. I looked back at her with each step I took.

19

Our Footsteps Stop Here

In August the setting sun embroidered the clouds with purple and golden edges. Tall poplar trees cast their shadows on the trails. At night, the full moon lit the country roads, pursuing me everywhere I went. I couldn't stop missing Mother. My heart followed her as the moon followed me. Once again, I was alone to face my uncertain future.

In the following weeks, my right hand recovered slowly. When the tree bark finally fell off, shiny scars covered the surface of new skin. Blue veins stood out like earthworms. The flames had sealed the skin's pores and damaged the sweat glands, so my skin couldn't breathe naturally. My hand hurt and turned purple when the weather changed.

My mood was low. The nightmare of the fire continued to haunt me. I would wake up suddenly at night and try to escape imagined flames. Sharp noises such as automobile horns brought me back to the accident scene again and again. I couldn't bear looking at transparent plastics, which reminded me of my skin sliding rapidly off my hands and arms in the blaze. I lived in constant fear. Even in the open wilderness under the enormous empty sky, I was afraid that something from above would fall and crush me to the ground. I saw houses along the road ablaze with swirling smoke and long tongues of ferocious flames. The psychological damage was far more lasting than the physical. For the rest of my life, I would have to live with the consequences of my youthful "heroism."

Reality changed me. More than ever, I wanted to protect myself so I wouldn't suffer other injuries. I began questioning my revolutionary fervor and its significance. Never before did I want so much to leave this place, which I regarded as a living hell. I wanted to go home, to study in a university, and to live like a real human being. But I knew it was only a dream, for thousands upon thousands of young city people were still being forced to leave their homes. To realize my dream, I must continue to pay.

In my diary, I wrote:

> I feel like a prisoner tightly bound to this land. My goal is as unseizable as smoke in the air. In the dripping rain, I look to the south, the direction where my home is. But apart from the mountains, forests, and this small village, I can't see anything clearly. The sky is overcast. Emptiness overwhelms me. My tomorrow is like the heavy weather — unclear and gray.

But honor sometimes comes hand in hand with suffering. On August 14, 1971, the elite Youth League associated with the Chinese Communist Party not only accepted me as a member but elected me one of its leaders. As a living heroine, I was sent to attend seminars and give speeches throughout the regiment and division.

Touring with me were other young people. One of them was a girl named Pan, who had fought bare-handed with a "class enemy" who tried to poison the livestock she was raising. The enemy hacked her ten times with an ax. Another was Zhang, who had fought with a wild hog that was charging a group of people he was in. He shouted to attract the beast's attention all to himself and drew it away in another direction. Another boy, named Hou, had jumped into a frozen river to rescue a drowning calf that had broken through.

Honor, like a yoke, pressed me so hard that I couldn't breathe. Shortly after Mother left, I returned to work. Unfortunately, there was no way for me to follow Dr. Ge's instructions to stay indoors for at least six months. When everyone else worked long hours every day to achieve another "economic miracle" in another large-scale political movement, how could I snuggle idly in bed? Whatever I did, I knew eyes were watching me. Once I rode the tiger, it was hard to get off.

Every day, I walked back and forth on the step-plank that I still dreaded, even though I had walked on it thousands of times already. The concussion I suffered in the fire caused me chronic headaches, and working on heights under stress made them worse. I never really overcame the acrophobia. Several times I nearly fell from the plank. But Yi refused to grant a transfer to another job. He had always said that the party trusted me, the revolution needed me, and my squad couldn't function without me as its leader. Now, as a heroine, I should do a better job of living up to the party's expectations. His tone seemed to suggest that as long as he was alive, I should never dream of doing anything else. I could see that he had honey on his lips and murder in his heart. Despairing, I even thought about running away to Shanghai, but the neighborhood administration would just enforce government policy and send me straight back. The company leaders would say that I had run away because I was afraid of frontier hardships. There was no road to heaven and no door into the earth. I was trapped. Yi was killing me with a soft knife.

Because of strong resistance from distraught parents, the government now modified its policies for assigning new middle-school graduates, who were sent to the suburbs rather than the frontiers. The news was bad for us, because we were still stranded here and our lives never changed. Often after night fell, when stars shone brilliantly in the black sky, someone would sing in a barely audible voice tinged with sadness:

> Missing you, dear mother!
> Thinking about you, my hometown!
> Our golden youth is gone forever,

And I cannot find the road ahead.
Oh, Mother! Oh, my hometown,
Our footsteps have stopped in this strange land.

Hands ceased what they had been doing. Ears listened. Tears flowed with the sentimental lyrics that returned us to our mothers' side, to our warm homes, to our days gone by, then back to the Great Northern Wilderness, back to the reality. Since we were just a short distance from the Soviet Union, a radio could easily pick up Radio Moscow, which played the banned "Song of Nanjing" almost day and night. Although listening to the station was a capital crime, many risked their lives to do so in secret. According to Radio Moscow the "Song of Nanjing" was like the Internationale to the workers of the world. And it was true that, by singing it, a youth could find friends and receive a place to stay and food to eat wherever he went in China. Yet Ren Yi, its author, had been arrested and jailed and sentenced to ten years for writing the song.

Missing you, dear mother!
Thinking about you, my hometown!

In the silence, the words lingered. When could we go home? In the darkness, we asked ourselves again and again the same question we had asked thousands of times before.

More than ever, I lost myself thinking about Tan, the flower in the mirror, the moon in the water. He was the inspiration for my life, my only consolation during these endless miseries. But as I made up my mind to leave, I vaguely felt that my love for Tan, though strong, was hopeless.

Snowflakes greeted the New Year of 1972. Storms wailed in the withered grassland. "Snow cannons" threw the world into chaos, making it impossible to recognize where the roads were and where the ditches and creeks. Still my squad collected rocks on the Mount of Cracks.

The symptoms from my fire injury lingered: an inexplicable fever, a piercing headache, skin pain. Now the trauma found an outlet in a carbuncle that grew on my waist. Within days it was the size of a man's fist. Even slight movement paralyzed me. I was forced to lie in bed all day and all night. The temperature outside dove dangerously low. The bitter northwest wind blew into the room through cracks in the door and windows. With nothing burning in the furnace, the room was like ice. Everything froze — towels, socks, and underwear, toothpaste, soap, even my sweat-soaked cotton-padded clothes and canvas rubber shoes. My breath made a white cloud. A thin layer of frost settled on my eyebrows, hair, and pillow. I buried my head inside the quilt and lay there counting the minutes, waiting for the one good thing that would warm me up — the hot noodles served only to the seriously ill.

Su came and set down a bowl of noodles beside my pillow. She felt my covering.

"Your quilt is paper thin. Didn't your parents know you were coming to China's North Pole?"

I was aware of the poor quality of my quilt. It was not only the thinnest in the whole dorm, but its old lining was also riddled with holes, which were growing bigger since my hands and toes poked inside them constantly. I should have replaced it a long time ago, but a new one would have used up my entire family's cotton coupons. Considering that my parents and brother needed the coupons for clothes, I couldn't make the request.

Su left the room. She came back shortly with a much thicker quilt, an overcoat, and the pelt of a dog in her arms.

"Look! Mine is as thick as the snow outside."

She spread her quilt on top of mine, then the dog skin on top of the quilt, and the overcoat on top of the dog skin. I breathed with difficulty under the weight, the bowl of noodles shaking in my hand.

"But how are you going to sleep?" I asked.

"Don't worry. We can share quilts."

★   ★   ★

Winter days were short. Like a young girl, the shy white sun was afraid to show its face for long. As soon as it hid behind the mountains, dusk fell like a velvet curtain. The stillness of the room was broken when the girls came back from work. The dorm bustled with noise, and body heat warmed the freezing air. At night Su came and slipped under the small mountain of covers. Inside, she took off her undershirt and helped me to take off mine. It was warmer wearing no clothes when sleeping, she said. Our faces were so close that we felt each other's breath. In her warm eyes, I saw compassion and friendship. I put my hand on her bosom and felt her heart jumping; she giggled without stopping. Su's sweet smiles were her best asset. In the battlefieldlike canteen, it was always a pleasure to see her grinning while serving meals. Her cordial greetings accompanied by straightforward laughter added a little flavor to the tasteless food all year round and brought a thread of reluctant smiles to the faces of her grunting customers.

Su's body heat warmed my stiff body. Even the tormenting carbuncle felt less painful. As if I'd smoked a pipe of opium, I relaxed from head to toe. Slowly Su's smiling face began floating, turning upside down and receding in the dizziness. Under the blue sky, Tan rode a white cloud and drifted toward me over the open land, extending his arms. . . . My heart melted. I leaned my head against his broad chest and listened attentively. Red and pink roses bloomed around him. A green laurel crowned him. Our bodies fused and became part of the green mountains, the rich forest, the thin fog, and the gossamer floating in the air. I felt liberated from the everlasting feeling of culpability, disgrace, and fear. Braving my shyness, I held Tan tightly. I hugged him as I embraced the sense of freedom. My feelings for him, which had been suppressed for so long, broke loose with such vehemence that it almost suffocated him. He cried. His tears dampened my lips. They were bitterly cold, freezing my heart.

But when I opened my eyes, there was only Su's pleasant face. My forehead was wet with sweat even in this coldest hour of the night. As I opened the quilts slightly to let the air cool my burning body, my heart stopped beating. In the moonlight flooding through the curtainless windows, Su's snow-white chest moved up and down with her even breathing. I felt a strong urge to hug her tightly, I so much wanted physical intimacy with another human being. While I was dreaming, I must have already hugged her unknowingly, thinking she was Tan. In the dead of night, solemn and tranquil, I was surprised to find that my feelings, like a clear spring running smoothly in the deep valley, came directly from the very bottom of my heart. It must be that the party's propaganda machines had forgotten this plot of primitive land. It was like a wildflower in secret bloom, pure and exotically fragrant, unpolluted. The sense of purity generated by physical closeness with another young girl was bewitching. For some reason, tears streamed down my face. I felt such self-pity. In this dreadful year, I had suffered so much — fire, injury, sickness, loneliness, depression, despair, fear. It had been the darkest time of my life, and I saw no hope of escaping the danger I had to face every day.

As I watched Su's face, like a sleeping lotus in full bloom, I calmed down. She gave me warmth. She gave me strength. In this peaceful moment of closeness, I felt as though I were sitting beside Mother at home, and chatting with Father. My younger brother Jie handed me a big apple. I even saw Ming. Our family hadn't been together for years. Now, as we gathered together again for the first time, laughter filled the small apartment. Home, what a lovely place. How safe I would feel at home!

The winter was long. Snowstorm after snowstorm, the immense whiteness frightened me. And the never-changing emptiness angered me. Could I suffer forever? Things had to change. I continued to work on the Mount of Cracks, drilling holes in the hard rocks and frozen land, burying explosives, lighting the fuses, then running on the meandering icy footpath along the cliffside to the bunker where our squad hid. Every morning, when I left for the mountain, I would glance back at the bed and think, Will I return tonight?

The Mount of Cracks had become the official graveyard for the young people in our Seventy-third Regiment. New graves kept being dug, for collecting rocks led to many accidents. I would often hear that falling rocks or explosives had killed or wounded young people in the regiment and would weep over these untimely deaths and injuries. My dear friends! You fell like tender melons off the green vine. When will I see your youthful shadows again and hear your songs ringing in the mountains? Is this the consequence of fighting heaven, fighting the earth, fighting with other people? Do we have to pay such a steep price for our ideals?

20

The Lin Biao Incident

In April 1972, when spring finally came to the mountain, when valleys were filled with pleasant dripping songs of melting snow running between the rocks, when the thawed earth sparkled under the gentle kiss of soft sunlight, our squad returned to construction.

A few days after we left the mountain, an appalling rumor spread like wildfire, burning through our company and regiment: "Chairman Mao's handpicked successor, Lin Biao, is dead! Lin Biao's plane crashed in Mongolia as he tried to flee to the Soviet Union!"

Commander Gao, who had just returned from her visit home in Beijing, first told me the news in a deserted corner of the canteen one night. I looked around carefully to see who was listening, since mentioning Lin Biao by name rather than the epithet Second Helmsman was a crime. Lin was Mao's unanimously acknowledged comrade-in-arms. During the Ninth National Congress, he had been officially designated Mao's heir and successor; this was even recorded in the Constitution of the People's Republic of China. It was Lin Biao who had said that he was the "most pious pupil of Chairman Mao. . . . Every word Chairman Mao speaks is the truth. Whoever dares rebel against him, the whole party will crush him. And the whole nation will rise to destroy him." It was Lin Biao who compiled and published millions of copies of the *Quotations of Chairman Mao* and transformed the nation into a red ocean.

"Are you crazy?" I murmured in fear.

"No! In Beijing it's an open secret. Only in this barbarous place are we still hoodwinked."

Gao began detailing what she had heard in the capital city. Word on the street was that Lin Biao had conspired to assassinate Mao by every means possible, including poison gas, bacterial weapons, kidnapping, urban guerrilla attacks, and even rockets. But Mao was always heavily guarded, and extremely careful. He never followed his schedule, and his special express train would change routes without warning. This last time, as Lin Biao prepared to murder him on his scheduled return to the capital, Mao had suddenly changed plans, returning to Beijing earlier than expected. Lin, his family, and his followers hastily boarded a military airplane and flew north to the Soviet Union. The rumors said that when Mao heard the news, he refused to shoot down Lin Biao's plane, which nevertheless later crashed in Mongolia. Lin Biao's betrayal was a fatal blow to Mao, his health, his ideological world, his aura of invincibility, and his Cultural Revolution.

Shocked, I walked out into the darkness, letting the chill air cool my confused head. I looked up at the sky searching for the North Star, which was said to be Mao shining in the night, giving directions to those who were lost in the darkness. But I did not find the bright star. Clouds obscured it, signaling an overcast day tomorrow. My heart was as empty as the Great Northern Wilderness beyond. The pillar of spiritual certainty had completely crumbled inside me. The belief in communism and my unwavering faith in Mao had collapsed. Lin Biao had proved through his dramatic escape and sensational death that he didn't believe in Mao and his revolutionary ideology at all. If Mao's most pious student and immediate successor didn't believe in him, why should I? Why should I? The scorched corpse lying beside his wrecked plane on the arid ground of Mongolia shouted at me: Do you know why I wanted so much to get rid of him? Because he is not God. He is a monster. The enemy of the Chinese people.

If Mao was wrong, then the Red Guard movement, the Up to the Mountains, Down to the Countryside movement, all my sacrifices for Mao, the hardships I endured here every day — in short, the entire Cultural Revolution — were scams. Before, I had blamed only the local leaders, thinking they had abused the power Mao gave them. But now, for the first time, I linked my sufferings directly to Mao, although in fear, shock, and disbelief. Question followed question. I had endless questions.

Gradually, through official and unofficial channels, we came to know the truth. In 1968, when Mao called upon the Red Guards to go to the countryside, the gross national product was only 86.6 percent of that of 1966, when the Cultural Revolution first started. Big cities had no jobs to offer the millions of baby boomers born in the early fifties, when Mao had urged increased reproduction, claiming that "with more manpower, there would be more strength." After Liu Shaoqi was ousted, the Red Guards and their violence were no longer needed. Actually, they were in the way of the Cultural Revolution that Mao was determined to see through to the end.

In his coup declaration, code-named Project 571, Lin Biao accused Mao of deception. The younger generation, he claimed, were Mao's biggest victims, both tools for his personal power struggle and scapegoats for the collapsing economy. The true nature of the Up to the Mountains, Down to the Countryside movement was a labor correction for massive unemployment.

Overnight, the Lin Biao incident turned the passionate generation of the Red Guards into the most cynical one on earth, critical toward any form of doctrine, religion, or teaching. Dismay filled our hearts. The meaning of life changed.

Under the warm spring sun, the snow on the roof melted and dripped down, at night forming jadelike icicles that hung from the eaves. Naughty children knocked them off and watched the icy sticks dripping in their hands. Soaked with melting snow, the once frozen roads became sodden. Layers of footprints covered the village's main street. Walking was difficult. Mud splashed everywhere. But it was a sign of change, for winter had indeed departed.

As the vehement criticism campaign against Lin Biao unfolded, our formerly overzealous company leaders became sluggish. These defenders of morality blinded their once snow-bright eyes and deafened their acute ears to the lovers' soft prattle that rose in the dusk. We couldn't forget that those eyes used to be more penetrating than daggers, and those ears sharper than needles. But, their beliefs dashed, the young people gave in to their natural desires. Boys and girls began to meet socially, even though dating was still regarded as evil and officially not permitted. It wasn't until 1973 that the State Council finally issued rules allowing marriages. That was in the seventh year after the first group of former Red Guards had arrived here. The eldest members had already reached the age of twenty-eight.

In anger, people escaped. The sons and daughters of high-ranking officials who were powerfully connected or still in power were the first to leave. Many supposedly sick or disabled people followed, arming themselves with so-called proof provided by doctors whom they went to see with knives and other weapons concealed beneath their clothes. Parents searched for city men who would agree to marry their daughters in the countryside. Some courageous people simply overstayed their leaves in the city and remained as illegal residents, without means of income or coupons for food. "Shrimp swim and crabs crawl." Everyone tried desperately to return home, but most could not.

Anger, great anger, mutated into a silent revolt. The endless waves of political movements that had tried to create miracles stopped. No one seemed to have the courage or strength anymore to get up in the middle of a sound sleep during the wee hours. We no longer observed the rigid morning and evening rituals wishing Mao a long, long life. None of us had enough enthusiasm to lift the little red book in salute before our chests. Confessions to Mao stopped. We began listening closely to our own natures.

Hard liquor, popular in the cold provinces, became the most sought-after treasure of the young men, who had never so much as seen it before. On the wall of the canteen someone wrote, "I would rather be drunk when everyone else is clearheaded than wide awake when everyone else is muddled."

In the sunset that dyed the treetops crimson, I stood with only my shadow comforting me. I stared into the swampland daubed with the colors of sundown, having no heart to enjoy it. I strolled in the village, hoping to see Tan. With faith broken and idealism lost, love seemed the only solace. How I wished to hold hands with him, to walk along the creek, to disappear into the evening haze. How easy it would be to settle down with Tan at the base of the mountains so that he and I would never separate for a day. But whenever I thought about college, I forced myself to resist. I knew very well that if I embraced him, I could never pass the party's strict political investigation, and I would be forever tied to this land. Since the party stressed "blood lineage" and "family connections," anyone linked with Tan, including his children and children's children, would carry the family stigma of historical counterrevolutionary. Our society was a class society. As Mao said, everyone was stamped with the brand of a class. Thinking of this, I lost all courage to look into Tan's eyes. I was afraid that the sentiment I found there would melt and disarm me, and I would throw myself into his arms. I must not do it. I must be emotionally strong. I had to leave this place, the sooner the better. The purpose of life should be more than just carrying a load heavier than myself until I broke my back or fell off the step-plank. It was a torment to a valuable life. It was a labor correction, a cruel physical punishment. I should be in college. I should be seeking an education at all cost. I must change my situation so I could live like a dignified human being.

Like the ever-beating evening drum in a monastery, the melody of Pushkin sang within me:

In this deep mine of Siberia,
Please continue to bear your hardship with pride.
Your painful work will not be in vain,
And your noble idealism is more than illusion.

Hope, the loyal sister of misfortune,
Is traveling beneath the dark tunnels.
She will awaken courage and joy,
And the day you've been waiting for will arrive.

Love and friendship will break the dark gate,
And come into your hearts,
Just as my song of freedom
Will reach you in this miserable mine.

Heavy shackles will fall
And the gloomy prison will crumble.
When freedom embraces you at the door,
Brothers will hand you their swords.

21

Marriage — Springboard Back to the City

In 1973 some girls, taking advantage of the government policy that allowed a woman to follow her husband wherever he worked or lived, used marriage as a springboard to return to their home cities. Marriage became an effective vehicle to bring girls out of hell.

My school friend Xue managed to leave the mountain village where she'd been sent three years ago. Her parents found her a forty-year-old peasant fiancé in the suburbs of Shanghai. She and the man had never met, but they soon held a wedding, which enabled her to quit Heilongjiang legally and forever. By the time of her departure, she could no longer walk on her own but had to use crutches. Rheumatism had disabled her.

My parents, feeling guilty that they lacked powerful connections to bring Ming and me home, urged me to consider "making friends" with Lon, my former squadmate, who was now a student at the Shanghai Foreign Relations University. He had been my deputy for two years, until the leaders sent him to college in Shanghai. Ever since Lon had left here in 1972, he had visited my parents regularly. We began exchanging letters.

Fate had somehow tied Lon and me together. In 1970 we actually rode in the same car of the train to Heilongjiang. But I didn't notice him until we arrived at Tashan. That night, inside the waiting room shrouded with pipe smoke, I looked around aimlessly. Among the exhausted young faces, my eyes stopped on a tall young man, the only person that night who wasn't wearing the poorly tailored green army overcoat that hid our individual characteristics. His frame was triangular: wide shoulders, broad back, thin waist, and long legs. When he turned in my direction, I noticed how strikingly handsome he was. His eyebrows were bushy and dark above piercing eyes. His nose was long and straight. Despite his youth, he had a mature face. But it was a gloomy face.

One day in April 1973, I received a telegraph from home urging me to take a leave back to Shanghai. Since I had been here for the required three full years, my application was approved at once.

The slowly rolling train threaded its way through the vast countryside. Like a bird out of its cage, my heart was light. In the brilliance of the spring, I saw hope in the budding tree leaves, in the bright blue sky, and among the million rays of the sun. I thought of the words of an ancient sage: "A common person must first go through unbearable physical and spiritual sufferings and frustrations before he is given an important task to accomplish in his life."

I raised my head. Silently I asked, Have I suffered enough yet?

Shanghai's North Train Station hadn't changed much over the past three years. The two red characters forming the word Shanghai still stood on top of the flat-roofed building and were still dust-covered. The long platforms were still filled with crowds of passengers getting on and off the trains. The familiar crisp Shanghai dialect rang in the air. Peddlers selling fried dough twists, red-bean and green-bean rice cakes, seaweed cookies, and spicy bean curd strips shouted raucously and banged their wooden stands. Sad parents said good-bye to their sons or daughters going to the countryside. The Up to the Mountains, Down to the Countryside movement was still going on. Middle-school graduates in great numbers continued to leave Shanghai for its suburbs and the nearby provinces of Jiang Su and Zhejiang.

My younger brother Jie was waiting for me. At eighteen, he was now a young man with a faint growth of mustache above his upper lip. Jie was lucky. He was assigned to a hospital cafeteria to clean tables. According to the more lenient graduation policy prevailing now, Jie was allowed to stay in Shanghai because both Ming and I were already peasants.

When I stepped into the tiny apartment, I saw tears in Father's eyes. Without saying a word, he took me to the window and examined me carefully in the bright sunlight. His eyes searched my face, his fingers touching gently the scars on the bridge of my nose, on my eyelids, and around the mouth. He inspected my scarred right hand, and asked if it was still painful. Then his eyes stopped at my hair, which already reached shoulder level.

"I wonder how you can continue working with all your injuries." His voice choked. He took out a handkerchief to blow his nose.

Mother said that I looked muddy, like an unearthed artifact. She complained that the dirt on my body formed a dark shell and obscured my true skin color; I must clean myself thoroughly from head to toe before doing anything else. She took me into the small bathroom, filled with white steam. A huge wooden washbasin brimming with hot water was ready, a green striped washcloth floating on the surface. Mother left, closing the door behind her. She came in again with a piece of strong soap and a bottle of medicinal shampoo to kill the lice living in my knotted hair. Taking a long nylon brush, she scrubbed me as if I were a pig ready for slaughter. She left again and came back with a small brush and cleaned my ears and hands. Mother threw away my green canvas and rubber shoes and soaked all my clothes in boiling water. She told me that white and red and black lice were crawling everywhere in my clothes and had laid eggs. I had become a real louse breeding center, raising probably the best lice in the world. She asked if I ever felt their existence. Yes: I pointed to the dense red bites, each the size of a needle head, spreading all over my limbs. But I was not particularly bothered. At night, whenever I lay down, I always fell into a sound sleep. During the day I had a lot of things to worry about other than the pests. Mother sighed. She put down the kettle and went to find an ointment to soothe the itching.

My parents ordered many dishes from a nearby restaurant: fish, pork, egg cooked with tomatoes, snow peas, fried dumplings, steamed dumplings, and boiled dumplings. It was the most sumptuous feast I had seen for a long time. I had eaten only boiled cabbage, potatoes, and salty broth for so long that the food dazzled me. Mother picked up a piece of pork dipped in red soybean sauce and put it into my bowl. The last time I had eaten meat was more than five months ago, when a horse had died from a disease. The leaders had decided to donate the carcass to our canteen. Strong young men cut up the horse, and the cooks boiled and served the meat. Commander Gao, the cook squad leader, grinned from ear to ear.

"Eat! Eat! Eat!" my parents urged. I devoured the food ravenously. I even bit my tongue a few times.

Sitting around the cleared table after dinner, my parents were ready to get down to "serious business." In 1972, after the Lin Biao incident, Father had been released from the Chongming Island labor farm and returned to Hudong University. But he was still a Kuomintang spy and a traitor, and the investigation into his past connection with President Liu Shaoqi dragged on. The inhumane living and working conditions on the island had ruined his joints. His fingers were red and swollen from arthritis. Under supervision, Mother cleaned bathrooms at her academy. But seven years into the Cultural Revolution, my parents had grown used to the tumultuous lives they were forced to live every day.

"The job you are doing is too harsh and dangerous for a young girl. As long as you are still there, every day we feel like we are sitting on pins and needles," Father said. From his anxious expression, it seemed that a terrible disaster was about to crush me right before his eyes.

"How is Lon? Do you have any contact with him?" Father asked.

"We exchange letters."

"He is a bright young man with a good future." Father knew that Lon would work in the Foreign Ministry in Beijing after his graduation. This had been decided the moment he enrolled at Shanghai Foreign Relations University.

"Lon is very gracious." Mother lost no time in agreeing.

In the eyes of my parents, Lon was an ideal future husband for me and the best son-in-law heaven could offer them. They were flattered and even grateful that Lon was willing to link himself with me — with my future still under a cloud. However, to me, the idea of marrying Lon in exchange for my return to the city sounded frightening.

One Sunday morning Lon came to visit. He no longer wore the green uniform as we did in the countryside. Since the Red Guard movement had died, the attire had gone out of fashion. Mao suits were in. That was the exact outfit Lon wore — a dark gray jacket with a short stand-up collar, padded shoulders, and four open pockets. He added a pair of spectacles with dark brown frames, conferring an air of knowledge and status in combination with his stylish garments. His appearance humbled mine. By contrast, eating huge amounts of Heilongjiang's corn bread and sorghum had made me gain weight. Mother said my waist was thicker than a barrel, my face as round as the moon: I was a real "rustic aunt." With my skin rough and dark from sunburn and from the hard-to-get-rid-of dirt that clogged my pores, I wondered what was it about me that Lon found worth looking at.

In the presence of my smiling parents, Lon held his back straight, nodding politely from time to time. He carried his chopsticks not too high or too low, but just at the right angle. He held the bowl in one hand and put it down when picking up dishes. He piled fish bones and meat bones carefully on the receptacle intended for them. Father kept on putting food in Lon's plate. Mother praised him for possessing an elegant manner. Although my parents often disagreed over trivial things, they worked in harmony in things like this. I was glad they played the major roles and did almost all of the talking. They still believed that, as far as marriage was concerned, I should defer to them. In the afternoon, as the sun threw bizarre shadows through the windows, they asked me to see Lon off.

When we were outside, Lon asked, "Why don't you ever respond to my letters promptly?" He stared at me. His eyes felt hot. "I've been nostalgic, missing the time we spent on the mountain carrying huge rocks. Do you remember that we built that hundred-foot-high chimney at the headquarters? The sun was under our feet, the clouds floated behind our backs, and people on the ground crawled like ants. I tried to forget you and leave Heilongjiang to history, so that I can make a new circle of friends. You know my classmates are all the children of powerful officials like the defense minister and vice premier, don't you?"

He paused to look at me. I nodded. His school was the famous nest for the children of high-ranking officials.

Then he became emotional. "But I don't know why I've been thinking of our past so often. It's strange. Maybe because you sponsored me to join the Youth League — that made my college education possible," Lon continued, "or maybe because you've been indifferent to me, even though we carried rocks together for years. You shouldn't be this proud. You know you're not beautiful, don't you?"

I licked my dry lips. I tucked strands of my thick hair behind my ears. I hid my dark hands in my pockets. Trying to avoid his eyes, I stared at the ground.

He tossed back the lock of hair that was slipping onto his broad forehead. "I know girls, beautiful girls, who admire me. If I smile at them, they'll be beside themselves." He raised his head to the sky, his comely face ivory under the sunlight. Then he leveled his eyes at me and opened them wide. I saw in them an arrogance that chilled me.

I didn't move. I didn't know what to say. My face must have been expressionless, for Lon said, "See, you're as cold as stone even now."

★　　　★　　　★

My twenty-day vacation passed quickly with the frantic purchasing of clothes for the peasant wives, who still regarded Shanghai as the "fashion center," even though the once trendy Shanghainese now wore only monotonous revolutionary colors. Hundreds of clothing stores lining Nanjing Road, the busiest commercial district in the nation, had nothing to sell but unisex garments in one style.

My parents saw me off at Shanghai's North Train Station one sun-drenched morning. Their eyes reflected deep sorrow. They worried about me, because they thought I was "overly impulsive," "overly enthusiastic," and "accident prone," although I had told them many times that ever since my belief died, I was devoted to nobody except myself. Having escaped from fire and blood, I had matured. I knew how to take care of myself. Half believing, my parents nodded. Departing was always sad, especially when my future remained a big question mark. My parents, like all other parents, worried that they wouldn't see me again. Loud cries could be heard above the din and bustle of the ever busy train station, which saw endless separations and reunions every day. The modern writer Lu Xun once said, "Having no emotion does not signify a real hero. Pitying the young does not signify weakness. Even the ferociously charging tigress looks back to its baby from time to time."

Trying to console my parents, I smiled hard while swallowing bitter tears. As the train moved away, I leaned out the window and waved broadly. Despite my uncertain future, I had already made an important decision — I was not going to use Lon as a springboard to return to the city. But I also knew that, other than Lon, my parents had no "back door" for me to go through. It was all up to me now — to win or die.

22

The Tide Turns

In June 1973, two months after I returned from my visit home, the Great Northern Wilderness beamed with wild lilies, which covered the rolling hills like the waves of a golden ocean. Mountains dressed in profuse green stood on the horizon. The wild geese migrating back to the north honked merrily, flying in ever renewed patterns across the blue sky.

Summer brought welcome news. At a meeting, the new college enrollment policies just issued by the State Council were read by the party secretary — not Yi but another retired army officer. During my absence Yi had been caught with a Beijing girl and asked to leave his position. This was good for me, since his departure opened a new door to my future.

According to the announcement, China's universities would formally admit students from among outstanding young workers, peasants, and soldiers with at least two years' practical experience. This was the first time in seven years that colleges had recruited students through open competition and entrance examinations. The Heilongjiang Military Farms, the largest operation of its kind, with about one million young people, would be a major source of candidates. Our village bubbled with excitement. We borrowed academic books and buried our noses inside them, trying to memorize their contents. We hoped to be like the fabled carp in the Yellow River: once it jumped over Dragon Gate, it would no longer be a small fish but a dragon, king of the universe, moving the clouds and stirring up the oceans. Beautiful dreams invigorated our lives. Laughter refilled the dormitories, and hope brought liveliness back to the village.

To eliminate corruption, so that a small group of unit leaders wouldn't have complete power to select whomever they preferred, the new policy laid down rules:

1. Every youth could apply.

2. General elections would decide the college candidates.

3. Local leaders could only conduct political investigations and family background checks.

4. Only politically qualified candidates could go on to take the college entrance examinations.

5. The college would make the final decision.

In less than a month, admissions representatives from various universities in the nation arrived at our Seventy-third Regiment. For the total of two hundred fifty young people in our company, the quota of college candidates was only four: Fudan University, Nanjing Technical Institute, Harbin Teacher's College, and Heilongjiang Academy of Agriculture. Since everybody wanted to go, the competition was keen beyond imagining.

I felt excited and nervous. This was the opportunity that I had prepared for politically and academically for so long. I was among the first to apply and often studied through the night. When I was too tired to read, I pinched myself so hard the pain would drive away the drowsiness. Sometimes I went to the well and drew a bucket of cold water to wash my face and refresh myself. The day when the company election was held, I was thrilled to learn that I had beaten all the other candidates and received the highest number of votes. Automatically, I would be qualified for the famous Fudan University in Shanghai if I passed the political background check and scored well on the entrance examinations. The first I did with ease.

The testing center was located in one of the office buildings at the regimental headquarters. I rose early. Humming, I skipped along on the newly graveled road, which, under the rising sun, seemed to be covered with golden bricks. As the morning mist gradually thinned, verdant sunlight-bathed mountains greeted the eye on all sides.

A roomful of boys and girls had already taken their seats. Some were cramming right up to the last minute, reading from scribbled notes in their hands. Others whispered in low tones. Among them I saw Wang Pei, our company's former deputy political instructor, who now worked in the regimental personnel division.

Suddenly a bespectacled middle-aged man in a light gray coat stepped into the room, squeezing a roll of test papers under his arm, a teacher's casual habit but always frightening to the students.

"Good morning, everybody," he said in Mandarin with a faint Shanghai accent. He explained that the examinations would last for three days and cover the subjects of the Chinese language, math, chemistry, physics, and politics (that is, knowledge about the current situation and the theories of Marx, Lenin, and Mao Zedong). I heard my heart beating. After the seven-year national ban on knowledge and education, today's tests signaled that China had restored normal education and revived its civilization. As one of the first college candidates allowed to compete academically, as regular students did everywhere else in the world, I felt proud of myself.

On July 10, 1973, I received the acceptance letter. But to my surprise, it was not from Fudan University but rather East China Normal University, a less prestigious institution located in Shanghai. What had happened? Who had made the change and why? There was no official explanation, but I soon learned that Wang Pei, taking advantage of her position in the regimental headquarters, had intercepted Fudan University and kept it for herself. Despite warnings from the State Council to abolish corruption, party officials at various levels didn't hesitate to disregard orders: "A waterfront pavilion receives the moonlight first." A common person couldn't challenge a party official, because the bureaucrats shielded one another. By struggling against them, I might have lost everything. So I accepted East China Normal University quietly.

But even this contentment was short-lived. As I packed my belongings, another political storm arose — the Zhang Tieshen incident, which soon shook the nation and postponed my departure.

Zhang Tieshen, who had failed his chemistry test, wrote a letter to the authorities. As an agricultural leader, he claimed, he had not been able to find the time to study because of hoeing season. He complained that it was unfair for his future to be decided on the basis of just one test. Unbeknownst to Zhang, this letter was passed on to Mao Yuanxin, party secretary of Liaoning Province and Chairman Mao's nephew. Soon the *People's Daily* published an edited version of it with the comment: "A small group of bourgeois intellectuals is using the college entrance tests as a weapon to prevent the working class from seeking higher education. This is leading to a slow capitalist restoration in our country." The target of this campaign was Premier Zhou Enlai, who had designed the new college admission policies and had demanded that all the college candidates take entrance tests.

The local leaders had to reevaluate us four prospective students according to new political standards. They found a problem with Hou, who was to study at Nanjing Technical Institute. The twenty-seven-year-old was one of the few who had completed almost six years of middle and high school when the Cultural Revolution started. Thanks to this elite educational background, he had achieved perfect scores on the entrance examinations. However, the leaders asked, if Hou was so good at learning, how would he have the time to develop his socialist consciousness? Indeed, Hou had been late a few times for important company meetings. He even dozed off once during a Mao study session. Without a doubt, the leaders preferred to send a socialist weed rather than a bourgeois seedling to college. A socialist "slow vehicle" was always safer than a capitalist "fast train."

So they replaced Hou with another young man. The school quickly approved the change and accepted the student without requiring him to take any tests, which the party had already revoked.

The Zhang Tieshen incident brought the incredible absurdity of the Cultural Revolution to another summit and altered the path of China's educational reform set by Premier Zhou Enlai in 1973. It was the prelude to a prolonged campaign targeting intellectuals in China's higher education. Zhang Tieshen — the student who had failed the chemistry test — was not only admitted to the university that denied him earlier but also became the school's party secretary, hailed as a "countertrend hero." After the Cultural Revolution ended, Zhang was sentenced to death for his prior role in the Revolution, but the verdict was overturned. He eventually served fifteen years in prison.

While awaiting authorization to leave, I submitted one report after another detailing my current ideological attitude toward Mao and the Cultural Revolution. But I knew that behind the scenes those in power were creating false excuses to disqualify the original candidates and replace them with either themselves or their relatives. Since foreign languages was the most popular discipline, a hot major desired by almost everyone, I worried that someone powerful would find fault with me, citing this or that unsatisfactory political behavior to discredit me. That made the wait even more miserable.

23

Farewell

Two months passed. In September a crisp coolness filled the air. The first frost fell, signaling the coming of the long, bitter winter. With each gust of northwest wind, autumn leaves withered, and the green mountains turned darkish brown. Wild geese, honking overhead, flew in ever renewed V-patterns southward. The red sun seemed to have turned gray, with a dark halo around it. Every day I waited impatiently, anxiously.

Then one day an official letter came. It was from the Party Committee of the Seventy-third Regiment and informed me that I had been cleared politically and was permitted to leave. Heart singing, I turned the letter over and wrote down the famous Tang poem by Du Fu:

> Tears wet my clothes at the news.
> Clouds of miseries disappear.
> Overjoyed, I indulge in books and poems,
> And drink until I get drunk
> And sing until
> Youth and vigor accompany me back home.

I packed immediately. I was afraid that something else might come up and trap me here forever. But anxiety gripped me, as though I had lost something invaluable. I realized that when I left Heilongjiang, I was also leaving Tan behind, the most desired but least attainable person in my life. I thought about him with a grateful heart. Feelings of romance overwhelmed me. I wanted to drive away his sadness like fire thawing ice. I wanted to hold his hand and climb to the summit of Yellow Mountain to watch the clouds flying in the twilight, then go to the East China Sea to listen to the spring tides singing. Soaked in happiness, I was almost beside myself. The moon will never vanish and the sky never grows old. With love, we are forever young. Hand in hand, we will race into tomorrow.

My heart beat wildly. Su, who was helping me pack, noticed my flushed face and unusual restlessness.

"You must be in love. Tell me who he is?"

Su was a seasoned hand. Since early that year, when dating and marriage were officially permitted, she had already found the right match and would soon marry a Beijing youth in the transportation company.

I blushed and became tongue-tied. So many tender thoughts were welling up in my mind that I really didn't know where to start. It was so difficult to open my mouth and express my inner heart. Ever since I was fourteen, I had been forced only to hide my affection and never to show or act on it.

"You're still old-fashioned. Open your eyes and look around. Who doesn't have a boyfriend or a girlfriend? Times have changed." Su recognized my embarrassment. She pretended to put her finger into my mouth to dig out my secret.

Closing my eyes, I blurted the truth about Tan and covered my hot face with my hands. But at the mention of his name, the usually exuberant Su froze, as if she had been nailed to the ground. I looked at her through my fingers and saw her shake her head sharply.

"It won't work. You know it won't work." She sounded a little reluctant, but she went on. "Pin fell in love with Tan the moment he saved her from the well. It's natural she did. Who wouldn't in her situation? But they began seeing each other only after college enrollment began. Pin told me the other day that they're getting married soon."

Su's words were like a thousand arrows shooting into my bleeding heart.

"Tan's family background is too dangerous for people like you and me. No one can live a normal life with such a heavy political burden. Pin and Tan are a good match. You know Pin's father was a Kuomintang spy before the Liberation, don't you? Who would dare marry Pin? Only Tan. Who would dare marry Tan? Only Pin. Right?" Su asked, but obviously didn't expect an answer. "For their children, having one historical counterrevolutionary grandparent or two or three won't make much difference. But for our children, having one or none makes a world of difference. Who wouldn't be frightened by that?"

I believed every word Su said. Pin was her confidante. They were both from Beijing and both had worked in the cooking squad for years.

Wiping her eyes, Su continued: "Tan is qualified in every way to attend a college, and he'll get elected for sure. But for him, election means nothing. How many times has he been nominated to be a party member? But he'll never be approved. That's why no one even mentioned his name for college this time. People have lost faith that he'll be given what he deserves and have started forgetting about him. He'll be the last one to leave this place. That is his destiny, and he can't change it."

I closed my eyes and let the tears flood my face. I hated myself for my selfishness and agonized over my helplessness in determining his fate. If I didn't have the courage to love him, then I had to lose him. Although subconsciously I had long expected the painful loss, for it to become a reality was too cruel to bear. Without Tan living within me, the world didn't seem to exist. I heard myself crying. But whom should I blame? It was no one's fault but my own. But did I have a choice? Why did such an innocent feeling entail such danger? Anger, like an invisible hand, strangled me.

But on second thought, did I really have the courage to bear Tan's family stigma forever? Was I prepared to undergo endless political investigations during my college years regarding my relationship with Tan? Maybe it wasn't so wise to meet him, since, knowing that I would never ever see him again, the sight of him would break my heart. Let me pretend instead that love never existed, as I had done all these years trying so hard to conceal my feelings from the outside world.

The pain must have distorted my face. Clapping me on the shoulder, Su comforted me: "Cheer up. You're like a golden phoenix flying out of this straw nest. Go and find someone in big Shanghai. College student! Are you afraid you can't find a husband?"

That night I saw Bei standing at the dormitory gate, as if waiting for someone. He was a shy young man with delicate features.

"Hi, do you have a few minutes?" he greeted me timidly.

He shifted his feet as if standing on glass. A child of divorced parents, he had grown up in humiliation, enduring verbal and physical abuse from peers and even adults.

The air bore a late autumn chill, and the intimation of a long and boring winter. A moment passed in silence before Bei suddenly thrust into my hand a diary.

"Keep it as a memento of your life here in Heilongjiang," he said bashfully, wringing his hands in front of him. Trees rustled; dry leaves went flying. The Great Northern Wilderness lurked in the sleepy darkness. Bei moved closer, his well-chiseled features becoming vivid, moonlight reflecting in his eyes.

He was no stranger. He had once saved my life, an act that minted a friendship. How could I forget? A wisp of chilly wind swept by and brought me back to the construction site.

I was carrying two high stacks of bricks while climbing up the step-plank. It was one of those days when I felt my body to be as soft as cotton and my legs like noodles. I pretended that it didn't matter.

This had happened many times before. I was young, and my youthfulness would conquer all odds. But halfway up the plank I wavered, hardly able to advance. The world seemed to go round and round and the valley below me opened its mouth, ready to swallow me up. Bei quickly descended from the scaffold, where he had been waiting to go down, and extended his hand.

Accepting the notebook, I felt the blood surge in my face and ears. When I returned to the dorm and opened the diary, a neatly written letter fell from between the leaves: "Could you write to me when you return to Shanghai? I don't feel that I have the right to ask you to. Just overnight, you have changed into a college student. We are no longer equal. I don't know what my future holds. My fate is out of my control. How can a sword cut water? How can it cut sadness?"

Teardrops wet the letter shaking in my hands. Hearing his cry of helplessness, I wanted to grab Bei by the shoulders and shout in his face, "Yes, we are equal! We are equal even if I am a college student!"

The dorm was quiet except for the rising and falling of the snores. The girls had already fallen into a sound sleep. Tomorrow, hard heavy work awaited them, and their lives would continue normally. I lay on my quilt with all my clothes still on, unable to sleep. The night was endless. From Bei, my thoughts wandered back to the day's farewell meeting. Saying good-bye to my comrades, with whom I had spent three and a half years, was not as easy as I had anticipated. Su wrapped her arms tightly around my neck, sobbing. I left her my two aluminum washbasins, considered valuable then, along with many other personal belongings. All these years, she treated me better than a sister. If she married, she would have to settle down here for a very long time. Distance would prevent us from seeing each other again soon. This departure might even be a farewell for life. I buried my face on her wide shoulders. When I lifted my head, I saw shining tears running down many faces. When will *we* go home? they seemed to ask. It turned out their wait would be long. While they waited, reluctantly, many of them assumed family burdens they had tried so hard to avoid at first, and in their arms they held crying babies. Their poorly washed bodies smelled. Their dirty, dark clothing was fastened with straw ropes, not with the awe-inspiring black leather belts. They rose at sunrise and retired at sunset; they drank from the well and ate what they grew. They lived like peasants, spoke like peasants, ate like peasants, and looked like peasants. In its vast bosom, the Great Northern Wilderness had assimilated these young people. But in their hearts, the longing to return home never died.

While the world tried to forget them, the 16 million no-longer-young young people repeatedly appealed to the central government, staging hunger strikes and holding mass demonstrations. Six years after I left, in 1979, the State Council, under enormous pressure, finally turned on the green light. In the following months, about 97 percent returned home. The tide receded as fast as it had risen in 1968, when the frenzied Red Guards pledged loyalty to Chairman Mao with their blood and rushed to the countryside in millions. Eleven years later, this massive return finally put an end to the long-lived Up to the Mountains, Down to the Countryside movement.

The next day, September 15, 1973, was the day of my departure. On my way to Tashan, I asked the truck driver to stop by the roadside. I walked into the endless fields, grabbed a handful of the Black Gold, and wrapped it with a piece of yellowed newspaper. My hands trembled, for the soil was soaked with my sweat and blood. In the afternoon I boarded a southbound train. At the sharp whistle, I surveyed the small Tashan train station for the last time. Flashing in my mind was the scene of three and a half years ago, when one thousand idealistic young people flooded the station. The tall trees were still there, the strong branches that held the company representatives were still there. Beside them, the tree stumps and huge rocks were still there. Everything was as vivid as if it had happened just yesterday. But no one could wade through the same river a second time. Today, there were dead, injured, and disabled among our number.

Slowly the train passed the stone-fronted ticket office, then the nearly empty platform lined sparsely with trees. Two thin donkeys stared in our direction. Falling leaves flew in the air. The vault of heaven was still cold, and the wild land beyond extended all the way to the edge of the earth. With misty eyes I caught a glimpse of a young man's lonely silhouette in the pale setting sun, the familiar black uniform, the full head with wavy hair, and the frame of medium build. I couldn't see the eyes, but I knew they stored unspeakable sorrow. It was my young hero, whom I had embraced thousands of times in emptiness and nothingness. My tearful eyes clung to him, my statue of glory. Out of the station, the train sped up and the statue gradually became a lucent dot, merging into the oyster-colored horizon.

> Like drifting clouds and scattered rain,
> We part from each other today.
> Do you know how miserable my heart is?
> See the willow weeping in the dusk.

For days the train rambled through picturesque landscapes as my thoughts surged ahead. The locomotive roared, passing tunnels, bridges, plains, and mountains with no fear. Before the rolling wheels, two silver rails shining under the bright sunlight extended far ahead, ushering the train to its destination. There Shanghai waited.

3

The Impenetrable Kingdom

24

A Student of a Kind

On September 19, 1973, beneath the hot sun, I arrived at the imposing iron gate of East China Normal University. Facing the main entrance, standing taller than the treetops, was a colossal statue of Mao in a heavy army trench coat, pointing his finger straight ahead. He was flanked by two long banners that hung down from the tall elm trees:

> Down with the Counterrevolutionary Scholars!
> Long Live Chairman Mao's Educational Line!

If it were not for the gigantic Mao, if it were not for the blood-red slogans calling for class struggle, the elegant campus would have been the poet Tao Yuanming's Garden of Peach Blossoms, a fantasy-land of peace far removed from the outside world. A zigzag stone bridge spanned a clear-water creek. Pale pinkish gray lotus flowers drifted lazily on the surface. Covered in the shadows of the swaying willow, huge elm, and pagoda-shaped magnolia, the angular red-roofed classroom buildings with their yellow facades looked more like pavilions and temples than the often dreary architecture of most other universities.

After several inquiries, I found my dormitory among a dozen pinkish buildings next to the school dining hall. In sharp contrast to the fantastic exterior, the inside of the residence hall was a world of raw cement. Concrete stairways ran all the way from the ground floor to the fifth. Concrete walls were painted with a thin coat of white-wash and still showed their rough texture. Concrete floors harbored hundreds of weblike cracks. Concrete sinks were iron-colored from overuse. But to me, fresh out of Heilongjiang, where our dorm's dirt floor was like marshland when it was drenched with soapy water, this building was clean, dry, and firm under my feet. The residence was alive with jubilant girls moving about in plastic sandals, dropping by each other's rooms, and chatting in various dialects.

Room 301 was already full of girls busily making their beds. I was actually the last to arrive. I sized up my new home; I would have to spend three years here. The room had three bunk beds and six individual desks, four in the center, two on the sides. In one corner stood a rack tall enough to hold six washbasins. A wooden bookshelf stood in another corner. At the foot of the wall, six red flasks were placed side by side. All the furniture was printed in white with PROPERTY OF EAST CHINA NORMAL UNIVERSITY.

The other five girls had already chosen their beds, leaving me with the top one next to the window, directly under the strong fluo-rescent light hanging ten inches overhead. While unpacking, I gauged my roommates from above.

A girl with a big face but small features got up from her bed below me. "My name is Juan Chen. Where are you from?" she asked, her voice low as a boy's.

"Fourth Division, Heilongjiang Military Farms," I answered proudly, knowing the power that the name carried.

"I am, too, but from the Third Division along the Ussuri River," Juan Chen said with equal pride. I noticed her strong arms, which were clearly used to lifting heavy objects, the familiar tanned complexion, and the callus-covered, solid hands.

"I'm from the Second Division," another girl in a fashionable light green coat cut in. Where is the Second Division? Xing'an Moun-tain in the northern part of the province. Endless mountain ranges and tall poplar trees. Siberian tigers, polar bears. Ginseng and wula grass.

The girl had bulging eyes that obscured the other features of her ruby-cheeked face. Her bangs were curled and her eyebrows shaped. She wore a pair of patent leather shoes, something we hadn't seen for years. The pink shirt peeking through the open collar of her light green jacket was arresting, like a rose against the leaves. In 1973, seven years after the Red Guards' "fashion censorship," society still shrank from bold colors. Smiling with closed lips, the girl introduced herself as Yun Yun, meaning beautiful flower.

Lifting her head from the book she was reading, the girl sitting at the corner desk introduced herself: "I'm Jing. From Division One."

Where is Division One? It is by the Black Dragon River across from Siberia. Wow! It must be very cold! The girl nodded. "Yes! Let me put it this way: Compared to my division, your Fourth Division in Tashan is a tropical resort." Jing smiled. Her sun-darkened face, small but bright eyes, and thin lips made me think of a sunflower seed. On this muggy day, Jing's long-sleeved shirt was still buttoned up to the collar. Seeing the small, dry hands and a portion of the long, thin neck, I could imagine her twiglike arms and bamboo-stick body, which had endured Heilongjiang's cruel winter for years.

I caught the timid gaze of a girl sitting on the bed above Yun Yun's, holding her chin and listening to us attentively. Her big eyes shone with curiosity.

"Where are you from? " I asked her.

"I am Cui, from Anhui Province," she answered with humility.

A poor place, I thought. Located on the north side of the Yangtze River, Anhui had long been prey to floods. In people's minds, Anhui connoted horrendous natural disaster and people driven from their homes. Peasants there ate sweet potato leaves year round. But when I saw how clean Cui's skin was and how tender her hands, I wondered if she had ever participated in harsh physical labor at all.

As if reading my thoughts, Cui pointed to the girl sitting beside the window. "Lang is also from Anhui."

I looked at this last girl. She had fleshy lips and two pitch-black eyes resembling dark purple grapes. Her flared nostrils suggested superiority. While her face expressed indifference, in reality she was listening to us attentively.

The sun sprayed its last rays on the green bamboo grove behind our building. Bright spots wavered on the elegant leaves, getting dimmer and dimmer as the huge sun set behind the silhouettes of the buildings in the distance. The loudspeakers all over campus boomed to life, blasting the music "The East Is Red" followed by routine editorials, criticisms, and songs of Mao's quotations. It was dinnertime. Supper served in the student canteen was rich: pork chops, boiled eggs, meatballs on top of green vegetables, and steamed fish. In the center of the canteen was an enormous pot of soup with pieces of fresh green onions floating on top. The soup reminded me of my past. I rapped my bowl lightly, bobbed my head, and hummed the soup song with Jing, who swore that she had drunk more soup than I had.

> Soup, I love revolutionary soup!
> Soup in the morning, I greet the sun.
> Soup at noon, I can't help lying down.
> Soup for dinner, I feel happy the whole night long.

After dinner we sat at our little desks filling out forms detailing every family member's ideological orientation and household income. Unexpectedly Lang, the girl with grapelike eyes, approached me and thrust her forms under my nose. I raised my head in surprise. Making sure I was watching her, Lang casually wrote down the numbers 38 and 28 in the slots that asked for monthly parental income. Then she moved away to show the numbers to everyone else in the room.

"Are those your parents' wages?" Jing asked in disbelief.

Lang wrinkled her nose and twisted her mouth scornfully. With everyone's attention focused on her, she slowly added a zero after the two numbers and displayed the forms again to every one of us. (The salaries were equal to about thirty-five and forty-five U.S. dollars, respectively, which was very high then.) When she saw how stunned we were, she doubled over and laughed herself breathless. Each of her parents, ranking officials of the former Shanghai municipal government, made about five times as much as a normal worker, who earned an average of only sixty-five yuan (eight dollars in U.S. currency) a month.

Several three-storied buildings were occupied by the Department of Foreign Languages at the far end of the campus. Unlike our bare-concrete dormitory, the classrooms were floored with hardwood. In every one of them, a color portrait of Mao hung in the middle of the wall, flanked by political slogans painted on red paper. At the front, near the podium, was a trunk-sized recorder along with a few reels of tape, each as big as a plate. The rooms were bright and adequately lit. Chairs and desks were in good shape and clean. The wall-sized blackboard had just been repainted. In every way the physical condition of the classrooms seemed ideal. One could sense an air of academic seriousness and formality that belonged only to the best universities.

But I soon learned that beneath the serious academic surface, East China Normal University was at the forefront of Mao's ideological war against Liu Shaoqi's "bourgeois educational line." And our Department of Foreign Languages was the point of crossfire. Jiang Qing's close ally Xu Jinxian, vice chairman of the Shanghai Revolutionary Committee, had criticized our department as a "haven for filthy intellectuals who were infatuated with the bourgeois way of life and worshipped nothing but things foreign." In particular, he accused the faculty and students of drinking milk instead of soybean milk and coffee instead of tea. They preferred baked bread to steamed bread and spoke Chinese mixed with English, French, German, Russian, and Japanese instead of just plain Chinese, as "real"

Chinese did. Worst of all, many of them secretly listened to the Voice of America, the BBC, Radio Moscow, and Japan's premier radio station, NHK, which were strictly prohibited. Xu declared that the Department of Foreign Languages was the nursery for "capitalist seedlings" and the hotbed for the "successors of revisionists."

An alumnus, Xu Jinxian often visited the university to implement Mao's educational reforms. In October 1973 Xu, looking like an intellectual in a gray jacket with four open pockets, came to speak to our class. We stood up and applauded him warmly. Xu smiled and waved for us to sit down. Without saying anything, he walked up to the blackboard and wrote "Mixing Sand" and asked if we all understood our historical mission.

"We are Chairman Mao's sands mixed in with the bourgeois intellectuals. Our mission is to abolish all the existing practices in this intellectual-occupied kingdom. We should not only attend the college but also rule and transform it," a student recited all in one breath as if reading from a textbook.

Nodding his approval, Xu moistened his lips and said, "It's important for every student to understand how in the past our universities created revisionists of Marxism, Leninism, and Mao Zedong Thought."

Xu stepped up to the dais. Elegant in appearance, he was in his early forties. His face was gentle and quiet; his manner was natural and unrestrained, like a liberal poet. No matter how he raised his hand or stamped his feet, he manifested charisma. When he spoke, words flowed like water running from the high mountains, smooth and rhythmic. His voice was mild but conveyed energy hotter than fire and stronger than steel. He was refined and charming without seeming to be aware of it. Girls in the class fixed their eyes on him, and, looking at him, it was difficult to believe he had been one of the rebel leaders during Shanghai's violent January Revolutionary Storm. It was even harder to believe that behind his cultivated surface lay a fathomless zeal and a fierce political ambition that drove him to persecute and destroy anybody in his way.

Pacing back and forth between the rows, Xu stopped in front of my desk.

"Do you all know the heroine Liu Lihua?" His eyes swept around the classroom and stared off into the distance beyond the window, envisioning the prospect of a struggle with his ideological enemies.

I held my breath. She was a girl I didn't care for. To me Liu, a Chinese-language major at our university, was a failure. When she couldn't keep up with her studies of Wenyanwen — ancient Chinese — she wrote a letter to the university leaders complaining that her professors used the ancient Chinese language as a weapon to attack her. The next day, *People's Daily* published Liu's letter. Its editorial praised her for challenging the reactionary trend that valued learning above all else and for single-handedly repelling the savage onslaught of the bourgeois intellectuals.

Taking off his glasses and cleaning them with the corner of his jacket, Xu went on, "The girl's letter is only a small pebble. But the ripples stirred up by this one pebble have spread, not only throughout this campus, but also to Fudan, Beijing, and Qinghua Universities, and all other institutions of higher learning in China. The significance of her action cannot be taken lightly!"

Xu waved his hand.

"The girl is just an ordinary student like you, but how then does she possess such a high level of class consciousness? The answer is clear: She's from the laboring people and loves Chairman Mao and our party. She is imbued with a spirit as lofty as the rainbow spanning the sky. With this spirit, we proletarians can conquer mountains and rivers." Xu's eyebrows shot up and his eyes seemed to emit flames.

He lowered his voice to emphasize the next points. "How long will we go on talking about the class struggle in higher education?

We'll talk about it every day, every month, and every year. We'll never tire of it as long as the influence of the bourgeois intellectuals still exists. You must smash any of the counterattacks devised by them. You must interrupt their speeches at any time by grabbing the microphones from them."

My heart trembled at his words. Snatching a microphone was symbolic of anarchy and chaos. It was a behavior typical of the Red Guards at the beginning of the Cultural Revolution. Images from those frenzied years flashed before my eyes: roaring Tiananmen Square, a sea of flying red flags, crimson armbands, waving leather belts, yin-yang heads, and parading victims on a fire engine. These events had happened seven years ago when we were still ignorant teenagers. Did we have to repeat history here? Were we college students or Red Guards all over again?

25

Professor "Rat Crossing the Street"

To learn or not to learn? Mao's revolutionary ideology was like clouds of a thousand shapes. They hid mountains and rivers, iron and swords.

I sat on my seat with a confused mind, waiting for the first English class to begin. A new rule in the department decreed that only a proletarian was qualified to teach the first class. The bell rang, deliberate and clear. In came a middle-aged man in faded blue overalls. His newly cut hair was jagged as if chewed by a dog; his shaved chin looked green under the light. On his chest was pinned a huge glowing badge of Mao. As the worker moved toward the center of the room, all eyes looked him up and down.

He stood before the podium and looked around the classroom solemnly before stating, "My name is Shi Jinbao —"

"Ha! Ha! Ha!" The class burst out laughing. His name meant "gold and treasure, please come my way." It belonged to the Four Olds — old tradition, old customs, old culture, the old ideas — and it was rare that such a feudal moniker could have escaped the Red Guards' name censorship in 1966. They must have forgotten to change it to Love the Party, Red Sea, or Against U.S. Imperialism.

"You may call me Master Shi as I have always been called in my factory. I am a Worker Propaganda Team member assigned to this department for four years. Like you, we are revolutionary sands mixed in the realm of higher education," Master Shi continued, ignoring the jeers. But his broken Mandarin, inflected with a heavy Shanghai accent, caused more uproar. Master Shi stuttered, his lower lip drooping. But he soon calmed himself.

"Today, we will learn two important English sentences. Please pay attention to how they are pronounced."

Master Shi walked to the blackboard and wrote slowly and carefully:

Long Live Chairman Mao!
Long Live the Great Proletarian Cultural Revolution!

His great respect for Mao saturated every stroke of his attentive writing. His hands shook with emotion, and he had to stop several times to calm them. Once finished, he read the two sentences with great sincerity. His face turned red, his voice trembled. I saw tears forming in his eyes.

We imitated him. The slogan Long Live Chairman Mao! was relatively easy. Almost all of us had heard it shouted over the radio or on the streets. Long Live the Great Proletarian Cultural Revolution! was harder, since there were so many multisyllabic words. The pronunciation of "proletarian" tripped up everyone. Students pppped and pooed, spitting everywhere. The air in the classroom was hot and Master Shi sweated profusely. He returned to the center of the room from time to time, opening his mouth wide to demonstrate. Taking out small mirrors from our pockets, we opened our mouths as wide as we could to match our tongue positions with his. I strained my cheek muscles trying to pronounce the word. Master Shi examined my tongue position and corrected it with his coarse fingers. Students called him from every corner of the classroom. Like a dentist, he checked everyone's mouth.

Master Shi's English was only slightly better than ours. So our real professor was Ms. Wu. A typical Western-educated Chinese woman, she wore tasteful clothes with elegant and subtle patterns and a pair of gold-rimmed glasses. Her short silver hair rippled slightly and was combed neatly to the back. To me, she seemed very "foreign." Even her soft Shanghai Mandarin sounded more like English. Her language training was strict and her oral drills mechanical. Above the chorus of our voices, Ms. Wu admonished over and over that only by listening and repeating the same language pattern could we use it without thinking. Not knowing what I read, I felt like a new monk chanting scriptures. I kept on moving my mouth and rolling my tongue until they lost feeling.

English was hard to learn. Many of the vowels and consonants didn't have Chinese counterparts. Some sounds, like "th," I had never heard before in my life. Ms. Wu did her best to demonstrate. She made as if to pronounce an "s" but placed her tongue between her teeth, resulting in the "th" sound. Imitating Ms. Wu, I tried to come out with "these" and "thirsty," while wondering why the English people risked biting their tongues off when they spoke.

My rusty brain, which for years had been used only for simple manual labor, was slow and stodgy when it came to the complicated foreign language training. What's more, since "the international class struggle was intricate and volatile," speaking with a foreigner was considered the behavior of a "national traitor." Listening to foreign broadcasts would land me in prison. Without an English-language environment, I turned to the China International Broadcasting Station, the only official English station, which praised the great Cultural Revolution and vehemently condemned the Kuomintang and Western imperialists day and night.

Also, I had no time to learn. Most of the day was still devoted to political activities. When I did squeeze in a little time to study, I felt enormous psychological pressure. Since learning was discouraged, I felt everyone could be spying on me and I risked being exposed. All day long, my head thumped with pain and anxiety and my heart pounded with fear. Soon I found that I couldn't sleep, and I couldn't think right.

The questions whether to learn or not to learn, how to learn, and where to learn plagued me. To calm myself, I took tranquilizers, lots of them. But they in turn paralyzed me. Staring numbly at Ms. Wu's sunken mouth and her churning tongue, I seriously doubted that I was capable of learning English at all. Language drills sounded like a cacophony of voice in my ears. I wanted to escape this place. Perhaps I belonged in a mental hospital.

But at night, when I heard deep sighs in the dorm and saw the haggard faces tortured by worries, I realized that I wasn't the only one suffering. The atmosphere was quiet but strained, like the tense calm before a hurricane.

It was a Thursday, another routine English class.

As usual, Ms. Wu introduced a new phrase, "sooner or later." She illustrated how it was used:

"Sooner or later, the rose will wither."

"The rose will wither sooner or later."

"The rose, sooner or later, will wither."

After leading the class several times through the examples, Ms. Wu asked Yun Yun to make up a sentence using the phrase.

Yun Yun responded, "We will wipe out the im-pe-li-sm sooner or later," struggling so with the word "imperialism" that she finished the statement with a nervous rising tone. The students broke out in laughter, eager to find amusement during the tedium of language training. Yun Yun's face turned bright red. Ms. Wu's eyebrows knotted, and she considered the class unhappily as she waited for order to be restored. She asked Yun Yun to repeat the sentence. "Im-pe-ria-lism," she said, pronouncing the word slowly for her to imitate.

Yun Yun stood there, unspeaking. Her face changed from red to purple. Suddenly she burst into tears and covered her face with both hands.

Ms. Wu, embarrassed, looked at the class and clearly didn't know what to do. She walked up to Yun Yun and tried to calm her. But the girl cried louder, shedding thick tears that spotted her light green coat.

Fu, the student Communist Party leader of the class, turned sullen. He fidgeted as he stared at Yun Yun's pink shirt exposed at her collar. As she kept on sobbing, his anger grew. He clenched his hand into a fist. Abruptly, he stood up and walked to the teacher's podium.

"I suggest that the English class stop for today. Instead, we should hold a criticism meeting. We have seen how the bourgeois intellectual uses English as a weapon to bully us. We cannot tolerate this practice, can we? We should never forget our mission," Fu concluded, pointing to Mao's portrait on the wall.

Ms. Wu blanched. Hands trembling, she took off her gold-rimmed spectacles and cleaned them repeatedly with a white handkerchief embroidered with tiny roses in pink and blue.

Yu, a male student with short legs, placed a chair in the front of the podium and bade Ms. Wu to sit on it.

Looking at the chair and then at the class, she appeared to hesitate: should she take it or refuse it? Sitting down was an insult. Everything was happening so fast. Ms. Wu's face was alive with fear. Her eyes fought back tears. She didn't grasp what she had done to trigger the incident. But Fu's words were clear and powerful. The iron fists of the proletariat were on the attack.

The bell rang to signal the end of the class. The hallway filled with talk and the patter of footsteps as students headed from the classrooms to the stairways. Yu moved the chair closer and spoke in a harsher tone. Ms. Wu took the seat reluctantly but held up her head and threw out her chest. I looked at her wrinkled face and slim eyes. She reminded me of Mother the day she was paraded around on the fire engine. Did Ms. Wu have children or grandchildren? Did this tragedy have to be repeated in another innocent family? I felt deeply worried for her.

Fu cleared his throat vigorously. The students began their denunciations, their emotions stirred up by Yun Yun's sobbing and Fu's instigation. Tongues lashed like leather belts. Words flew like cannonballs blasting relentlessly at the old lady. Ms. Wu's head sank as her confidence dwindled. Her chin finally touched her chest. All I could see was her silver hair, now disheveled. Her world of sustaining dignity and authority had collapsed. When hundreds of fingers pointed at one's nose, no one could resist the immense pressure. This was the insurmountable power of Mao's mass movement. Ms. Wu broke down in tears and wiped her eyes with the embroidered hand-kerchief, which she clutched as tightly as if it were a life-saving rope meant for a drowning person. She seemed to ask, "What are you going to do with me?" Although at this stage of the Cultural Revo-lution corporal punishment was not as prevalent as during the Red Guard movement, Jiang Qing and Xu Jinxian were not against the use of violence in higher education. Intellectuals had become their major targets.

Meanwhile, the pressure built for those of us who had remained silent. Authoritatively, Fu's smoldering eyes swept around the class-room. He especially focused on me, whom he had recently hand-picked to join the party. He had already looked at me several times, as if urging me to speak out. What should I do? Should I tell the truth? What was truth anyway? Had not Liu Shaoqi abandoned his truth and yielded to Mao's charges that he was China's Khrushchev? Had not my parents succumbed to the "truth" that they were Capitalist Roaders? History was repeating itself in my classroom, and I had to face it. My breathing became difficult, as if a heavy stone pressed my bosom.

As I struggled within myself, I heard Fu call my name. In my ears, his voice rang as loud as thunder. Like everyone else, I had to make clear where I stood on this case of class struggle. I should say what I was supposed to say, for the party always trusted me as its loyal follower born with pure communist blood. I should pick up another rock to drop on Ms. Wu, who had already been pushed to the bottom of the well. Yet, despite this reasoning, the words I uttered were:

"Today Ms. Wu was simply performing her duties as a teacher."

My pronouncement met with dead silence. Ms. Wu stopped sobbing, raised her wrinkled face, and looked at me through tearful eyes. Students sat stiffly on their seats. They were shocked to hear something so contrary. Fu lowered his head. His face turned red with anger. He hadn't expected me, his handpicked party nominee, to openly challenge him, the party leader in the class. I saw him clench his teeth to suppress his rage.

As if relieved of a heavy load, I breathed more easily. My heart was as light as a small bird. I wasn't sure how much I might have helped Ms. Wu, but at least no one spoke after me. The criticism meeting was hastily adjourned.

But for Ms. Wu I paid a high cost. The student party group treated me as a "traitor" and canceled my party candidacy. The department party secretary took the matter seriously. She scolded me for standing on the wrong side of the class struggle and asked me to hand in page after page of self-criticism for sympathizing with the filthy intellectuals. But considering that this was my first offense, and that I was still a good member of the proletariat, she said that she wouldn't make a permanent record in my file.

Bars of winter sun glimmered on the walls of our classroom. The portrait of Mao smiled splendidly from its lofty perch. Master Shi came to replace Ms. Wu temporarily, but the department soon sent our class Professor Zhu, a pale-faced scholar in his early forties. This gentleman gave us an easy time. He didn't want to hurt or embarrass the students and never asked for any individual activities. Instead he treated the whole class as one person and let it drill together and answer questions together. In the spirit of collectivization, everybody was equal. In the chorus, no one could tell a good student from a bad one. Any lesson that might possibly reveal the students' academic differences was prohibited, including examinations and tests in any form, which were branded cruel weapons to persecute the students. Professor Zhu believed that if he corrected no one, then he offended no one. Everyone should be happy. However, his way didn't last long. The students resented this collectivization. Fu cautioned us that the class struggle was complex. Sometimes, the bourgeois intellectuals attacked only in disguised ways.

Professor Zhu left and the grim-looking Professor Lu replaced him. The lanky new teacher quickly earned himself the nickname Old Number Nine, since he favored the smartest students in the class and worked only with them. He tried to avoid the academically poorer students, regarding them as "sleeping lions" that he wanted at all costs not to disturb. Of course, the smarter students were active, and everything went smoothly at first. But the rest of the class wasn't sleeping. The students' eyes were smoldering with anger. A volcano soon erupted.

Another criticism meeting was held. This time, the target was my roommate Jing, the soup girl. She was hated because she was the apple of Professor Lu's eye. Juan Chen, my bunkmate, said that Jing put learning before everything else. She said that Jing practiced English with an imaginary conversational partner while opening a window, mopping the floor, eating meals, or sewing on a button. In fact, Jing practiced so much that she once walked into a tree and bumped her head during the morning study period. Juan Chen spoke with such passion that her shoulders shook. She reminded the class that Jing's head injury proved again that studying blindly without following Chairman Mao's political direction, even when walking on a level road, would expose us to hidden danger.

The sun had already set and the classroom was cold. Jing's pointy face sagged. Her small dry hands nervously pinched her own legs. I tried to avoid her eyes by looking at the ceiling, concentrating on the spiderweb hanging loosely in the corner, swaying in the air. Why does everyone condemn learning? Studying isn't a crime. Even a three-year-old toddler knows this. Are people crazy? Do they really not know the truth? Looking at the serious faces of my classmates, I felt I didn't understand them at all. But I knew I had better keep my mouth shut. I had already taken the wrong side once. I couldn't afford to stand up and fight the trend again. After all, I shouldn't have opinions of my own anyway.

26

The Punishment of Knowledge

*A*fter the December criticism meeting, Jing stayed in bed whenever she could. From time to time she made noises in Chinese to prove that she wasn't studying English.

"What are you doing up there, Jing?" the inquisitive girls often asked her. Standing on tiptoe below her bunk, they peered through the white mosquito net.

Jing poked her head out, her eyelids heavy and her voice flat. "Taking a nap." She yawned.

The girls turned to other matters.

But I knew everything Jing did inside her net, since my bed was level with hers. Jing had gone underground. She continued reading and talking in English with her imagined conversational partner, but only under her breath.

The crusade to punish the acquisition of knowledge swept university campuses across the country. Our school rigorously condemned academic activities and penalized anyone who wanted and dared to teach and anyone who wanted and dared to learn. Bulletin boards were erected along the main boulevard running from our living quarters to the classroom buildings. There large-character posters listed all kinds of behaviors that should be denounced as "putting learning first." The party group of our class wrote a short play criticizing a student who was seen reading in public *English 900,* an American textbook. Ironically, the play was supposed to be performed in English, and somehow

I was selected for the principal role. I stuck out my forefinger and pointed it at the nose of the offender, who was holding the book in both his arms as though carrying an infant. Pressing Chairman Mao's *Quotations* tightly to my heart, I gave him what for:

"Little Zhang, it's wrong of you to study *English 900!* This capitalist cultural trash is poisoning your brain! We have to save you before it's too late!"

I stepped forward, grabbed the textbook from the remorseful student, and threw it offstage. Little Zhang accepted the red volume of the *Quotations* from my hand, his eyes wet with grateful tears. In the background, my energetic classmates tore the textbook apart page by page.

Many believers in the doctrine that "the more educated one is, the more reactionary one becomes" completely abandoned their academic studies and went days, even weeks, without touching their books. In the dorms, girls knit sweaters, sewed new clothes, and washed their bedsheets repeatedly. The boys were active on the sports grounds, playing volleyball, ping-pong, basketball, or soccer. In the chilly winter wind at night, some students simply ran laps in the moonlight, one circle after another. Their legs became like those of deer, thin, flexible, and powerful. They ran to exhaust themselves, to burn up their energy. My head grew dizzy following the white lines painted on the ground, watching the students turning like tops. What should I do? I looked at the dark sky, so deep, so unfathomable. The questions still gnawed me. To learn or not to learn? How to learn and where to learn? Xu Jinxian made it clear that we should always remember how the universities before the Cultural Revolution created generations of capitalist successors. Students then studied all day and half of the night to realize their ambitions. We, Mao's new type of students, had a different historical mission. We were sent here to abolish education. Was it not clear that to raise an ignorant generation was the purpose of Mao's educational revolution? Education was enlightenment and enlightened minds were not obedient. They should be eliminated. But my conscience told me otherwise: "I want to learn."

I searched for secret places to study. The ladies' room, with a dozen individual squat toilets, was quite safe. Once I locked the door and squatted down, the continuous sound of running water drowned my soft voice and drove away the fear within me. This lavatory was totally mine. I could read and write anything I liked on my lap. If somebody was waiting, I simply put the book into my school bag, flushed the toilet, and left without causing the slightest suspicion. But the squatting made my body sore and my legs tired, and the stench was sometimes unbearable.

The other place to study was on my bunk. No one could see what I was doing within my dark green American military mosquito net, which I had brought from home. The dark green color obscured the view from outside. The girls frowned at the ugly net, which made them feel hotter in summer and colder in winter.

"Where did you get that 'treasure'?" they asked sarcastically. They hated my bed and seldom lingered in front of it.

By the pillow I kept a medium-sized shortwave radio and piles of books and dictionaries. When I climbed up into my net and put on the earphones, I immediately shut out the outside world. Here I could read anything, from the banned *English 900* to Bei's letters. My feelings toward Bei had deepened through the year's correspondence. Under my net, I relished his every word without fear that I would be discovered reading a love letter. At nearly two thousand miles' distance, I could kiss only his letters. I often fell asleep with them lying on my chest.

After the overhead light was turned off, I switched on the flashlight under my quilt so that no one in the room would know I was still reading. I read until my eyes became sore, then I turned on the radio and listened to any foreign channels I could pick up.

The reception of the Voice of America and the BBC was terrible, since the government rigorously interfered with the signal. But the English-language broadcasters from South Korea, Japan, and Germany were more audible. They reported the continued decline of China's gross national product, the ongoing power struggle in the top leadership, the activities of the Gang of Four headed by Mao's wife, the persecution of many of the overthrown party officials and intellectuals, and other issues we heard little about officially.

I loved my bed, which became an oasis in the desert, a safe harbor in the treacherous sea, a heaven on earth.

But before bedtime, when all the girls were back in the room, I often sat at my small desk reading loudly from Marx's *Communist Manifesto:* "A specter is haunting Europe — the specter of Communism. All the Powers of old Europe have entered into a holy alliance to exorcise this specter."

Or from Mao's *Poems:*

It is easy for humans to get old while it is hard for heaven.
Cong festival comes every year, and now it is here again.
The yellow flowers blooming in the battlefield are excep-
    tionally fragrant.

"Yes! Yellow flowers are fragrant but it is late now," someone would always remind me. That was exactly what I wanted: to be urged to go to bed. Then I would set my book down reluctantly and climb into my little heaven.

Over the months, the campaign to criticize learning heated up. Editorial after editorial lambasted intellectuals. Xu Jinxian made one speech after another urging educational revolution. Old professors left and new professors replaced them. Then, in September 1974, the first day of our second year, we got Professor Wang. The slightly plump teacher wore a faded brown jacket with concealed side pockets and a tiny standing collar, the kind often worn by rural people. Despite his plain appearance, behind the plastic-rimmed glasses shone a pair of small eyes bright with wisdom, cleverness, and vehemence.

"What kind of family are you from?" a student asked Professor Wang.

"It's a little above the lower-middle-class peasant. But it is still accounted in close alliance with the proletariat," Professor Wang said humbly.

Professor Wang was a revolutionary professor. He taught differently. In class, he never opened the textbooks once. He said he was going to break the "textbook-centered phenomena" popular under Liu Shaoqi's rule. In his English drills, he replaced common everyday words with fancy revolutionary expressions. Thus the student, instead of reciting, "We not only speak English but also write English," would shout the slogan "We worker-peasant-soldier students not only study English but also criticize Confucius."

One day Professor Wang walked in with urgent steps. He looked around the class solemnly and declared that he was going to revolutionize a formality that had deeply bothered him for a long time. From now on, every student should remain seated when answering questions. The feudal regulation that created class differences in the classroom must be eliminated.

Ironically, this ancient custom had taken deep root in our blood. Although we were the ones who were supposed to make the classroom revolution, we were simply unable to break with tradition. Remain seated while answering the teacher's questions? Unheard of. It was the behavior of traitors and heretics. It was the worst possible offense. Even the rebellious Fu looked cowed at the thought. So whenever we heard our names called, we continued to spring up as if prodded with an electric charge.

"Sit down! Sit down, please! We cannot afford to be only oral revolutionaries. We must act like real revolutionaries — going into the mountains, even though there are tigers there." Professor Wang's witty eyes twinkled behind lenses thicker than the bottoms of glass bottles.

"In the classroom, we must get rid of what is bourgeois and

promote what is proletarian. Although it is true that I'm your teacher, you are also my teachers outside class. Why do you have to stand up since we are all equal? Let us break the barrier between us. Let us be one!" Professor Wang said, his hand hacking the air.

Several months passed, and Professor Wang, heavily armed with Mao Zedong Thought, continued to lead us. One school year passed, and Professor Wang still stood before us, making one classroom revolution after another. In this way he escaped the fate of the filthy intellectual, who was like a "rat crossing a busy street" that anyone could beat and kill.

27

Open-Door Schooling

In January 1975 Shanghai's weather was dry and cold. The sky was leaden. Shriveled climbing vines clung to fences, shuddering spiritlessly in the winter wind. All the colorful birds had disappeared and only the dull-looking sparrows were left. People wore several layers of sweaters and cotton-padded coats, puffing up like balloons. They tried to avoid going outdoors. But our school campus was full of activity. Flags flapped. Loudspeakers thundered. Car engines roared. We bustled around, loading our luggage into open trucks. We were preparing to brave the winds and walk to the Number Three Silk Factory in Shanghai's Yangpu industrial district, where we would practice Mao's Open-Door Schooling for a month.

For thousands of years the Confucianists had held that those who worked with their brains ruled and those who worked with their hands served. People trusted that "in books are buried gold and beauty." In pursuit of these ideals, generation after generation of young scholars slept on brush and tasted gall, digging and trudging in oceans of books. Rarely in China's five-thousand-year-old civilization had the belief that "books are above all else" been challenged. Now Mao broke with tradition; he claimed that students trained under Liu Shaoqi knew nothing else but book knowledge. The students were unable to understand the working people they had to serve after graduation. Thus the students were useless to the proletarians. Mao called for an end in all schools to the Three Centers — textbook, teacher, and classroom. He said that the only antidote to the Three Centers was regularly to move the classroom out of the school and into the countryside, the factories, and the barracks of the People's Liberation Army.

The Number Three Silk Factory was crowded with rundown workshops with low ceilings and dim lights. Everywhere ran bright industrial water that dyed the factory roads the colors of the rainbow. Aged textile machines reverberated in three shifts. They never stopped making silk unless they broke down. After the January Red Storm, the Shanghai industrial workers had quickly returned to work at the urging of Premier Zhou Enlai. They became the national models for "continuing production while making revolution."

Our classroom was set up in a tool room between the bleaching and textile workshops. Deafened by the noise of the old machines, I could barely hear Professor Wang's desperate voice. He didn't speak, he shouted. His face was red. Veins protruded on his neck, and he looked miserable. He wasn't teaching. He was struggling for life. Open-Door Schooling was his opportunity to show his support for Mao's educational revolution. But despite Professor Wang's efforts, his weak voice was inevitably swallowed up in the sea of noise and its message lost to us. Besides that, the strong chemical odor made me want to vomit. The food smelled of bleach, and the soup tasted of machine oil. I wondered why our classroom had to be put in the noisiest and smelliest part of the factory. But the department said that the closer our classroom was to the workshops, the closer our feelings for the workers and the redder our hearts would be.

Since Open-Door Schooling meant that everything taught and learned here had to be about factories, workers, machines, and silk, our assigned textbook was inappropriate for the new situation. Professor Wang had to compile his own teaching materials. This was to break the center of books. At night I would operate the textile machines. Only by working shoulder to shoulder with the workers could I understand their feelings and care about them. This was to break the center of classroom. Knowing nothing about making silk, I often broke the old machines, and the shuttles would sever the brilliant silk threads like cutting grass. Whenever this occurred, a young girl would have to bend over for hours or days trying to reconnect the broken threads. At the end of the month, she lost her title of model worker. I felt guilty when she cried.

While we took classes, the curious workers, who wore knee-high rubber boots and reeked of machine oil, would linger in front of our classroom and watch through the doorway, which had to be kept open since this was Open-Door Schooling. They listened with puzzled looks on their faces. The younger ones laughed with understanding when they heard the name of Chairman Mao. The young girl I worked with took me to the factory's showroom, a fanciful world of bright silk with designs of phoenixes, dragons, and exotic flowers in silver, gold, green, purple, and red. She pointed to her proudest achievement, a silk painting with a tremendous red sun rising above tall mountains and shining over long rivers. A work of art, this imitation of the famous Chinese brush painting *How Splendid Our Land Is* was gigantic, covering the center wall. The girl said it had taken her two years to complete the job. Next month she would send it to Chairman Mao in Beijing, because he was the red sun in the painting and in her heart.

The factory Open-Door Schooling session ended in February, on the eve of the Lunar New Year of 1975. But when the warm spring decorated our campus with lively colors and we had discarded the layers of thick winter clothing for lighter attire, it was time to move our classroom for another month-long session, this time into the barn of a people's commune in Qingpu, a suburb of Shanghai.

Qingpu was a beautiful and fertile rural county with a network of lakes and rivers. During the 1950s this area had suffered an epidemic of snail fever that wiped out village after village. The first day, my hostess, an old peasant wife, asked me to fetch a bucket of water from the river to boil for drinking. At the riverbank, a farmer next to me washed his mud-stained feet in the turbid water. Across from him, a woman cleaned a basket of diapers. A young man not far away splashed water on the farm tools at his feet. I decided to wait. But when the farmer beside me left, a granny came with a wooden toilet in hand. She bent down and began scraping it vigorously with a brush made of thin strips of bamboo. I closed my eyes and filled the bucket. On my way back, I saw villagers with big bellies and rodlike legs who had contracted snail fever from the water.

At night Professor Wang stood in a torn blue shirt at the center of the barn, his feet buried in husked grain, and conducted the evening English class. I sat on a grain mountain, my face swollen from mosquito bites. While swatting mosquitoes with one hand, I tried to copy the English sentences written on the makeshift blackboard: "The countryside is a vast sea for the fish to swim in. The factory is the high sky where the bird flies. I am the fish. I am the bird."

In the night mist, bats coasted below the eaves of the houses. Frogs croaked in the nearby paddies. Mosquitoes chased us wherever we went, circled our heads, and even crawled into our nostrils. The peasants said that the bloodsuckers loved strangers, for their blood smelled fresh and tasted sweet. After the English class came the "re-education" session. This was the most crucial part of Open-Door Schooling — to learn about the complicated class struggle waged in China's vast countryside.

Sucking a long pipe held in a knotted hand, our host Yao, a sixty-year-old farmer whose weatherworn face sagged with loose skin, started things off. Villager Chen once stole a mother hen from villager Li in the dead of night. It was the mother hen's twenty baby chicks that found her in Chen's house. Villager Tang married his sixth niece who gave birth to a poor girl whose heart had a coin-sized hole. Villager Kan often beat his wife with a red-hot iron rod, because the one-eyed woman dared to talk back to him. Villager Du caught his young wife with her lover in their outhouse. I nodded mechanically every half minute, smiling faintly. My mind was revolving around the full moon, trying to figure out why its deep shadows were thought to resemble a rabbit pounding medicinal herbs in a mortar with a pestle. I saw the beautiful daughter of Heaven Emperor dancing in her long silk gown and flying across the starlit sky toward our world, searching for a human husband. Our class had fifteen young men. Was she willing to join us in our Open-Door Schooling? She was certainly welcome here.

Lines of strain crept across Yao's shriveled forehead. The loose skin moved with the movement of his mouth. Bowing his gray head, showing his thin hair, the old man talked about his old landlord, who used to own most of the land and livestock in the village. He said the landlord had been a good man, who helped the needy and relieved the distressed, giving the villagers silver and copper coins when their children were sick. During the Land Reform Movement, which reached here in 1951, all his property was distributed to the villagers. But those who had received his goods returned them to him in the evening. This angered the Land Reform officials, who tied his legs to two donkeys and drove the animals in different directions.

Yao took the pipe from his mouth and knocked out the ashes on the bottom of his cloth shoes.

"You see, the class struggle is always cruel. We must talk about it day after day, year after year."

28

Nipping the Bud of Love

Not long after we returned to campus, July arrived. In July 1975, Bei came from Heilongjiang to see me. According to a beautiful legend, lovers should gather on the seventh evening of the seventh moon of the year because, on this night, the parted Cowherd and Weaver Maid meet on the bridge made of a thousand magpies in Heaven. It was a time of reunion.

Peering from behind green leaves, the shy faces of little red flowers shone like a thousand ruby eyes. I dreamed about the moment when Bei and I would meet. I imagined showing him around and introducing him to the other girls. But walking on campus with a young man would tarnish my brilliant image as a worker-peasant-soldier student. Living like monks and nuns, we students weren't the source of many romantic stories. So far our department had caught only one couple, who had the habit of trysting in the girls' dorm on Sundays when everybody else went home. A student who returned unexpectedly caught the two stuck to each other as if glued, rolling on a bunk bed. The university accused them of damaging the bed, the state's property, and the couple was dismissed from school. Afraid I might be caught committing a serious "moral offense," I asked Bei to visit me at home.

It was a Sunday afternoon when the grinning Bei showed up on my doorstep, his head and shoulders glistening with tiny beads of rainwater. I invited him inside. My parents rose slowly from their chairs and shook hands with him politely but remained silent afterward. My usually active parents became unusually quiet that day. I sensed cold-ness behind their courtesy. But their indifference gave me the opportu-nity to be alone with Bei in the other room for some private time.

Sitting side by side on the edge of the bed, we could hear each other's short breaths. My heart filled with sweetness. I wanted to tell him how he had changed from a young boy into a man. He was a real man now. His ropelike muscles bulged. Biting his lips while carrying loads heavier than himself had already carved wrinkles on his face, making his once delicate features rough and strong. His body was so muscular that his unfashionable green uniform clung to him tightly.

"Would you show me your hands?" I asked.

Bei tilted toward me, extending both of his hands. They were not handsome. The palms shone with yellow calluses. The backs were chapped from the cold, with cracks here and there, healed and unhealed, each like a small mouth. But it was this pair of hard hands that had pulled me out of danger. Again, in front of my eyes he rushed down the shaking step-plank to drag me to safety. I was lost in the past for a moment, wondering when he would be liberated from the sentence of harsh labor and return home. I sighed with emotion. Abruptly Bei withdrew his hands and hid them under his thighs. Burying his chin inside his collar, he fixed his eyes on the cement floor. The room was quiet except for the tick-tock of the small table clock. Leaves flying in the rain patted the window. Presently Bei raised his head and turned his face to me, his eyes pleading.

"Let's think only of the present."

He grasped my hand and held it tightly. He drew it to his cracked lips and kissed. My heart melted. He held me in his arms, pulling me close to his chest, his fingers trembling. His black eyes became limpid lakes, as smooth as mirrors. The water was so clear that I could see to the bottoms. There lay a miserable heart. I felt my long-repressed desires revived. My lips went under his chin. My fin-gers smoothed his dark hair, which smelled of youth. I longed. It was

a carnal desire. This little room was my home. It was safe. No one
would report me. For the first time, I began tasting the sweetness of
love with my whole heart and soul. We clung together, treasuring the
moment that we knew would soon end.

The door pushed open. Horrified, Bei quickly unlocked my
arms from his neck.

Carrying a small black-and-white television, Mother stood
smiling in the door. "Don't want you to get bored, so I think TV will
help while away the time."

Bei blushed. He stood up, took the television from Mother, and
placed it on the desk near the window. He knelt on the floor to plug
the short cord into the outlet behind the desk. Mother sat on a small
stool that she placed against the open door and started watching the
model Peking opera *Harbor,* which everyone in the country had seen
at least fifty times. While the woman wearing a wicker helmet on her
head and a white towel around her neck stood in the morning harbor
and sang at the top of her voice, I grew angrier and angrier, wondering why Mother was being so insensitive.

Bei watched me nervously. We could say nothing. Mother asked
Bei which of the eight model Peking operas he liked best. Maybe
Harbor, he answered absentmindedly. A small worry crept to his face.
He moved away from me and sat at the far end of the bed, kicking
gently at the chair legs in front of him. Mother remained quiet,
guarding the door. I felt her eyes watching us closely, like beams from
a searchlight. After enduring an hour of this, Bei stood up. He
thanked Mother for letting him watch *Harbor,* and said he had to
leave. Mother made an effort to stand up from the low stool. "Leaving so soon? Why don't you stay a little longer?"

Outside, the rain pelted down. There were pools deep and shallow on the roads, reflecting the dim streetlights. We walked side by
side under the same umbrella. Before we reached the crowded bus
stop, Bei stopped and turned to me, his eyes misty.

"Would you come for dinner with my mother and elder sister next Sunday, before I leave? I hope . . ."

He stopped, looking at me timidly. I understood. He feared I might meet someone else on campus who was already a college student and already in Shanghai. I explained to him that this university was like a battleground, and I only wanted to escape. Smelling the scent of ammunition every day, who had the desire to be romantic? I told him I would always remember that he had saved me. Bei seemed convinced. A faint smile rose to his eyes.

The green-and-white bus came, its wheels splashing water on the people waiting at the stop. The wet crowd flooded into the vehicle. The door shut behind Bei, catching an edge of his army coat. I watched until the bus disappeared around the corner. I found myself standing alone in the rain. Joy tempered with sorrow always accompanied partings and reunions. In recent years, I had experienced too many of them. Yellow streetlights twinkled on the wet pavement, and a stirring strain written by the Tang poet Li Shangyin played in my mind:

It is difficult to meet
And it is difficult to part.
The east wind is weak
And the flowers wither.
A spring silkworm stops spinning silk only when it dies,
And a candle ceases shedding tears only when it runs to ash.
Under tonight's cold moonlight,
I see that sorrow has aged me.

I jumped over the puddles. Along the way, I stopped at a small department store and selected two notebooks with colorful covers as souvenirs for Bei when we met next Sunday.

My heart almost froze when I saw my parents' long faces at home. Mother looked cold as frost, her smooth smile all gone.

"What are you going to do with those?" she asked, when she noticed the two notebooks.

"I'm going to give them to Bei when I meet him next week for a family dinner," I answered honestly.

Mother exploded. In a fit of rage, she grabbed the notebooks from my hand. "No, you can't give him anything," she shrieked.

I was stunned by her sudden anger. What happened to Mother? Choking back tears, I stared at Father. But his face was even icier.

"Bei is still in Heilongjiang, and his future is unknown."

"Of course, I know that," I retorted.

"If you marry him, are you going to follow your husband back to Heilongjiang again? Or are you two going to live two thousand miles apart from each other for the rest of your lives?" Father's voice was severe. Abruptly he stood up and began pacing, his hands behind his back. "Do you know how difficult it is for men like Bei who have no Shanghai residence to return home? Do you know that in China, separation between husband and wife is lifelong?"

Mother cut in. "How is Lon? Do you still have any contact with him?" She never forgot my former squadmate.

I had nothing to say about Lon. We hadn't been in touch with each other since I returned to Shanghai.

Mother shivered, looking around the small room as if searching for something handy to hit me with.

Father continued. Despite the fuss, his voice was devoid of emotion. "Marriage is not a joke. If you can't face the consequences of marrying Bei, you shouldn't continue the relationship and give him an empty hope that can never be realized. The hurt to him will be a lot worse than it is now if you don't stop the relationship today."

At his words, I couldn't keep from crying, "No! I can't break with Bei!"

"To do anything in China, you need to exert more reason than feeling. Romance does not belong to your generation. It is a luxury that you cannot afford."

"Why? Why? Why?" I shouted, tears flooding my face.

Father didn't answer. He avoided my angry eyes. I hated him but knew he was right. I saw the bloody body lying in the white snow. Saw Tan's lonely silhouette lingering on the platform of the Tashan train station. Heard the trembling voice of the Shanghai "traitor" over the loudspeaker asking for one last candy before he was executed. Then I heard Bei's heartbroken words, "We are no longer equal. I don't know what my future holds. My fate is out of my control."

Father patted my twitching shoulder. "Lon is a promising young man. He must have graduated by now and be working in the Central Government."

I wiped away my tears and looked at him angrily. "You look down on Bei because he's still trapped in Heilongjiang and has no hope of returning soon. You love the haves and hate the have-nots!"

Father's face became pale and flushed by turns. He was mute for a long while before he replied, "I don't love the haves, but I love my daughter. I saw you narrowly escape from the lair of the wolf, and I will not let you fall from there into the mouth of the tiger."

The raindrops tapped against the windows. The white curtains fluttered as though moved by a hidden hand. The dripping of the rain sounded like a girl's weeping. Without my being aware of it, night fell on the city. I was exhausted. I knew I could not change my parents. Once they had made up their minds, nine bulls and two tigers could not drag them my way.

Father spoke again. "Instead of pursuing some unrealistic thing in the clouds, you should keep your feet firmly on the ground. Look at your elder brother Ming and the millions of other young Chinese still toiling and struggling in the countryside with no hope of return. With what you have today, you should be very happy."

The wall clock struck nine times. Mother offered to go with me to call Bei from a pay phone inside the neighborhood committee building. She was determined not to let the matter outlast the night.

"Bei should have no illusions about continuing his relationship with you," Mother said firmly.

"I can't say this to him. It will hurt him badly. The conditions in Heilongjiang are already cruel enough."

"You must call him tonight and tell him that you cannot attend his dinner."

I didn't budge. I knew that if I called Bei, I would never see him again. We had hardly even met before we had to say farewell to each other forever.

Mother knew she had to act quickly, before the attachment grew too strong to sever. She yelled, pounding her chest with her fists and gasping for breath. Her face was pale and her eyes watery. She even staggered as she moved about the apartment. This frightened me. She had developed a heart condition because of her travails, and I was afraid our argument would trigger a crisis.

Father urged me to obey. "She is not going to stop. You don't want your mother to die for you, do you?"

I took an umbrella and went to the door. Father followed me.

In the dreary office of the neighborhood committee, four black public phones were placed in a line on a long table. The woman on the night shift was dozing, her head nodding back and forth with her breathing. I picked up a phone and dialed the number Bei had left. A man's thick voice answered. He wrote down my phone number and asked me to hang up. He would deliver word of my call to Bei's home.

In about fifteen minutes, one of the phones rang. I picked it up reluctantly. Bei greeted me on the other end.

"Hi! What is it you need to talk to me about this late?" he asked, sounding full of uncertainty.

"Bei, I won't be able to attend dinner with your family. I . . .

I . . ." I choked on my words, unable to go on. Big tears rolled down my cheeks.

There was dead silence on the other end. I felt the world around me had frozen. Then came Bei's broken voice. "I understand everything. I wish you well."

My heart was torn into pieces. Bei, aware of his difficult situation, had told me many times in his letters that he didn't have the right to love me. If for any reason I felt reluctant about the relationship, I could stop it at any time and he wouldn't blame me.

He did what he had promised.

I don't remember who hung up first, he or I. I don't remember how I got home. Where was Father? What did he do? I only remember lying in wet clothes on my bed like a corpse. Tears kept flowing until there were none. For weeks and months, my soul followed the silver rails all the way to Tashan and traced the dirt road to the earthen room where Bei lived. It hid in the dark corner and listened to his wounded heart weeping. It saw the last hope vanishing from his eyes like the flame of a torch going out. I lived as in a trance. With Bei gone, the secret castle in my heart, which used to be bathed in streams of golden sunlight, collapsed. For a long time, I was racked not only by the loss of a precious love but also by an enormous guilt. I had abandoned him when he was most in need of me, when he was still struggling in hopeless Heilongjiang without knowing when he could come back home. We would never live together in this world.

Bei never wrote me again. Long before, he seemed to sense that our separation was inevitable. Looking back, many of the poems he enclosed in his letters were about sentimental farewell. One was the famous Tang "Crane Pavilion":

> My friend flew away on a flying crane,
> And left empty the Crane Pavilion.
> The flying crane will never return,

Leaving the white clouds here
Floating lonely for a thousand years to come.
. . .
Where will my home be when the sun sets?
Drifting on this misty river worries me.

29

A Slip of the Tongue

My roommates, who knew nothing of Bei, thought I must have come down with hepatitis. They said that my face was sallow and my eyes were dry. The emotional anguish had turned me into a "yellow-faced woman" at the age of twenty-two.

To add frost to the snow, one Sunday morning in September 1975 a mailman came to my home and handed me a letter. It was a brief note written on a piece of toilet paper: "Peasant girl, please come see me at Luonghua Hospital ASAP! Shen." I was shocked to learn that Shen, the daughter of a family friend, was in Shanghai's psychiatric hospital. She had been a French major in the elite Beijing Number Two Foreign Languages Institute and a promising future diplomat for China. But in 1969 she was jailed in Beijing for making the "slanderous" comment that Mao's wife Jiang Qing was China's Hitler.

Why was Shen now in Shanghai? Was she insane? Prison life must have driven her crazy. I sighed deeply, feeling for her, for she had suffered so much for a slip of the tongue. But after reading her simple letter again and again, I found that her writing was clear. She didn't seem confused. What had really happened to her? Why had she addressed me as "peasant girl"? Was she hinting that I should disguise myself as a peasant? She must have something to say that she couldn't write in this note, which she knew would be censored.

I took off my glasses and combined my two braids into a thick one at the back of my head. I covered my head and half my face with a bright green-and-yellow-checkered scarf. The day was not as hot as usual; a cold front had arrived in the city, and it had rained heavily the night before. In my hand I carried a bamboo basket of fresh green vegetables with a few brown eggs on top. Dressed in this fashion like a peasant girl, I left home and took a bus. After several transfers, I got off at the hospital, which was at the southern edge of the city. I adjusted my scarf so it shielded half of my face again, took the basket in my right hand, and walked with small steps up to the security gate. The guard glanced at me and quickly waved me in.

Chinese parasols, silhouetted against a glowing sky, stretched evenly on both sides of the walkway like big umbrellas. After the night rain, blossoms dropped their petals like snow to the ground. Big-bellied golden bees buzzed around. On the fourth floor of the inpatient building, amid hysterical shrieks, I found Shen sitting in a cagelike room with iron bars on the door and windows. In a white-and-red-striped hospital gown, she stared blankly at the wall, her eyes showing more of the whites than the black pupils. She recognized me only after I called to her several times and woke her from her numbness. She was just twenty-nine, but she looked like withered grass. Colorless hair, hollow eyes, and drooping skin all conveyed her unimaginable sufferings.

"You've come," murmured Shen. She smiled at me, stretching her mouth wide. It was a bitter smile, lacking inner happiness.

The nurse on duty opened the door and let her out of the cell. Since she wasn't allowed to leave the floor, we walked up and down the gloomy hallway. Amid the patients' wailing, Shen whispered in my ear that the doctors had repeatedly electroshocked her. This treatment would eventually wipe out a healthy person's memory and deaden her normal mental ability. She was resisting desperately by faking incapacity and drug-induced apathy. She took the tranquilizers that the nurses gave her, but as soon as they left she poked her fingers into her throat to vomit everything.

"Who sent you here?" I asked, for I didn't believe in the least that she was insane.

"I was abducted."

"Abducted? But why?"

She told me that earlier this year, after six years in prison, she had been released. Though prison life had transformed her into a pale-faced, gray-haired old woman, and poor lighting had seriously weakened her eyesight, nevertheless she had been looking forward to a new life. At the Beijing train station, Shen was told that she would get a good job in her hometown of Shanghai, one that would utilize her knowledge of French. She was excited. But as soon as she stepped off the train, four men snatched her and carried her upside down to a car with tinted windows that was waiting outside the station. Because her head was only a few inches above the ground, no one could see her face clearly, even though the abduction was conducted in broad daylight and in the most crowded area. The men shoved her into the car's trunk and took her to Luonghua Hospital.

Shen wanted me to be a witness in case something happened to her.

"If I die, it'll be because they persecuted me to death. That's what they're doing now, slowly but surely. I will never shut my eyes and allow death to carry the wrongs they have done me into the grave. Never believe that I've committed suicide. I will never do it. I'm not crazy. Can you see that I'm not crazy?" she asked. Her sunken eyes searched my face for an answer, imploring me to confirm that she was normal. Living with the mentally ill and being treated as mentally ill every day, she had begun to question her own mental balance.

"Shen, don't doubt yourself. You're not crazy at all. You're as healthy as I am." Looking at her pleading eyes, I cried in my heart. How easy and how fast the Revolution could turn a human being into a living corpse.

Shen scribbled down the name of an important official on the Shanghai Revolutionary Committee and said that he was the mastermind behind her kidnapping and torture. But she added that Mao's wife, Jiang Qing, was the main culprit. Shen asked me to keep the slip of paper until the day when it might be needed to clear her name. She was desperately afraid that she wouldn't escape the doctors' careful and persistent "treatment."

"I have no one to turn to but you. My father died and my mother is still in detention." She sniffled. "My fiancé has broken off our engagement. He can't bear any more of this. It's just too much for him." Shen's lips jerked. She burst into tears, wiping her eyes with her veined hands. It must have been a big blow. Their relationship had lasted for eight full years, surviving even her jail time. But as her persecution intensified in Shanghai, Jiang Qing's stronghold, the man was afraid that he himself would soon be targeted.

"You must leave now. If someone recognizes you, you'll be in big trouble." Shen stopped weeping and started hurrying me after I hid the slip of paper in an inner pocket. Her fear was contagious. I looked around nervously, my scalp tingling. Visiting Jiang Qing's enemy in a mental hospital was already enough to incriminate me. I could be sent here too. I quickly pulled up the scarf, picked up the vegetable basket, and walked toward the stairs. Shen's big hollow eyes followed me closely. When I was down at the main gate, I stopped and looked back at the inpatient building. Behind one of the porthole-shaped windows, I saw a shadow standing motionless, the hands grasping the iron bars. My throat tightened. But for my own safety, I never went back. Shen continued faking apathy and survived the "medical treatment." But she remained in the mental hospital and wasn't released until two years after the end of the Cultural Revolution.

The following Sunday, when I returned to school in the evening, the dorm was stifling. Concrete construction that absorbed the baking sunshine during the day released the heat relentlessly during the night. Lang, the girl with grapelike eyes, was the only one in the room. She lay on her bamboo-mat-covered bed reading English.

When she saw me, she instinctively put away the textbook. I left the door open wide, sat at my small desk, and opened Mao's *On Practice*. Since the other girls would be returning to school as well, it was best for me to be seen reading Mao.

Lang moved her chair next to mine.

"Would you sponsor me to join the Youth League?" she asked nervously.

I agreed at once, since developing new members was part of my duties as a Youth League leader. Lang was overjoyed, her smooth face radiant with a smile. She began searching for words to thank me. Unable to find any, she started talking about her parents and family. Like unpredictable weather, her mood changed instantly from happiness to rage, from delight to hysteria.

"That bitch Jiang Qing is like a dog threatening people on the strength of its master's power. Who is she? A third-class actress and semiprostitute wandering on the banks of Huangpu River before she seduced Chairman Mao." Her snow-white complexion reddened, her face stern, her dark grapelike eyes wet with tears. As she continued cursing, I learned that Jiang Qing's men had once burst into her home and beaten her father almost to death.

"The bitch has tortured so many of us." The circle of people she was referring to were Shanghai's famous movie stars, artists, and writers as well as some senior officials who were Jiang Qing's severest critics and staunch enemies.

Lang's explosive attack on Jiang Qing was frightening. I felt cold with terror on this hot night. Our school was Jiang Qing's private empire, and her "comrade-in-arms" Xu Jinxian kept a close eye on the ideological orientation of students and faculty. It was his supreme duty to carry out her plans and root out her critics and punish them. Among the many victims in Shanghai, the celebrated actress ShanGuan Yuanchu, who knew Jiang Qing's sordid past during the twenties, was forced to jump from a building. Zhao Dan, China's movie king and Jiang's onetime costar, had been jailed and was dying from cancer. Xu Jinxian had already turned Shanghai into a hell for Jiang Qing's enemies. Didn't Lang know that denouncing the great banner-holder was a "heinous crime" that could lead to a life sentence or even death? Did she know of my friend Shen's tragedy? Did she know that if I repeated what she had said to the authorities, not only she but also her entire family and her circle would all be destroyed overnight?

In a panic I jumped up from my chair and locked the door. Now Lang became even more unbridled. Angry denunciations of Jiang Qing gushed out. Whether her confession was prompted by political naïveté or recklessness I didn't know, but I was deeply moved and flattered by her openness. She must have taken me for a reliable friend who would never betray her under any circumstances. I felt I must return her trust. I stood up from my chair. My short-sleeved shirt was soaked through. I told Lang of the August night in 1966 when I watched Father collapse onstage, blood staining his clothes. My words calmed her. With tears in her eyes, she nodded in sympathy and listened with great attention. At that moment, our two hearts beat with the same rhythm.

30

Down with Deng Xiaoping

Only one month later, at my recommendation, the elite Youth League admitted Lang as a member. But before the sound of my congratulations had died, Lang's warmth toward me vanished. She turned her face away. She laughed and talked vivaciously to others, trying to be popular among the students, and quickly gathered a small group of girls around her, but me she tried to isolate. I could see that hate, like poison, grew quickly in her heart. Since she had become a Youth League member, I was of no more use to her. In fact, I was in her way. With graduation only months away, everyone was trying by whatever means possible to impress the department leaders so as to win a favorable job assignment.

In January 1976, Premier Zhou Enlai passed away. His first deputy premier, Deng Xiaoping, succeeded Zhou as the acting premier. In the name of commemorating Zhou, people gathered to express their anger and grievances at the prolonged Cultural Revolution, which was entering its eleventh year. Thousands of wreaths piled up in hills in front of the Monument of Heroes in Tiananmen Square, already an ocean of white flowers. White and dark banners wrapped the trees and poles. The distraught Beijingers, wearing black armbands, covered their faces and cried. Students and intellectuals were roused to action, writing heartrending memorial poems and reciting elegiac couplets to disparage the present. Tiananmen Square was sleepless, boiling with anger. In the cold wind, Beijingers lined up on ten-mile-long Changan Street to pay their last respects to

Zhou's remains. Zhou's death was tragic. The rumor on the street was that Mao had ordered the medical treatment of Zhou's prostate cancer to be withheld and then delayed. Fearing that his coffin would be opened and his corpse whipped for political reasons, Zhou had asked that his ashes be spread over China's rivers, seas, and mountains.

As spring returned, the days became longer. In the warm breezes and rain, bare trees burst into life, putting out tender leaves overnight. However, a restless wind that presaged a storm swept East China Normal University. The school, which had been criticized for becoming lax in its political progress, began enforcing a new schedule. A typical day started at 5:45 with military training on the sports grounds. After breakfast, morning classes and political activities began at 7:30 and ended at 11:30. During the afternoon, more activities until 4:30. Then military training again. In the evening, small political study groups from 7:00 to 8:45. At 10:00, all lights on the campus went out. At the curfew bell, everyone was ordered to bed.

Military training was intended to discipline us to be as obedient to orders as soldiers and as courageous in fighting ideological enemies in the classroom as the soldiers were on the battlefield. Soon several counterrevolutionaries hidden in the student body were discovered. The bunkmate of a Russian-language major reported him for listening to the Voice of America a total of fourteen times and Radio Moscow twenty-five times. The exposed student was sent to work on a farm outside Shanghai. One night he was found hanging from the iron flush chain fixed high on the wall in the men's room.

The restless wind, after swirling the dry leaves from the coarse cement roads, ceased suddenly. For days the sky was black and low with cheerless clouds. The Russian major's photo was posted on bulletin boards across the campus to remind the students of his "crime."

Fear filled my heart: would I be caught like the Russian major? Listening to the truth over the foreign stations had already changed me. I realized that the Cultural Revolution was an immoral political massacre. Under Mao, the country was a shambles and my future was hopeless. A human being without the freedom to think, speak, and express herself was a slave. Living with a bloody sword hanging over my head was not only tragic but shameful and unbearable. Yet if I ever contemplated daring to speak my mind, Zhang Zixing would serve as my warning. Her story made my heart bleed. Zhang, a young provincial employee, had been accused of anti–Cultural Revolution comments and ideology. For her crime, she was jailed in Liao Ning Province, one of the harshest places for political prisoners. She was thrown into the men's prison to be raped repeatedly by the savage inmates before she was eventually executed.

The atmosphere on campus had never been this tense. Leaders at all levels were closely monitoring our ideological orientation, and everyone was afraid. Yet the thoughts that the Cultural Revolution must end and the tyrant must be overthrown burned within me, angering and depressing me. I dreaded that one day I wouldn't be able to help betraying my true self in public and would be ruthlessly discovered and brutally punished like Zhang Zixing.

To survive, every day I had to mouth things that I didn't believe and even despised. I had to disguise myself as well as I could, telling political lies, big and small. I particularly dreaded the "attitude check," an exercise during which everyone had to exhibit his or her attitude on every single political issue. We sat in a circle face to face, listening, observing, and analyzing each other relentlessly. Performing like this under fault-finding scrutiny, I couldn't help stuttering, sweating, and flushing. Living as a double-dealer left me exhausted. I had one nightmare after another. Passing the wall-sized bulletin boards on the side of the road, I saw my own name crossed out. I heard my fellow students shouting slogans at me. To calm myself so I would look normal and perform normally in the vigilant crowds, I became addicted to tranquilizers, which I hoped would eliminate the deep fear within my heart. Once again, survival became my primary concern.

★ ★ ★

One night in April, long after the lights-out bell, an urgent voice called over the loudspeakers: "Every student, please get up and gather at your department classroom building immediately."

Who had been overthrown this time?

I quickly put on my clothes and rushed outside. The weather was mild. The air was fresh with the smell of new grass and new leaves. The spring night was deep with tranquil stars. The flash of a meteor shot across the sky in the distance. I shivered. It was an evil omen.

As a former Red Guard, I was all too familiar with these midnight rites — celebration of the destruction of another of Mao's enemies or the publication of an important editorial by the *People's Daily*. I listened to the familiar and powerful voice of the male anchor from the Central Broadcasting Station and felt goose pimples. If this particular anchor was on the air, it was nothing trivial. The man's voice was smooth as silk, noble as gold, and tough as steel. It was the same strong voice that had broadcast the May 16 Statement that formally proclaimed the beginning of the Cultural Revolution. It was the same strong voice that had declared Liu Shaoqi the country's biggest traitor and China's Khrushchev. It was the same strong voice that could shake the heart of every Chinese. Father once said that just hearing it would trigger a heart attack. I stretched my neck and listened attentively.

"Deng Xiaoping is behind the counterrevolutionary riot in Tiananmen Square. . . . The People's Liberation Army has successfully crushed the rebellion. . . . For his monstrous crime, the Central Political Bureau has unanimously decided to dismiss Deng Xiaoping from his current post." The ominous words used in these denunciations were vague despite the severe tone, and from beginning to end, the broadcast failed to tell what really happened. How had Deng Xiaoping rebelled? Had he and his followers taken up arms or simply expressed their opinions? How many people had participated in the so-called riot? How was the coup smashed?

225

But one thing was sure. Memorial activities in Tiananmen Square were being repressed in the crackdown and Deng Xiaoping, the acting premier, had been expelled again. Disappointment gripped me. The people's plea for the end of the political massacre was quashed. And with Deng's ouster, his third since the beginning of the Cultural Revolution, the Four Modernizations — of industry, agriculture, science and technology, and national defense — were being aborted almost before they had begun. During the dark years when speaking of "economic reconstruction" was a punishable offense, Deng had been the symbol of China's economic restoration. To the miserable Chinese, his name meant modernization, whereas Mao had pushed the country to the verge of bankruptcy.

I mourned secretly in my heart. The Chinese people had lost another opportunity for progress. How long would we have to remain in this chaotic and disastrous situation? When would this nation step up from poverty and become strong?

A huge crowd of students had gathered in front of the foreign languages building. The anchor from the Central Broadcasting Station repeated the denunciations. The tone became even harsher, like a knife peeling everyone's heart. It seemed to suggest to the whole nation that those who supported these actions would prosper, those who resisted should perish. Chills ran down my spine. The department party secretary, whose face was panic-stricken, asked each class to hold a "thoughts unification" session before we hit the streets to show our massive support. In our classroom, the chairs were rearranged in the shape of a full moon. Moths darted through the wide-open windows to the white fluorescent lights. The anchor's powerful voice crept in. Excited, sleepy eyes refilled with the fighting spirit. Words, like cannon rounds, exploded. Full of the smell of ammunition, the classroom became a battlefield again.

Since this was the most serious political event that had occurred while I was here, I knew I must act quickly. Yet I couldn't open my mouth. Indignation was not with me. But sympathy for the people protesting in Tiananmen Square and for Deng was dangerous. It could kill me and bury me. I had to whip up my feelings to great rage at once. I must echo the strong voice, the voice speaking on behalf of Mao.

I raised my head nervously and met the grapelike dark eyes of Lang staring at me, pitilessly hard and cold. Although she had been trying to avoid me, she had never really ignored me. Silently she had been watching closely as if waiting for something. I could feel her smoldering hatred. Now Lang had already given an excellent performance in denouncing Deng, and she was waiting to see mine. Although I didn't believe a word she said, just as she wouldn't believe anything I said, Lang was a much more talented actress than I. She was so angry when she criticized Deng that her facial muscles bulged, and sparks of indignation danced in her eyes. Where did she find all those feelings?

Like a cornered beast, I had no way out but to match her.

"Down with Deng Xiaoping!" I heard myself shout hysterically, my voice trembling, cutting off one of my classmates who was in the middle of his criticism. He raised his hand in a fist and shouted along with me. The whole class joined in:

"Safeguard the fruits of the Cultural Revolution!"

"Protect our great leader Chairman Mao with our own lives!"

Fu, the student party leader, nodded to me. But Lang sneered. From her cold eyes, I felt a chill running through my body.

31

A Stab in the Back

Two weeks later I was among several veteran Youth League members nominated for Chinese Communist Party membership. We were praised for our "outstanding performance during the political struggle." This was my second nomination. The title of Communist Party member was not only an honor in name, it also promised real benefits in the future. It was a gold key to privilege and a life among the elite.

As a routine procedure, a party representative came to the class to collect opinion. When accepting new members, the party was open-minded and ready to listen to all kinds of opinions, negative or positive. It encouraged people to expose each other. It had to separate pearls from fish eyes, for it wanted only the real communist, not a fake one, to be its new blood.

One morning after class, Master Shi, our worker teacher and also the department's deputy party secretary, asked me to stay behind. I looked at his face expecting a smile of congratulations, but instead it was shadowed by a look of melancholy. I sensed something was wrong. But what could it be? The classroom was bright. A young light-green vegetable butterfly fluttered to a perch on the windowsill, glowing in the sun. Master Shi, whose faded overalls were spotted with dark grease, grabbed a chair and sat next to me, his fingers leafing through Chairman Mao's *Quotations*. He looked at me sullenly and seemed to hesitate before opening his mouth.

"During our investigation regarding your party membership, a student said that you are against the Cultural Revolution."

His words, like thunder, almost knocked me down. In a school infamous for its leftist polarization, they carried the weight of a death sentence.

"A student said that your home was searched, your father beaten, your mother arrested, and you and your brother suffered in the working class neighborhood. The Cultural Revolution has done a lot of harm to you. It's logical that you should hate it." Master Shi stretched his thick fingers one by one while stating the accusation.

I was struck dumb with fear. I knew at once that Lang had reported me. She had betrayed me! She had stabbed me in the back. But at that moment, even if I grew one thousand mouths, I still couldn't explain clearly what had really happened between Lang and me on that crazy night. Suddenly, I lost my sense of hearing and all feeling. I was preoccupied with one thought only: Why? Why did she do this? Why did she want to ruin me?

When Shi was through with me, I dragged my heavy legs down the stairs and out of the building. It was still a bright day outside. The sun was golden, shining over the treetops. Its light settled on the smooth boulevard that glistened all the way to the other end of the campus. But for me, it was a dark day.

I returned to the empty dorm. I hid inside my mosquito net. I wept quietly, thinking about the words of the Han dynasty poet Cao Zhi:

> The burning beanstalk is boiling the beans.
> The beans are crying in the pot:
> We come from the same root.
> Why press so hard?

I wanted to ask Lang, "Why press so hard? Why do you want to push me onto the death road?"

Other girls came and went, but Lang never showed herself. I lay on my bed, soundless and motionless. Like a wolf waiting for its prey, I waited for Lang's return. After the lights-out bell, I was still waiting, rolling and tossing on the mattress. I pushed my head out of the mosquito net and looked at Lang's bed again. It was already past midnight, but her bunk was empty.

Lang didn't show up the next day nor for many days after. No one knew where she was.

Meanwhile, the party organization put a stop to the procedure for accepting me as a new member. I knew the authorities would never let me get off without severe punishment. I prepared for the worst. I stopped listening to foreign broadcasts. I shut myself in the women's lavatory and cut Bei's letters to pieces, flushing them down the toilet. As the water swirled the shreds of paper away, I couldn't help sobbing. I missed Bei badly. I threw the *English 900* textbook behind the deserted utility building. If found in my possession, the book would prove that I worshipped capitalism and had become its shameful captive. As an unspoken rule, one person's crime was always the crime of the entire family. Everyone in my family would be tainted by this. But the person who would suffer most was my younger brother, Jie. He worked in a hospital canteen doing everything from washing and sorting vegetables to cleaning tables. Because of my political "crime," his ambition to attend a medical college might never come true.

In less than a week, Master Shi came to the classroom again and waved me out. My legs felt leaden, and I walked with difficulty. I followed him to his office on the second floor. There, behind the desk, sat a long-faced, stiff-postured army officer. He was motionless. I bowed my head low in silence, like a war criminal waiting to be sentenced.

Master Shi leaned against the desk. His torso tilted forward. "Do you understand who has given you everything that you have today?"

"Chairman Mao and the Chinese Communist Party," I answered mechanically.

He nodded. "Lang and you had a long conversation. Is that true?"

"Yes."

"It stands to reason that you couldn't have just started talking all by yourself. What did Lang say that night? Her father, you know, is not a small fry. Now he's under intense investigation. This army officer here would appreciate any information you can provide to facilitate that investigation."

The officer, who introduced himself as a member of the Army Propaganda Team of the Shanghai Revolutionary Committee, looked at me eagerly.

Finally, a perfect opportunity for revenge! I was thrilled. Lang's life was now within my firm grasp. I felt so powerful. The officer took the cap off his pen and displayed the paper pad in front of him. Master Shi's body relaxed. Yes, I would tell. How relieved I would feel if I could tell it all. How sweet would revenge taste. Lang deserved it. It was she who hated the Cultural Revolution. It was she and her circle who wanted to hang Mao's wife with their own hands and inflict a thousand cuts on her. The words were on the tip of my tongue. Yes, I would tell, tell now!

But somehow the words failed me. I felt a sudden uneasiness that was like a cat's claw tearing my heart. Could I live the rest of my life with a mind at peace, knowing that Lang, her family, and her entire circle were all cruelly persecuted because of me, because I wanted revenge? After all, those people were as innocent as I was. Did they deserve punishment simply for expressing personal opinions divergent from the orthodoxy of the Cultural Revolution? Did they deserve severe punishment simply for criticizing an individual such as Jiang Qing? No! I would not be used as a political tool. I simply couldn't repeat what Lang had said the other night. It was too scary to tell it all; the name of Jiang Qing was too horrible to pronounce under these circumstances.

The thrill of revenge disappeared like a wisp of smoke. I bit my lower lip and locked my tongue tightly behind my teeth.

Master Shi's body stiffened. His furrowed face looked grave but not formidable. He seemed to understand me and didn't ask any more questions. I saw a look of sympathy in his eyes.

In the stubborn silence, the glow of curiosity in the eyes of the army officer dimmed. The anticipation on his stern face departed little by little. He put the cap of his pen back on and clipped the pen in his breast pocket. Pushing the pad away from him, he picked up the sagging army hat, stood up swiftly, and left.

Master Shi poured two cups of water from the red flask on his desk and put one on the edge of the desk near me. He made a slurping noise while sipping. He was thinking, long and hard. A huge knot moved between his eyebrows. His apprehensive eyes told me that his mind was in conflict. He had to decide what he was going to do with me. Master Shi knew our class very well. For almost three years, he had been our political advisor and followed us everywhere, whether in the fields, the workshops, or the soldiers' barracks. Never a good farmhand, he had lagged behind in harvesting crops. I had often helped him.

"I know you are a good comrade. We want you to be our party's new blood. But this is unfortunate," Master Shi said, his fingers tapping the side of the enamel mug.

My cold heart was warmed. Good words spoken in hard times were like the spring wind thawing the frozen land. Tears were gathering and running down my cheeks in rivulets. I tried in vain to hide them. Master Shi wiped his eyes. Then he spoke with a muffled voice.

"We won't report your case to the upper levels. But your party membership has been permanently denied. You will receive an internal warning. Your Youth League membership and your leadership position in the League will be suspended until your graduation. A fall into the pit, a gain in your wit. Remember!"

With tears of gratitude, I made a deep bow to him and left the office.

The sky was bluer, the grass was greener, the flowers were redder, and the sun was brighter. Even studying in the women's lavatory seemed much easier to endure. Life was a lot more pleasant after the disaster.

But Lang, who returned to school ten days later, became more and more restless. I could tell from the anxious look in her pretty eyes that followed me everywhere: Why were no mass criticism meetings held? No orders to dismiss me from the university issued? No arrest as she originally expected? She tossed heavily on her bed at night. I heard her sobbing off and on. When our eyes met accidentally, she looked afraid.

32

All Rivers Flow to the Sea

*T*he first of June came. Noisy children, wrapping their heads with cooling wet towels, waited patiently under the hot sun in front of the iron-gated swimming pools, which opened today for the season. The timeless evening scene of summer resumed on the streets. After the last golden rays of the scalding sun vanished into the western horizon, the residents moved small tables, bamboo beds, and reclining chairs outside to take the air. Every lane and street of Shanghai reverberated with the sound of the wooden slippers that people old and young wore as they moved about on the concrete sidewalks, playing in the special live orchestra every Shanghainese was familiar with.

During the eleventh summer of the great Cultural Revolution, graduation also arrived. In accordance with Mao's theories, we, his new college graduates, were returning to where we came from — to the countryside, to the mountains, and to the frontiers. Writing pledge after pledge, we vowed to go to the farthermost corners of the earth, to places where there was no water, no electricity, no shelter, no hospital, even to the Arctic if Mao commanded us to do so.

As the big day approached, I was deeply worried. With a record of suspension, I wasn't optimistic about my graduation assignment. While I longed to leave the university, which was hardly any better than a prison, I feared being sent back to the northern frontier. Whenever I thought about the Great Northern Wilderness, my heart turned icier than the stormy weather there. The thought of the huge rocks, two times bigger than myself, and the long bed, colder than a coffin, made me tremble.

Silver-haired, wrinkle-faced grandmothers swaying on small bound feet and haggard-looking grandfathers moving slowly with the aid of bamboo canes filled the hallways of our class building. The elderly came to persuade the department leaders to consider their poor health and keep their grandchildren from going back to the rural areas. Grandpa Wang said he had lung cancer and wanted his granddaughter to take care of him until his dying day. Grandma Zhang said her blood was cancerous, and she would like to have her grandson be with her. Almost all of them said that their old bones were brittle and they needed their grandchildren to look out for them. At first the eyes of the departmental officials were wet with sympathy, for the Chinese have always respected the elderly. Soon, however, they became indifferent, as their ears grew calluses from hearing similar stories repeated hundreds of times a day. On the door of the department office, a note was posted: NO ELDERLY, PLEASE.

Unofficial news travels fast. Just before graduation day, rumor had it that Jing, my roommate, would stay on to teach in the department. The news stunned the class. Wasn't Jing the capitalist seedling who cared about nothing but book knowledge? In selecting her as a future faculty member, what message did the Department of Foreign Languages want to send? For three years, it hadn't allowed foreign language studies and vehemently advocated that politics should always be the most important measure in evaluating a student. White clouds changed into gray dogs. How could the changes take such freakish forms? How could academic competence become important all of a sudden upon graduation? Mouths agape in wonder. Frozen facial expressions. Jittery eyes, glaring eyes, and fierce eyes. Feeling deceived and betrayed, the class was in an uproar. I kept silent, worrying about my own situation. It was said that politically tainted students often received delayed graduation assignments because no units wanted them. Would I be assigned? Would I be assigned on the same basis as the other, politically healthy, students? Bearing the heavy rock of suspension on my back, I was pressed down a head shorter than my classmates. Politically, I was inferior.

The classroom boiled with pent-up fury. The temperature inside rose higher than outside. Cicadas among the thick leaves beyond the windows droned, drowning the campus with their clamor. Fu, his face contorted with anger, growled louder than the crazy bugs.

"This graduation policy is against Chairman Mao's rule that politics should have priority in everything we do. We must overturn the decision."

With graduation less than twenty-four hours away, no one needed to pretend. The department officials had already decided the destiny of every student behind closed doors. Like birds, we would soon fly in different directions. Lies and disguises were no longer necessary. Masks were torn up. Hatred streamed from the miserable hearts like magma bursting out of a volcano.

The wounded Jing stood up, turned her small nose up to the ceiling, and, carrying her thin body stiff as a rod, walked out of the class meeting. She shut the door with a bang. The summer air was muggy. The cicadas almost shouted their song. Yu, the shortest male student, picked up a chair and threw it at the huge tape recorder. Another student dumped the plate-sized tapes into the trashcan behind the door. Others vented their anger at Professor Wang.

"This must be Wang's idea! Let's go and get him!" Several male students dashed out of the classroom.

Fu's eyes were burning with a wild expression. His fingers nervously drumming the desk, he looked at the students, who were also looking at him. His hard jaws clenched. In just one step, he hopped to the teacher's podium and took out a roll of paper, an ink box, and brushes. The class immediately knew his intention: to write large-character posters, the sharpest and the most effective weapon in a class struggle.

Standing in a corner of the classroom, I calculated what impact the student rebellion might have on me. Five years after he had received the fatal blow from his former successor Lin Biao, Mao's health was deteriorating day by day. He could hardly walk without assistance. His sagging face was sad and dead. His wife, Jiang Qing, and Xu Jinxian seemed to have loosened their grip on Shanghai and our school, their ideological fortress. This might explain why our department dared to go against its longtime policies and drive the "capitalist fast train" rather than the "socialist slow wagon." I welcomed the change, and hoped that my political suspension would be forgotten and my academic progress, achieved after years of studying under difficult conditions, be recognized. In the student rebellion, I should therefore not support my classmates. I should refuse to sign on the petition.

Soon Fu completed a ten-sheet-long large-character poster and the students scrambled to sign it. No one noticed me standing quietly in the corner. In the chaos, I slipped out of the classroom into the women's lavatory. When I emerged, the students had already hung the poster in front of the classroom building, drawing a huge crowd of students. Shouting in unison and demanding the reversal of the graduation decision, they stormed the department office. Looking over bobbing heads and shoulders, I saw the woman party secretary ashen-faced, her usually authoritative eyes registering fear. As more and more students rushed in, she agreed to hold talks with Fu. The crowd pushed me outside the building.

Rose-tinted clouds floated by. The flowers drooped in the heat of the setting sun. Dragonflies hovered only inches above the ground, signaling the coming of a thunderstorm. As late afternoon grew into evening, an exhausted-looking Fu emerged from the office. He raised his arms to declare a victory — the department had canceled its original assignment of Jing. I lowered my head.

The following morning, our graduation ceremony was conducted in the huge lecture room, which was jam-packed with graduates, teachers, and Worker Propaganda Team members. Soldiers guarded the door, keeping order. The event attracted a lot of attention, since it was the first graduation assignment of newly minted college students in Shanghai and the country. Although crowded, the lecture room was dead silent.

My heart beat unevenly, as if waiting for a death sentence. Nervously I reached for the hand of Jing sitting beside me. It was clammy with cold sweat. She was deeply worried too. Where would she be reassigned?

At nine o'clock sharp, the party secretary stepped onto the platform. On her chest a badge of Mao's head glittered like a gigantic red diamond, making her look more like a real revolutionary. Surveying the room with authority, she cleared her throat a few times. My heart jumped wildly at each movement of her mouth.

The party secretary announced that my roommate Lang would go to one of Mao's war preparation districts in a mountainous part of Guizhou Province, in China's deserted southwestern region. With tears in her eyes, Lang reluctantly stepped onto the stage to receive the students' applause. She smiled in embarrassment, her mouth falling. The red paper flower pinned on her bosom highlighted her face. She waved mechanically to the students, who were cheering their own luck at not having her job. The smiling party secretary exhorted Lang to make revolution in the mountains for the rest of her life. Lang's forced smile looked worse than crying.

Fu took Jing's teaching position in the department. My three other roommates, Juan Chen, Yun Yun, and Cui, were among the many students who would go to the suburbs of Shanghai to serve the rural areas, where English was not used at all. Good news for Jing! She would teach in an academy. Her nervous hands relaxed. She unbuttoned her collar and sleeves to cool herself down. Jing whispered that the assignment was better than she had expected. But I wasn't in any mood to celebrate with her.

Where will I go? Why hasn't she called my name yet? I asked

myself, growing more and more anxious. It must be the suspension. My bad-mouthing the Cultural Revolution is much more serious than Jing's. It's a political crime. It is anti–Cultural Revolution. Anti–Cultural Revolution is anti-Mao. I'm already lucky I'm not in prison. What else should I expect?

The party secretary continued reading names. I was almost in tears. Now she came to the last piece of paper, seeming to confirm my worst fears that the department delayed assigning the politically problematic students. My heart dropped. As I began taking this in as my destiny, I heard her calling my name.

"Shanghai University," she pronounced, character by character, her face indifferent, her tone matter-of-fact. But to me, her dry voice was the joyous declaration of a promising future.

"Over! It's all over! An old road has ended and a new journey begins," I heard myself saying.

Jing grabbed my hand and shook it. "Congratulations! My sincerest congratulations. We should celebrate our good fortunes."

I felt so numb that I didn't know what to say. Automatically, I answered, "Yes, we will! We will!"

I should throw a party. Didn't the great Tang poet Li Bai say, "When it is time to celebrate, don't let the golden wine cup face the moon empty. Spend all the gold, for it will return, for Heaven must have a use for me."

Let me raise the wine cup and drink a toast. Let me indulge in festivity, for gold spent would come back, for Heaven must have had a purpose for me when it gave birth to me. After the nightmare, here was the new day. But at the moment, my hands covered my face. Warm tears trickled from between my fingers, running down my elbows.

Years passed filled with dangerous pitfalls,
Rights and wrongs have been judged at last.

Don't say the floating clouds can forever shield the sky,
Bursting are the buds when spring comes.

Floating clouds cannot block the sky forever. No, they cannot.

Immediately after my graduation, on July 28, 1976, a powerful earth-quake registering 7.8 leveled the ancient city of Tangshan outside Beijing, killing nearly 250,000 people, injuring 170,000, and wiping out 7,000 entire families. Soul-stirring cries resounded above the debris of the city day and night. The shock waves also rocked the capital city. Buildings shook. Furniture danced. Rivers, reservoirs, and wells dried up. Frightened Beijingers refused to return to their houses and made the streets their temporary homes. Then a gigantic meteor fell in Jilin Province in northeast China. People claimed that heaven was trying to send China a message. In the stifling summer night, Shanghai was still as hot as a steaming pot. Residents, as usual, streamed into the streets and onto the sidewalks to get some air. Smoking pipes and waving banana-leaf fans, old men with silky goatees pointed their fingers to the sky. They said that the wrath of heaven and the resentment of men foretold that the world was going to change. "It should. Almost eleven years!"

Other people silently agreed.

On September 9, 1976, the scent of golden osmanthus blossoms perfumed the autumn air. The flaming crimson leaves of maple trees on Beijing's Western Hill danced in the sky. But Mao could not climb the magnificent rostrum of Tiananmen. His heart had stopped beating this day. God had died. The usually strong, harsh voice of the Central Broadcasting Station became softer than silk, gentler than water, laden with great sorrow: "The Himalayas stand in silent mourning. The pine trees bow their heads. The Yangtze River has ceased running, and the moon and stars have stopped shifting." Sorrowful funeral music hung in the air. Mao's soul lingered. It didn't want to leave his vast empire, where the great leader had killed more people than Hitler and Stalin combined.

My countrymen wept sweet tears. Everywhere jubilant voices celebrated the people's emancipation:

> Good wine flowing,
> Happy songs flying.
> My friend! Let us toast!
> Let us toast!
> The joy of victory can never be forgotten,
> And cheerful tears fill my cup.

Only those who had been shackled like slaves could weep like this after regaining their freedom. On October 4, 1976, only twenty-six days after Mao's death, Jiang Qing and her Gang of Four were arrested. The coup officially ended the Great Proletarian Cultural Revolution, which purged, beat, tormented, exiled, injured, or killed approximately 100 million innocent Chinese, changing forever everyone's life in this nation. In 1978 the Chinese Communist Party itself admitted that the Cultural Revolution had led to domestic turmoil and brought enormous catastrophe on the party, the state, and the people.

People wiped away their tears, buried the dead, and cleaned the bloodstains from their clothes. They began building a new country on top of the ruins.

33

Flight to Freedom

After the death of Mao, the political winds changed overnight. Whoever had profited during the Cultural Revolution was ousted and whoever had lost was in power. Mao's Worker Propaganda Teams, which had been stationed in every educational institution, went back to the factories, and the downtrodden intellectuals recovered their academic positions. Hudong University returned what remained of the goods that the Red Guards had confiscated from our home in August 1966. The charges that Father was a spy and a traitor were dropped automatically. Mao's wife, Jiang Qing, shouldered all the blame for Father's sufferings. He not only got his original position back but also received a promotion: he was now in charge of the Shanghai Party School, brainwashing those Shanghai officials who had worked for the Gang of Four during the Cultural Revolution. Our family moved into a spacious new home. Since Mother suffered from a heart condition and a mental disorder, she could no longer work. She retired early with full benefits and a significant increase in salary. My now twenty-two-year-old younger brother Jie, who had never stopped studying privately, took the first national college entrance examinations, restored in 1977, and was admitted to Shanghai Medical University. In 1979 my elder brother Ming, thirty-two, finally returned home from Heilongjiang. To realize his dream of going to college, he had refused to marry his battalion commander. But he had tasted the bitter fruit of his scorn. His requests to leave had been turned down. His rank as sergeant had been taken away, and he had been relegated to blasting rocks in the mountains. His request to transfer to another regiment had been denied and his repeated applications to attend a college thrown away. But in 1979 the State Council permitted the former citydwellers to return home and everyone fled, forming a huge tide surging back to the cities. Only then did Ming's battalion commander give up her punishment of eight years. The same year, Ming took the college entrance examinations and was admitted to Shanghai Industrial University, his first step to becoming an electrical engineer.

Ming had left Shanghai in 1968 as one of the first batch of Red Guards sent down to the countryside. When he appeared before my parents in 1979 with luggage in hand, Mother's slim eyes blinked nonstop, tears springing out by themselves. During his absence, his gorgeous youth had died, squandered in resisting the omnipotent party official's power. Time had left its ruthless traces. His thick black hair was thin, already salt and pepper. Wrinkles recording untold miseries were imprinted on his once smooth forehead. But Ming was home at last, ending the family separation of thirteen years since that August night in 1966. In jubilant toasts, my parents' wounded hearts began slowly to heal. With all three children in Shanghai's popular universities, a rarity then, Father could walk with his back straight, his chest stuck out, his eyes bright with pride. He was glad that we had followed his guidance to educate ourselves even during the most hopeless hours in our lives. History had proved the truth of his words that the day would surely come when education was important again.

However, while our family celebrated, I fell into the dark canyon of distrust and disgrace. We, once Mao's glorious students, were now denounced as the "small running dogs" of the Gang of Four. Suddenly we became politically dangerous and academically worthless and were purged from our various positions. My classmate Fu was removed from his teaching post at East China Normal University, when our former professors became important departmental heads. Fu was bitterly remembered for his radical past. Living like a "rat crossing a busy street," he died young. As the purge continued, I, like other former Red Guard leaders working in Shanghai University, was placed under extensive investigation. Those of us who had committed serious violence were expelled from the party and even imprisoned if their victims insisted on the penalty.

My three-year college degree became virtually worthless. Worse, instead of an honor, it became a humiliation. As the new college graduates with formal four-year degrees came to teach, I was shunted aside and at any time could have been asked to leave. My career path came to a dead end.

In 1980 I was twenty-seven. But I was still single, scorned by society — a real "old girl" in the eyes of the Shanghai people. Gossip insisted that I must have a physical problem, since I couldn't get a man to marry me. In fact, my problem wasn't physical, but I did suffer from fear in dealing with men. Mao's enforced asceticism had left deep psychological scars and made it hard for me to function normally as a woman. Although the atmosphere was much more relaxed during the 1980s and no woman would be persecuted for talking to a man, I still feared being watched, criticized, or punished. I still cursed myself for evil thoughts — dreaming about men, longing for physical intimacy, wanting to have children. Although the external fetters binding my hands and legs were smashed when the Cultural Revolution ended, I still lived in a prison of spiritual torment and couldn't achieve inner peace. My parents blamed each other for being unable to find me a desirable husband.

Memory often carried me back to Tan. I couldn't forget the last silent moment when I saw him at the train station. His transportation squad often worked in Tashan. Had he come to see me off? The answer was not important, but the warmth would always live in my heart. How about Bei? He must have returned to Shanghai and married. Guilt still haunted me whenever my heart went to him. I also thought of Lon, whom Mother never forgot to mention. But all that had become history. As youth departed from me little by little, I wanted more than ever to get married and have a family of my own. I wanted to live like a real woman.

In 1981 several teaching groups at Shanghai University were combined to form the Department of Foreign Languages. With this merger, I met Wei, a lanky young man in his early thirties with a submissive appearance but an inwardly indomitable personality.

Wei's desk directly faced the door. Every morning when I stepped into the office, he was the first to greet me. He would say hello as he raised his face, then quickly bury his nose in his books again. His life path was similar to mine: a senior Red Guard received by Mao several times in Beijing, a toiler in the Tie Li Independent Regiment of Heilongjiang Military Farms, and a worker-peasant-soldier student at Shanghai University, he had remained to teach upon graduation. I could see that Wei suffered too when talking with members of the opposite sex. His face would turn purple. He didn't know where to look or how to place his hands. His body became stiff like a tree trunk. He must be fighting bitterly with his own "dirty" self.

Life continued without a ripple. One year later, both of us were well past the special minimum marriage age imposed after the Cultural Revolution in order to control the population explosion: twenty-five for a woman, twenty-eight for a man.

Then one day a coworker in her forties joked with us: "Our ancestors believed that a man should get married when he comes of age and a woman when she's fifteen. Neither of you is as young as that. Do you guys want to be a monk and a nun for the rest of your lives?"

The sun's rays flamed in the window. A fitful breeze blew in and lifted my hair. Her words were like needles pricking my heart. She didn't seem to be mean. But when she said "nun," was she hinting I would never get married? It was scary to hear that truth. I lowered my head. Did Wei despise an "old girl"? Nowadays single men wanted to marry women under twenty-five. And there was a sea of younger women in Shanghai. Without wanting to, I raised my face and met Wei's gaze, which flashed with bashfulness mixed with warmth. I looked at him. His eyes were not mocking. For the first time, I looked at him boldly. The spiritual walls inside me, once firm and cold as an iceberg, melted suddenly, streaming like spring water. In the silence, I flung aside all my worries and fears. As we embraced with our gazes, we honestly revealed to each other our longing for companionship and intimacy. My sleeping soul awoke all of a sudden: he was the one.

This feeling, without the shock of electricity or flare of lightning, came like soundless spring rain, penetrating and nurturing the withered heart. It was a love with understanding, a love requiring no conditions, and a love that would endure all misfortunes. With the infinite power of love, we quickly changed from "cowards" into "warriors." Like teenagers first awakening to love, we walked shamelessly hand in hand in the vegetable fields behind the university, in the park by the Huangpu River. We sat eye to eye in the empty teachers' office at night, engaging in endless talks. With Wei, sorrow departed from me little by little. We met almost every day, chasing after our disappearing youth and trying to catch its tail.

Now there was only one hurdle I needed to overcome, and that was the one I dreaded — obtaining approval from my parents. When they heard about Wei, their faces went expressionless like a dead pond. Then Mother sighed, her face long. She still felt I should marry Lon. Father studied me for a while.

"Like attracts like. He is a worker-peasant-soldier student, isn't he? Why don't you find a formal college student like your brothers?"

Then Father said he should meet Wei, but he didn't want Wei to visit at home in case he didn't like him.

At the sight of the gray-haired man with critical eyes coming into our office, Wei, who had rehearsed for Father's visit for days, jumped up from his desk and pumped Father's hands without stopping. That day, despite the warm weather, Wei wore two thick sweaters under his coat so he would look strong. Smiling, he showed Father around the office and accompanied him on a walk around campus. They finally stopped at the school canteen and ate lunch together. Wei told Father that since his home was close to Apricot Restaurant, famous for its artistically shaped meat-and-egg moon cakes, he would happily bring him several boxes to taste. Father smiled from ear to ear but quickly swallowed his grin so that he'd look more serious. Thrown off guard, he said that he wanted to invite Wei to a family dinner to talk about our relationship, but Wei didn't need to bring anything when he came. Wei replied that he had already stood in line half the night to buy the moon cakes. Father's eyes opened wide in disbelief.

"Was the line that long?"

"Not that the line was long. It was because the restaurant didn't open till seven o'clock. I just wanted to be first."

In June our simple wedding ceremony was held in our office with some hard candies and green tea. Our coworkers were our witnesses. The school let us borrow a dormitory room facing north. Though it was dark and small, we were satisfied. The economy was still recovering. The stalled construction industry couldn't keep up with the baby boomers' robust demand for housing. Flames swayed on the red candles, casting shadows on the wall. The small room was filled with the intoxicating fragrance of wine. I was drunk with happiness. I had been dreaming of this day ever since I was fourteen, fantasizing in front of a mirror, longing to be a bride. But when the moment came, it was sad to find out how ignorant and clumsy we were in the forbidden zone of intimacy. Neglecting our needs and repressing our desires for long years, we found that sex was too strange for us. My husband was as naïve as I was. Don't blame him, I said to myself. It isn't his fault. It's not easy for a young man to go through the era of asceticism, when there were so many so-called "rapists" among the young who were executed. Our joyfulness on this wedding night vanished. Left was the heavy burden of overcoming our "abnormality." We consoled each other: if the cavemen could do it, we could too. But we were no cavemen. I forgot that they had never gone through what we had.

Early fog invested the city the next morning, hanging a cloudy curtain outside the window. The white pillowcases embroidered with the red characters for "double happiness" seemed ironic. The new quilts with colorful lovebirds playing among the jolly flowers appeared to be mocking us. But, as if awakening from a nightmare, I suddenly recalled reading a news item saying that many newlyweds in Shanghai flocked to see doctors after their wedding night. Many others had suffered from the same problem. We were not alone.

For me, unsecured as a small boat rocking in a wild sea, marriage was like a safe harbor. Soon, it rewarded me with new life, and I reached another milestone in a woman's journey. During my pregnancy, I often sank into deep reflection, thinking: My dear child, I hope your life won't be like ours, full of twists and turns. Yours should be as bright as the warm sun, and smooth as the blue sky. The road ahead of you should be broad and straight, covered with red roses. May you live happily and worry-free, as a child should. Our past should never happen to you. Never!

In only six weeks the baby's heart began beating, and in twelve weeks its brain had developed. In the warm womb a single cell, nourished by its mother, became a fetus with tiny hands, feet, head, and body. I talked to the baby with my heart, comforting it by caressing my belly. Its every stirring would make my heart sing, about a new life, about my motherhood. It was my happiest moment in life.

After nine months came labor. Cramped abdomen. Waves of pain. The wet of amniotic fluid. Wei rushed me to the nearby hospital.

I was put on a bed in a big room where at least one hundred prospective mothers waited in various stages of labor. It was the peak season. The ward, even the corridor, was filled with pregnant women who groaned, screamed, and wailed. Doctors and nurses threaded among the beds like diligent bees working among the flowers.

Amniotic fluid continued to flow. As lubrication, it would help carry the new life out of the womb and into the world. The baby within me rolled restlessly. I could feel its legs kicking and arms knocking, attempting to gain freedom. My womb contracted in cooperation with the baby's movement. Pain, unspeakable pain, spread all over. I groaned through clenched teeth, but enormous delight overtook me. For my baby I was willing to bear any suffering. How eager I was to meet it, already ten days past due. I knew it was naughty; it kept a close watch on me. When I was in a low mood, it would roll and toss in protest. When I listened to beautiful melodies, it would stay as quiet as it could to enjoy them with me.

The ward became unbearable. Shrieks rose and fell, turning the place into a slaughterhouse.

"I want to have a C-section! Please! The pain is killing me," one crying woman begged.

Sweating doctors and nurses admonished: "Don't scream! You're not a young mother. Of course labor will be difficult! We can't slice open every belly. You have to be patient!"

Waves of excruciating pain tortured me hour after hour. For some reason the baby couldn't get out. It was like a small animal trapped in a closed cave, tumbling and struggling to break through. Twenty-four hours passed. When the second night came, the amniotic fluid had long stopped running. The baby was supposed to have been born by that time. Yet it still struggled within me. Tortured by the killing pain, I wailed myself hoarse. Over the next day, I was moved several times to the delivery bed. The medical staff, who insisted on natural delivery, surrounded me, urging me to hold my breath and use all my strength to push the baby out. At one time the baby's hair was spotted. Doctors and nurses applauded, believing my labor would soon finish smoothly. However, the small head got stuck. After a desperate struggle, it disappeared. The disappointed medical staff moved me back to my bed. Layers of my womb muscles were torn up. The pain never stopped for an instant, and the child never ceased fighting. It was determined to break through all obstacles and enter the world. Another twenty-four hours passed. Gradually, the pain subsided. The baby became docile, kicking only sporadically. On the third morning, all pain was gone. There was no movement within me. I lay weak on the bed, completely exhausted. Soon I remembered nothing. But a doctor's scream startled me. I opened my eyes and saw her listening through a funnel-shaped instrument placed on my belly.

"I can't detect the baby's heartbeat," she cried in alarm. Soon followed an oxygen mask, paperwork, and a signature from my husband, who had been waiting for long hours in the safe zone where men could hear and see nothing of the women's world.

I was placed on the operating table. Disinfection. Local anesthesia. A knife cut open my abdomen and womb. Pain, sharp pain. I screamed in pain. "More anesthesia!" the surgeons shouted. Another injection. My lower body became numb but my mind remained clear. I heard distinctly knives and scissors slicing open the muscles like cutting layers of thick rubber. My abdominal cavity was exposed.

"We'd better hurry. The baby's already turned blue from lack of oxygen." As though lifting a small bundle, the doctors took my baby out of me. It was passed to the nurses. The sound of slapping. Silence. More slaps, and more. My chest tightened. I'd expected to hear the first cry as the child entered the world, but it didn't come. The baby was mute. Slapping continued.

"Wa — wa — wa — " Finally the resonant crying broke out, immediately driving away the black cloud shrouding me. To my ears it was a song, the most beautiful melody in the world.

"What caused my labor to be so difficult?" I asked the doctors later.

"Your pelvic basin has been severely deformed, making natural delivery impossible. Unfortunately, we weren't able to detect the problem earlier," the woman surgeon said.

Carrying excessive loads at the age of only seventeen had distorted my skeletal system, and now I had to reap the bitter harvest.

Four years later, 1986. A landmark year for China. After much hesitation and debate, the government decided to loosen its rigid restrictions on study abroad, realizing that the outward flow of talent would eventually benefit China and speed up the process of its industrialization and modernization. In response, the United States and other Western countries welcomed China's students with outstretched arms. Hundreds of thousands of scholars left to seek further education overseas. On a momentous day in March, I received a letter from the chairman of the Speech Communications Department at the University of Georgia in Athens. He wrote that the department had accepted me as a graduate student and awarded me a scholarship to study in the United States. I immediately accepted the offer and boarded the ship of opportunity that time had provided.

With the roar of its engines, the Boeing 747 of China International Airlines nosed into the skies. In the twinkling of an eye, Shanghai became a small, colorful map lying below. Through tears, I looked down to take in a last glimpse of the huge city, wondering when and whether I would come back again. The plane continued to climb until even this tiny map faded. All I could see now were the cottony white clouds with gold and silver borders floating leisurely against an immense blue velvet.

My heart still bled. It was torn apart by the sharp cries of my four-year-old son fidgeting in my husband's arms as I waved goodbye at the gate of Shanghai International Airport. Over the monotonous drone of the airplane I could hear my son's voice begging, "Mom, don't go! Mom, don't go!" His little bony hands grasped my collar tightly and wouldn't release their hold. He closed his eyes, and tears covered his delicate face. He seemed to sense that I would be gone a long time and completely brushed aside the initial thrill he felt when I had promised him I was going to buy a huge ceiling fan so he could watch it turn round and round. His tears became mine now, and kept trickling down my cheeks.

"You must already be homesick?" a man sitting next to me asked.

I nodded, then shook my head, unable to explain.

"You're going to study in the United States, aren't you?" asked the man, pushing his heavy spectacles back up the bridge of his nose.

"Yes."

"Which school?"

"The University of Georgia. And you?"

"The University of Texas."

I turned toward him. He was not as young as I first thought. Like me, he was in his early thirties. Gray hairs already showed in his sideburns.

"Are you one of the Three Old Grades?" I asked.

"Class of Sixty-nine. Red All Over," he promptly replied.

Almost two decades had gone by since the era of Up to the Mountains, Down to the Countryside, but the special terms sounded all too familiar.

"Where did you go?" I asked, brushing my fingers through my hair.

"Jiangxi Province, the Red Army's base during the civil war. Still a very poor region even today." His tone sounded heavy. His eyebrows knitted. Then he lifted his head and asked, "Where did you go?"

"Heilongjiang Military Farms," I answered. Huge snowflakes flew in front of me.

A terse silence followed. Then he said:

"Now, like we did sixteen years ago, we're leaving our families behind, facing the unknown, and starting from nothing. In a sense it's another Up to the Mountains, Down to the Countryside." He looked at me as if to seek agreement.

The dim lights brightened suddenly, and there appeared beautiful stewardesses, whose smooth faces radiated the natural blush of youthfulness. Smiling pleasantly, they began serving wines and soft drinks.

"What would you like to drink?" a thin-waisted girl asked, stopping her cart beside our seats.

I chose a cup of green tea while the man asked for a glass of red grape wine. The cordial service of the attractive girls roused the dormant cabin. Passengers became alive and filled the air with dynamic conversation and laughter. A tall, sturdy American man with a shock of brown hair walked up and down the aisle, holding a glass of light green liquid. While sipping from the long-stemmed glass, he spoke loudly so all of us could hear his pure American English. He stopped beside a girl.

"It seems to me everyone on this plane must be attending a school in the U.S.A. Miss, if you don't mind, may I know which school you'll be attending?" he asked.

"Of course not," the girl said, chuckling. Her English was automatic, bearing a faint accent typical of the northern Chinese. Then she remained silent, slowly enjoying her red wine. The American was embarrassed. His gray eyes showed confusion. His fingers started tapping the glass unnaturally. Presently another girl answered, "She will attend Harvard."

All eyes fixed on the Harvard girl. Her plain face was slightly flushed from a few swallows of red wine. Holding her head upright, she obviously liked the attention. Her thick eyeglasses revealed the great efforts she had expended behind books.

My green tea gradually cooled down. One refill, then another. After a thirteen-hour flight over the vast Pacific Ocean, the airplane brought us to the city of San Francisco. Looking down, I saw the Golden Gate Bridge and the silhouettes of skyscrapers. This was the gate to the United States. From there I would take another plane to

Georgia, into the heart of the South — my final destination. As the plane descended like a huge eagle with opening wings, my heart beat wildly. Once we landed, I would begin a new life. No one could take me back to the past, which I had left behind forever. When my feet reached the firm ground, I bent down to touch the carpeted floor. I asked myself, Will my new life begin now?

I looked around. Faces of all colors in the crowded airport answered resoundingly. Yes! It begins right here in this free land.

On the north campus of the University of Georgia in Athens, I found the Speech Communications Department. Guided by the hospitable secretary, who walked like a flying butterfly, I knocked on the office door of Dr. Dale Leathers.

"Come in."

I pushed the door open and was met by a pair of spirited eyes. Dr. Leathers stood up promptly from the big armchair behind his broad desk and extended his hand warmly. His light brown hair shone under the bright fluorescent lamp overhead. He was as tall as a small hill.

"Welcome, welcome! You are finally here!" he said, signaling me to sit on the sofa while measuring me as if I were from another planet. After we had spoken for a while, the professor removed a pile of letters from his drawer. I recognized my application and other correspondence I had sent from Shanghai. He said that some of the envelopes had obviously been opened and resealed.

"Do you think they went through some kind of censorship?" he asked.

I nodded, not surprised.

He sank into a brief silence, then raised his head. "Maybe we should find time for you to talk about the Cultural Revolution."

"So you know about it?" I was surprised the phrase had jumped out of the mouth of an American professor.

"It was quite a miserable time for the Chinese people. But what we know is very superficial. Tragedies like that belong to all mankind." Dr. Leathers looked at me earnestly. "You will tell us more about it, won't you?"

At age thirty-three, I became the oldest graduate student enrolled in the department that year. In 1987 my husband Wei and my son came to join me. After an absence of a year, my son of five didn't recognize me at first. He looked thin and was ill-dressed, wearing a girl's green-dotted garment and a pair of oversized sandals. Obviously, Wei didn't know how to dress his son. The boy's shining eyes looked at me suspiciously, then he turned to his father, his two hands tightly clinging to Wei's neck as if he was afraid of being snatched away. He turned his small back to me. He looked at me again only when he heard that I would take him to watch many ceiling fans turning round and round all at the same time.

In June 1988, in the favorable academic atmosphere, I completed my graduate studies and defended my master's thesis. That day, when the professors on my committee shook hands to congratulate me, exaltation filled my heart. From my dark green mosquito net in the East China Normal University to the bright classrooms of the University of Georgia, from the banks of the Huangpu River to Georgia's Stone Mountain, I had never ceased fighting. Only through struggle could I realize my life's true value. Only in struggle could I win today and have a tomorrow. When my joy gradually settled into tranquility, I heard a voice inside me say, Nothing in this world can bring you down! Nothing! Except yourself.

Outside, Georgia's pine trees, hung with ropes of ivy, reached to the blue sky. A hundred flowers smiled under the bright sunlight. A shiny red and white school bus stopped in front of our building. Students of all skin colors filed out, bringing with them youthfulness, vigor, and hope. Life was beautiful. I flung myself into the arms of the future. A new road stretched ahead.

34

A Calling

After fifteen years of living in America, I feel myself to be a part of this great democratic system. When she angers, I yell; when she mourns, I weep; when she celebrates, I sing. America is my homeland. But my Chinese background also links me closely with the ancient land lying on the other side of the Pacific. My aged parents and relatives still live there, and thinking of them often induces homesickness.

In 1997 I went back to see my professor, Dr. Leathers. I didn't visit him in his office but in a funeral home. He had died from a heart attack at the age of fifty-eight. In the well-lit, spacious memorial hall, the professor rested amid colorful flowers and fresh bouquets. His thin brown and gray hair was neatly combed to the back; age spots dotted his face. While paying my last respects, I thought about the day eleven years before when I reported to the department upon my arrival at the university. In mourning, I saw Dr. Leathers vividly rise up from his big armchair to shake my hand.

"You are our first student from communist China. I've heard about the Cultural Revolution. It was quite a miserable time for the Chinese people. . . . You will tell us more about it, won't you?"

My eyes stopped at a drop of moisture rolling down a delicate petal. His soul would soon return to the long river of history. In this bright drop, I saw the preciousness and brevity of life. Human beings come and go. Only the river of history we create is ever-flowing. In that moment, I decided to write about my past. I felt it was my responsibility to tell about our unique experiences. I believed that the world should know and remember our stories. Our power to face, endure, and survive in times of immense human tragedy should be praised as exemplary of the universal spirit of mankind. The human spirit could be tortured, misused, and persecuted, but it could never be broken.

The same year, I visited Shanghai for the first time since my emigration. The yellowish Huangpu River, which used to wash away my tears and nurture my adolescent dreams, rolled unhurriedly to the East China Sea. Thousands of willow branches rippled in the air. The gentle breeze escorted me all the way home. Deng Xiaoping's economic reform had brought great changes to Shanghai, my once gray-faced, poor hometown. With the influx of foreign investment, skyscrapers had risen from the ground. Old, narrow streets were being widened and resurfaced. Neighborhood after neighborhood of low hovels, homes for many Shanghai residents, were being bull-dozed flat for new construction. The markets were spilling over with red tomatoes, orange peppers, chives, white Chinese cabbages, shining purple eggplants, yellow soybean sprouts, brown and hairy taro, and black pickles. The days were gone when every daily necessity had to be rationed, when people had to carry around coupons for grain, meat, eggs, fish, bean products, oil, sugar, cotton, and cigarettes. Men and women, old and young, wore colorful clothing. They had bid farewell to the monotonous revolutionary colors of black, blue, and brown. Cranes clanged. Bulldozers raised clouds of dust, obscuring my vision and coating the heads of pedestrians. The market economy and the capitalistic incentives were reshaping the country. A powerful China was, as Mao had once said, "like a vessel navigating in the sea. Its masthead is already in sight of the shore. It is like a rising morning sun in the East. The boundless radiance piercing through the clouds has been seen on the summit of the mountain. It is like an almost mature fetus moving restlessly in the womb. The infant is ready for delivery."

A Pekingese dog barked at me, waggling its short tail. The tiny bells hanging from a red string fastened around its neck made bright noises. Children kicking a ball in the tree-lined courtyard looked at my suitcases and asked where I was from and who I was looking for. They laughed and whistled when I said in the pure Shanghai dialect that I was returning home. At the sound, my parents came to their door.

"This is my daughter living in America. She hasn't been back for eleven years," Mother explained proudly to the inquisitive neighbors, who set down baskets of groceries and helped me carry my suitcases.

"A good daughter! You are back home to see your parents," they said. Their familiar hometown accent warmed my heart.

As he had many years ago when I returned home from the frontier, Father took me to the window and looked at me in the daylight, examining me from head to toe. His hair had turned thin and silver.

"Time hasn't changed you much," he concluded.

In a minute, the table was covered with steamed dumplings, deep-fried twisted dough sticks, sweet-rice cakes in green, and yellow, creamy soybean milk — the home food I had seen only in my dreams.

"Eleven years!" my parents said with bright tears in their eyes.

"Yes! Eleven years!" I answered, a wandering child returned home.

"You are no longer young."

"No!"

"What a generation!"

My parents complained that they had indeed grown old and were suffering from this pain or that, this ailment or another. Aged and ailing like candles guttering in the wind, they said. Every day was a struggle with past wounds and new diseases.

Father's desk was piled with rice paper, wolf-hair brushes with heads as big as lotus buds, stone ink slabs, colorful inks. On the walls hung ink paintings of galloping horses, gorgeous peonies, elegant bamboo groves, green mountains with maroon pavilions. One painting in black and white caught my attention — an old man with a huge bamboo hat sat on a lonely boat, fishing in a frozen river lined with steep, snow-capped mountains. Ever since Father had retired in the late 1980s, he had sought peace in Chinese traditional painting. He lived in seclusion, totally shunning politics, in which he had been involved all his life. Other times, Father liked to sit in a rocking chair and think. When he looked back on his life, painful memories came to him. His grandfather, a landlord, had been executed beside a ditch in the Land Reform Movement in 1949. One of his sisters had been branded a rightist during the antirightist movement, in which Mao had denounced 550,000 enemies among the intellectuals. Father shivered when he mentioned the great famine that followed the Great Leap Forward. He stood up, pacing the room with his hands locked behind his back.

"When the famine struck in 1959, you were only six and Jie was hardly four."

In the man-made famine that starved to death forty million people, several of Father's relatives in his rural hometown had died from eating grass roots, poisonous plants, and Buddha dirt, a fine whitish soil. In the Cultural Revolution, his mother had died. The hospital had refused to treat the wife of a capitalist and industrialist. Thinking about the pain hurt Father even more. Scars left by the Red Guards shifted with the wrinkles that had amassed on his face. But Father said that he never resented them.

"No! It is not the Red Guards. The young people are innocent," he said.

Mother too said she had long forgiven the Red Guards. Maybe it was because both Ming and I had also been Red Guards, doing the same thing to other people to "protect" Chairman Mao. But after thirty-one years, the past was still vivid. Mother drew me into a small room and in a hushed voice told me that Ming and his fellows had hurt several of their high school teachers and kicked to death a school librarian. During the national purge following Mao's death, the families of the victims had come looking for Ming while he was still trapped in Heilongjiang. Even my younger brother Jie, only ten years old at the time, had been a Little Red Guard, joining with his pals to beat his school principal. Our hands, when they were still young and tender, when they should have been holding pens to write poems and equations, were stained with innocent blood in the fierce power struggle.

"When you get old, everything in the past comes back to you," Mother murmured, her slim eyes blinking. "What chaos then, when you went out to torture others and others came to beat us."

Suddenly she changed the subject.

"I want to leave your father forever and live alone! I have had enough of him!"

"How many times have you said that, Mother! You should have done it earlier, not in your seventies," I joked, already having heard the same wish pronounced hundreds of times before. I knew that mentally she was still a little unstable. My parents had quarreled throughout their lives, often over such issues as in which direction a chicken feather had flown in the kitchen and who should pick up the garlic skin on the floor. Miraculously, their lifelong battles never seemed to do them much harm. I guessed that their habits had sharpened their wits, animated their lives, and helped to relieve their fears and stresses, especially during the Cultural Revolution. Like two fighting cocks, they were ready to go to war at any time. Father once said that if he didn't hear Mother's yelling, he would feel restless — that something important was missing from his life. Today, with all the children gone, they went on as usual. The fuel for their wars was still the chicken feather and the garlic skin. Their voices were louder than ever, but the two "warriors" still hung together after a marriage of fifty-one years.

My elder brother Ming had married in 1983 when he was thirty-six. It was an arranged marriage. His wife was the daughter of one of

Mother's old colleagues. In 1989 Ming came to the United States to study electrical engineering. He has since been living in Kansas.

After receiving his medical degree, my younger brother Jie worked in Zhong Shen Hospital in Shanghai. Jie married in 1992. He had once secretly fallen in love with a classmate, a girl from Xinjiang Uygur Autonomous Region, but since she would have to return to Xinjiang following graduation, he had to forget about her in order to avoid a marriage in which the couple would live separately for their entire lives. Father was right when he said that the price of romance was too steep for our generation.

In the mid 1990s, as foreign technology continued to invade China's market, penetrating each household, state-run enterprises and factories either closed their doors or laid off workers in great numbers. The economic revolution, for the first time in New China's history, produced a huge army of the unemployed, most of whom were over forty with neither adequate education nor special skills. These middle-aged men and women were the sacrifices of China's industrialization. For them, many of whom had been heroic Red Guards during the Cultural Revolution, the massive unemployment was not new. Always the victim whenever the country was plagued with disaster, they asked themselves why ill fortune followed them every step of the way.

Every day, the lanes and streets outside my parents' home in west Shanghai bustled with primitive commercial activity. Sallow-faced men and women cried their wares — plastic sandals, pink and green cotton underwear, socks, towels, and other small merchandise of inferior quality — which were displayed on a plastic sheet spread on the ground. Shouting in the Shanghai dialect, they solicited pedestrians, bargaining vehemently, sometimes even begging.

"Look at the pants. They're made of pure cotton! Very warm in the winter. Sister! Buy a pair for yourself." A woman in a shapeless flowered shirt waved the pants in front of my eyes.

I stopped and selected two pairs of the thin pants. After I handed her the money, the woman opened her heart to me, words gushing out like water.

"These things are close-outs from our factory, given to us as unemployment compensation. The factory went bankrupt and has no money to pay us," she said with a bitter smile. "When you buy my pants, I can buy a few eggs today for my teenage boy. He has had noodles, nothing but clear noodles for days. The boy is growing fast at his age. He needs meat. He needs nutrition." The woman rubbed her dry eyes and brushed back her hair coated with dust kicked up by passing vehicles.

The man selling next to her approached me with a pair of plastic sandals.

"Young sister! Buy a pair. They're pretty comfortable," he urged. The man was wearing a huge straw hat.

"But *Jienfang Ribao* warned yesterday that some sandals sold on the streets were made from poisonous industrial plastics and already killed a dozen people who wore them."

"No! Not mine! Mine definitely won't kill anyone." He looked humiliated. Quickly setting down the plastic sandals, he picked up a pile of towels with colorful stripes. "How about the towels, ten for five yuan? Use them as hand towels, dish towels, whatever you want. Feel them. They're soft!" He thrust the towels, as thin as paper, into my hand, his dirty fingers trembling slightly. I bought twenty. With the pants and towels, my hands were full.

I guessed they were only one or two years older than I, so I asked, "Where did you go during the Up to the Mountains, Down to the Countryside in 1969?"

"Not sixty-nine but sixty-eight," the man corrected me. "Why? No one ever asks this question anymore. It was almost thirty years ago. Who cares about our past?" The man pushed up the straw hat that almost covered his eyes and replied, "I went to the grassland of Inner Mongolia. The song 'Horses Are Running under the White

Clouds' makes me dream about the place. I stayed there for ten years raising horses."

"I went to the Yuan Nan Mountains to cut rubber trees. My mother volunteered to retire early so I could come back to take her place in Shanghai," the woman said.

A group of middle school students passed by, jumping and pushing each other. The man and woman started crying at the top of their lungs, "Good pants! Please buy a pair! Towels! Soft to the touch!"

Sirens of ships sailing on the Huangpu River resounded. Another oceangoing ship entered the harbor. The "Big Ben" on the customs building blocks away chimed every half an hour, loyally reporting the passing of time. As I watched the man and woman extending their dusty hands to the pedestrians, the burden of history came back to me. With these same hands, we wielded wide leather belts, whipping Mao's enemies. And also with these hands, we gripped hoes and sickles hopelessly, reaping the bitter harvest in the far corners of the country. For one man's political ambition, we had already given too much and paid too dearly. Still, ill fortune was not over. My contemporaries struggled yet.

"Buy a pair of cotton underwear!" The woman shouted again, trying to stop a young man, who avoided her outstretched hands. There were too many of the unemployed crowding Shanghai's streets. People were tired of them and the inferior goods they were selling. I put down the pants and towels and took out two hundred U.S. dollars, equal to one thousand six hundred yuan. If a laid-off worker was lucky enough to receive cash, the monthly unemployment compensation was less than three hundred yuan. I handed the money to the man and woman. Although we had never met before, we shared a common past. We were brother and sisters. Because of their votes, their raised hands, I was able to attend a college in Shanghai while they themselves struggled for six more years before returning home.

The man stood woodenly and didn't know what to do. The look on his face was complicated. I understood it had to do with the ego, a man's ego. The woman's initial reaction, as a normal Shanghainese's would be in this situation, was to decline.

"No! No!" She wanted to push my offer back, but her hand stopped in midair, then quickly took the money and put it in her pocket. As a mother, I knew that every minute she had her only child in her heart: he was growing fast, and he needed nutrition. She would not let her child suffer. Otherwise, a Shanghainese would not accept money this easily.

"Where do you work?" she asked.

"I teach in a college."

"You're lucky."

"But like you, I went through it all." I showed her my right hand, red and scarred from the burns.

"Where did you go?" she asked.

"Heilongjiang Military Farms."

"My brother went there too!"

"Almost every family in Shanghai had someone there."

Gazing at my hand, the woman said suddenly, "We were born untimely."

"But we're the happiest generation on earth, aren't we?"

"You must know the popular saying?" she asked. I shook my head. She looked at me strangely.

"Tell me, please. What is it?"

"Listen!" She began in a soft tone: "I was born in New China and grew up under the banner of Mao Zedong Thought. When I was in kindergarten, I starved in the man-made famine. In middle school, we beat teachers instead of seeking education. When I was seventeen, dating was a crime. At twenty-four, marriage was illegal. A new law enforced late marriage, so when I was thirty-one my son was only two. Then came the forced family planning, one couple, one child only. Now in my prime years, I have been laid off. My husband will soon be jobless. When that happens, we could have only the north-west wind to drink!"

Her voice cracked, hurting my heart and leaving my eyes moist.

I patted her on the shoulder. "Can't you go back to work when the economy gets better?"

"Not at my age. I'm forty-five. When there are so many young girls under thirty, why would businesses want to hire us?"

She was right. For us, youth, the biggest asset a human being has in life, was long ago used up during those frantic years. Today everyone sought young people. Shanghai's newspapers were full of help-wanted ads, many of which were placed by big companies from the West. In this, the most populous country on earth, with infinite labor resources, those international companies from democratic countries openly set age limits and gender, political, even physical preferences in hiring. In one such advertisement I saw, the company not only asked for girls who were attractive but also set specific height and weight requirements. At first I thought it was a personal ad seeking a mate. Many of those companies indicated that they wanted only women under thirty and men under thirty-five. They preferred men to women in many jobs and favored Communist Party members, who were known to work harder. The younger genera-tions growing up in the post–Cultural Revolution era received an uninterrupted education and job training and were well prepared for their working life. On the disadvantageous job market, the former Red Guards, all in their forties, had lost the edge of competition. Many didn't even have a middle school diploma. Nobody wanted to hire them.

Everywhere in the city, the unemployed were looking for ways to make a living. They had aged parents and young children to care for. They had to work and were willing to do anything. It made me think of John Steinbeck's words in *The Grapes of Wrath:* "They streamed over the mountains, hungry and restless, restless as ants, scurrying to find work to do — to lift, to push, to pick, to cut —

anything, any burden to bear, for food. The kids were hungry. . . . They were hungry and they were fierce."

The sun had moved to the middle of the sky, throwing short shadows from the trees to the bare ground. The woman half closed her eyes. Her lean face was dark from exposure to the sun. Now she gazed at me and I saw hopelessness in her eyes. While millions of people like her struggled, official corruption ran rampant. Those in power embezzled money and materials, indulging themselves in novel ways. Understanding that power could go as quickly as it came, they used every means they could to milk it to the fullest extent for their personal gain. When it was exposed publicly, the wealth accumulated by the deputy mayor of the city of Harbin shocked the nation. In Wang Lin's home, money, all in big notes, was hidden between the pages of books, in desk drawers, boxes, and trunks, inside pillows and quilts, and in every container that could possibly be used for the safe storage of money. Expensive electronic products such as televisions, VCRs, and cameras were stacked from floor to ceiling, like the inventory of a good-sized department store. Once in a while, a corrupt official like this at the local levels of the county, city, or province, but never the central government in Beijing, was sentenced in order to appease the rage of the disillusioned people. It was widely believed that Mayor Wang was only a drop of water in the sea. Many, if not all, officials in his position had a huge amount of money deposited in foreign banks — commissions they received from big foreign companies for giving them favors at the expense of the people and the country. Officials purchased luxurious apartments and cars, visited prostitutes, and supported multiple lovers, throwing money around like dirt. When a man gets to the top, his friends and relatives, even his dogs and chickens, get there with him.

"Buy a pair of cotton pants. They're comfortable!" the woman cried to the pedestrians. Seeing no buyers, she turned to me.

"Do you practice Falun Gong?" she asked.

"No. But I do Tai Chi," I answered. When learning Tai Chi, I was taught to think about Dantian, my lower abdomen, to protect the air stored there, which was said to be important for curing ills.

"I practice Falun Gong in Bade Park close to my home. Gong allows me to seek spiritual faith and help from another world, the world in space, the world of truthfulness, benevolence, and forbearance." She struck a mystic tone.

Forbearance! Forbearance! What kind of Gong are you learning in order to forbear? I cried in my heart. How long would she have to forbear? Was the endurance of hardships for thirty years not long enough?

Hearing our conversation, the man with the big straw hat cut in: "At first, I didn't believe in Falun Gong at all. My faith in anything died long ago. Now I'm jobless and I'm angry." He pushed his straw hat up again. "But concentrating on Falun Gong has helped me cope with misfortune while remaining kind to others." His voice was calm.

Wherever I went in the morning, in every park or on any strip of open ground, I could see people, an ocean of people, most of them middle-aged women, maneuvering their bodies and limbs. Closing their eyes, some raised their arms in front of them or above their heads with palms facing the sky. Others meditated, sitting on their legs as portable radios played mystical music, lingering and soothing as if coming from outer space. In the morning, it was the world of Gong everywhere in Shanghai.

"How does the Gong work?" I asked the woman.

"When you stick to it wholeheartedly for some time, you will feel a wheel rotating in your abdomen. That is the Falun Wheel, or Space Law Wheel," the woman explained to me, pointing to my stomach. "The turning Falun Wheel will absorb energy from the universe and relieve the body of bad elements such as anger, depression, and sadness, in this way treating ills."

At her words, I drew in a deep breath and held it in my Dantian, imagining a wheel turning there.

"When the wheel is constantly rotating day and night" — the woman's forefinger made circles in front of me — "you are cultivating Truthfulness-Compassion-Forbearance. It is the supreme nature of the universe. With this spiritual involvement, you will feel full of power."

While they talked about Falun Gong, the faces of the man and woman took on a pious appearance, reminding me of the faces of churchgoers in the United States.

One drizzly day, I visited the Shanghai Woman's Association. Since women over forty were the first to be laid off, they comprised the bulk of the unemployment army. In an elegant building located in Shanghai's best residential area, I met with a woman in her late thirties, a senior official of the association. Holding a teacup with both hands, she greeted me in the parlor on the ground floor. In stark contrast to the jobless women on the streets, she appeared relaxed. She sipped green tea from time to time from the refined cup with the delicate designs of a chrysanthemum.

"I can't think of a way to help at present." She began listing the numerous reasons why the Shanghai Woman's Association couldn't assist women: they were short of hands, lacked funds, lacked space. She apologized that, since she had just come back from a trip to Western Europe, she didn't know much about the current domestic situation. She went on and on before she stopped to correct me about the unemployment statistics I'd heard in the United States.

"Unemployment is not as serious as they say there. That's a deliberate exaggeration intended to slander our country," she warned me. I knew that, as the association's senior official, she enjoyed a limousine with a personal driver, a spacious house provided by the government, a salary many times higher than that of the ordinary worker, and many other benefits and privileges that had to be kept secret. Her smooth complexion, the expensive light green dress, and the refined teacup forever in her hand all told how different her life was from those of the unemployed women, with their young children, searching for ways to support their families. When I left the Western-style building, I let the fine rain wet my face. I walked slowly along the street lined with luxurious French parasols. Muddy water splashed on my pants and soaked my leather shoes. I was irritated and deeply disappointed. The hope that one individual could make a world of difference had to die within me.

Three years later, in spring of the year 2000, I visited Shanghai again. Peach trees blossomed like burning flames, pear trees like leaping snowflakes. Under the pale clouds, brilliant skyscrapers and lavish apartment buildings stood like bamboo shoots after the spring rain. They sprang up on both sides of the river. The glory of modernization and capitalism was mirrored in the sky. On webs of brand-new highways, automobiles ran ceaselessly like the ever-flowing Huangpu River. Dazzling neon lights flickered day and night in the commercial districts. Narrow muddy lanes of the kind once found everywhere in Shanghai had been turned into wide boulevards. The city, formerly called a concrete forest, was dotted with verdant bushes, lawns, and flowers. Food spilled out of the markets. Western-style clothes beckoned people from the tall shop windows. For a moment, I almost had to wonder where I was. Capitalism had worked miracles in Shanghai and turned it into the Paris of the East, a splendid pearl on the East China Sea.

However, behind the booming surface lurked a crisis. New waves of unemployment continued to rack this industrial city. The gap between the rich and the poor grew daily. The very rich drove Mercedes Benzes and Lexuses and carried handbags made from snake or crocodile skin. They wore garments made in Italy or France and sent their children to elite private schools in London and Paris. The poor, whose monthly income was less than the cost of one dinner in a luxurious restaurant, struggled to feed themselves and their families. Each time I went out, Mother would caution me, "Be careful of your purse. Nowadays, even the workers steal. Men, women pass in and out of buses, train stations, markets, and other crowded places to pick pockets."

Mother said that a dying girl's father, who was a worker, had appeared on television, begging the person who took his bag to return it. "It has my daughter's cancer medicine. Please save my daughter." His tears must have moved the thief, who returned the bag with a note: "I'm sorry, brother. I was also a worker before I was laid off. I also have a daughter at home who has to eat."

The narrow lanes outside my parents' home were all gone. In their place was a park. Schoolchildren, red scarves around their necks, played near the fountains. Grandparents sat chatting on the stone chairs, basking in the sun. After the residents had complained about the peddlers and their cries, which used to start as early as dawn, the city had cleared the streets, prohibiting any unlicensed commercial activities. I still visited the parks in the early morning. However, the Falun Gong people were nowhere to be seen, nor was their space music to be heard. Other people had taken their place — the group in black uniforms practicing morning drills, the group in loose white uniforms maneuvering the wooden Tai Chi sword. On the strips of open ground where Falun Gong people used to gather, young men and women danced in pairs like swirls of wind. As more and more hopeless people had turned to Falun Gong to seek spiritual strength and physical health, the Communist Party felt threatened. In China's long history, there are many examples of angry masses coming together and using their power to end an old dynasty and establish a new one. In July 1999, President Jiang Zemin ordered armed police to arrest Falun Gong leaders all over the country, declared that Falun Gong was an "evil cult organization," and banned the practice of Falun Gong anywhere in China. Innocent people have been rounded up and subdued for choosing to believe in "spatial law" instead of communist doctrine that has no more meaning for them. They have been harassed, sent to labor camps, beaten, exiled, jailed, forced to commit suicide, or killed. The ban was soon extended to Tai Chi, one of China's proudest cultural achievements, and a strict size limit placed on gatherings of its practitioners. In the face of this repression, the unarmed Falun Gong refuse to yield. Among these brave people, many are women who are my contemporaries. They are fighting for a basic right as human beings, one that many in the world have long taken for granted: the freedom to believe.

The bloody sun was sinking slowly in the west. Standing at the front window of my parents' apartment, I looked down at the streets streaming with people painted with the golden redness, flowing like a crimson river. People! There are always a lot of people wherever you go. China has one-fifth of the population on earth, the country's biggest asset. The black-haired and yellow-skinned people are honest, working hard to survive. They are clever, having created a splendid civilization of five thousand years. They are kind, knowing how to endure, and to endure for a long time. I closed my eyes and prayed: May some day come when kind people won't suffer and their children won't go hungry. May some day come when people live happily in this vast land, free from any form of persecution.

"Come and see my new creation!" Father's voice sounded behind me. He led me to the television room. On the front wall was a new painting, a long scroll hanging from the ceiling to the floor. It was colorful: a fleet of ships soaring on the silver Yangtze River, on its banks new trees, with honeysuckles, azaleas, and lilies covering the mountain slopes of the Three Gorges. On the top right above Father's scarlet seal were verses from another ancient poem in his vigorous calligraphy:

A thousand sails pass by the shipwreck,
Ten thousand saplings shoot up beyond the withered tree.

Chronology of Events

Nanjing, 1953 — Author's birth
Mao's nationwide elimination of counterrevolutionaries.

Harbin, 1957 — Age four
Mao's antirightist movement.

Harbin, 1958 — Age five
Mao's Great Leap Forward campaign.

Harbin, 1959–1961 — Ages six to eight
Three-year man-made famine caused by the Great Leap Forward campaign.

Harbin Industrial University, 1960 — Age seven
Mao's Lushen Mountain Conference against rightist-deviationist thinking inside the party.
Father is demoted and criticized.

Shanghai, 1961 — Age eight
Father transferred to Shanghai.
Author's family leave behind the ongoing famine in Harbin.

Shanghai, 1964 — Age eleven
Mao's Four Clean-ups Socialist Movement, the prelude of the Cultural Revolution.

Shanghai, May 16, 1966 — Age thirteen
Official start of Mao's Great Proletarian Cultural Revolution.

Shanghai, 1967 — Age fourteen
Author becomes a junior Red Guard leader.

Shanghai, 1968 — Age fifteen
Mao's Up to the Mountains, Down to the Countryside movement.
Brother Ming leaves for Sino-Soviet border.

Shanghai, 1970 — Age seventeen
Author leaves Shanghai for Heilongjiang Military Farms on Sino-Soviet border.

Heilongjiang, 1971 — Age eighteen
The Lin Biao incident shakes the country.

Heilongjiang, 1973 — Age twenty
Author chosen to be one of Mao's worker-peasant-soldier students at East China Normal University in Shanghai.

Shanghai University, July 1976 — Age twenty-three
Author becomes an English teacher.

Tangshan, July 1976 — Age twenty-three
Earthquake levels the ancient city, killing 250,000.

Beijing, September 9, 1976 — Age twenty-three
Death of Mao.

Beijing, October 4, 1976 — Age twenty-three
Arrest of Mao's wife, Jiang Qing. End of Cultural Revolution.

Shanghai University, 1978 — Age twenty-five
Nationwide purge of former revolutionary rebels, Red
Guard leaders, and worker-peasant-soldier students ("run-
ning dogs" of the Gang of Four).

September 1986 — Age thirty-three
Author leaves Shanghai for the University of Georgia.